Field Guide to

Leadership and Supervision

in Business

Second Edition

By Carter McNamara, MBA, PhD

AUTHENTICITY CONSULTING, LLC

MINNEAPOLIS, MN USA

For reprint permission, more information on Authenticity Consulting, LLC, or to order additional copies of this or any of our other publications, please contact:

> Authenticity Consulting, LLC
> 4008 Lake Drive Avenue North
> Minneapolis, MN 55422-1508 USA
>
> 800.971.2250 toll-free
> 763.971.8890 direct
>
> http://www.authenticityconsulting.com

Trademarks

Authenticity Circles, Free Management Library, and Free Micro-eMBA are service marks of Authenticity Consulting, LLC, Minneapolis, Minnesota. "Leveraging the Power of Peers" is a registered mark of Authenticity Consulting, LLC, Minneapolis, Minnesota.

Credits

Cover design and illustrations by Erin Scott/Wylde Hare Creative, Woodbury, Minnesota.
Photographs © 2010 Photos.com, primary cover photo; © Teri McNamara/Impressions & Expressions and © Erin Scott/Wylde Hare Creative, secondary cover photos.
Clip art by Nova Development Corporation Art Explosion 750,000 Images.
Printed by Graphic & Printing Services, Big Lake, Minnesota.

Manufactured in the United States of America
First Edition April 2002
Second Edition March 2010

Waiver of Responsibility

Various Web addresses are referenced in this book. The author and publisher have no legal responsibility or liability for the currency or accuracy of these Web addresses or the content at these addresses.

Publisher's Cataloging in Publication Data

McNamara, Carter, 1953 -
    Field Guide to Leadership and Supervision in Business
        / by Carter McNamara
    ISBN 13: 978-1-933719-27-6
    ISBN 10: 1-933719-27-3

    1. Leadership development. 2. Supervision. 3. Business. I. Title

FSC
Mixed Sources
Product group from well-managed forests and other controlled sources

Cert no. SW-COC-004306
www.fsc.org
©1996 Forest Stewardship Council

Table of Contents

Table of Tables

Introduction

Critical Need for This Guide

There has been an explosion of books about leadership. Many explore grand concepts, such as embracing "The New Millennium" and adhering to the values in "The New Paradigm." In our experience, when leaders struggle, it is rarely because they do not understand such grand concepts. Rather, they struggle because they have not mastered – or they have gotten away from – the critical fundamentals of leadership and supervision. Of course, businesses can – and eventually should – pursue more leading-edge concepts in leadership, but before they do, they should establish the basic foundations of effective leadership to ensure the current stability and health of the organization.

Many business leaders have long tolerated their Board members as some kind of necessary evil – a group of people who the leaders have to deal with because the law requires corporations to have Boards. That perspective is changing. Leaders of some of the world's largest corporations have been convicted of crimes – crimes that likely would not have occurred if those corporations had independent, engaged and diligent Board members. The public has become very impatient with Boards where members were selected primarily because the members were good friends of the Chief Executive Officer.

Another reason that Boards are being taken more seriously is because wise leaders are recognizing that Board members – members selected for their expertise and independent judgment, rather than for being friends of the CEO or employees of the organization – can be an invaluable asset to the organization. Those members are not to be shunned; rather they are to be celebrated.

Those are the reasons that this Guide is so critically needed.

About This Guide

Focus of Guide: All Areas of Leadership and Supervision

Simply put, leading is setting direction and influencing others to follow that direction. You can lead yourself, others, groups and the organization. This Guide is useful for leading all of these areas of focus. Supervision is overseeing the productivity and progress of employees who report to you, that is, leading those employees – this Guide is for supervisors, too.

Note that this Guide does not address specifics of certain management functions, such as administration, financial management and facilities management. You can access a large amount of that type of management information by referencing our Free Management Library^{SM}, one of the world's largest collections of well-organized, free resources about personal, professional and organizational development. The Library is described in Appendix B of this Guide.

While this book does guide the CEO and employees to more effectively appreciate and work with the Board, this book does not go into depth about the development and operation of a corporate Board of Directors. Readers with that interest are encouraged to read some of the books about Boards as listed in the Bibliography.

Nature of Guide: Highly Practical Tips, Tools and Techniques

This Guide is written in a highly practical, how-to style that is immediately useful to businesses, especially those that are new and have limited resources. The Guide includes tips, tools and techniques, rather than general discussions, concepts and analyses. Thus, this Guide is customized particularly to the real world of the extremely busy Chief Executive Officer and other leaders in the business world.

Usually there are many approaches that can be used to address a particular challenge, for example, approaches for successful time and stress management. This author strongly believes that leaders can benefit most from consistently applying almost any one of these approaches, rather than gathering more and more of them. Consequently, this Guide generally provides one set of time-tested and useful tools, rather than many.

Audiences

This Guide is written for you if you are a:

- Founder or Chief Executive Officer

- Member of a Board of Directors

- Leader, manager or supervisor

- Management consultant

- HRD professional working with businesses

- Someone who aspires to be successful in business

We recommend that each leader and supervisor have his or her own copy of this Guide.

This Guide is particularly useful for small to medium-sized organizations that place priority on establishing or maintaining the fundamental systems for effective governance, leadership and supervision. Medium-sized organizations might be viewed as those having one to several business units, or separate major areas of products and services, and an employee headcount of several thousand. Note that new departments in organizations of any size will also benefit from this Guide by following its guidelines to establish the fundamental systems needed for effective leadership and supervision.

The Guide includes occasional references to USA-specific and Canadian-specific information, which are marked as such. There are differences between various countries regarding employment laws and those laws are highly relevant to the practices of leadership and supervision of employees. Therefore, you are advised to establish an up-to-date set of personnel policies with the guidance of an expert in local regulations and norms. Guidelines to do this are on page 171.

How to Use This Guide

Leaders of small to medium-sized businesses rarely have sufficient funds for professional development. However, in our firm's experience, that is not the biggest issue in developing leaders. The biggest issue is that leaders seldom seek help and, when they do, they rarely can use that help to its fullest advantage because the help is not customized to the nature and needs of small to medium-sized businesses. This Guide is customized to those needs.

Do not be concerned about the large size of this Guide. It is designed to be a reference manual. Refer to each topic in the Guide as you need it in the day-to-day activities of leading in your organization. Each topic includes references to Web addresses that provide additional free information.

Here are some suggestions for the best way to use this Guide:

1.   Ensure that each leader and manager has a copy of the Guide. This is usually much cheaper than hiring an expert to conduct one-shot training sessions – sessions that often result in unused materials, left to collect dust on shelves.

2.   Schedule one hour a week to read the Guide until it has been read cover to cover. As you go through the Guide, complete a calendar of the activities that you plan to conduct from referencing the Guide.

3.   Refer to the Guide whenever your organization is engaged in an activity that is addressed in this Guide. Post a copy of this Guide's Table of Contents on the side of your desk or somewhere accessible for easy reference.

4.   Schedule half an hour per month to discuss a topic in this Guide with the rest of your employees or with a group of peers in other organizations.

5.   Be sure that you have mastered use of the guidelines in PART III: Core Skills for Leading and Managing! Those are the skills that are most important in being an effective leader, yet those are the skills that are most frequently forgotten.

6.   Any guidelines in this Guide are superseded by the organization's personnel policies. You should review your organization's personnel policies and compare them to guidelines in this Guide. If the organization does not have an up-to-date set of personnel policies, then develop them as soon as possible. More information about developing personnel policies is included in this Guide in the section, Personnel Policies in PART VI.

Frequently Used Terms in Guidebook

The following terms are used frequently in this Guide and with the following definitions:

Customers

The people or groups of people who directly benefit from the products and services of a business.

Board of Directors

The group of people who are legally charged to govern the corporation. The term "Director" is not used in this Guide as it is in many other books that include information about Boards. The term can be confusing because it can apply to members of a Board of Directors or to the Chief Executive Officer. The Guide instead refers to "Board members" or "members of the Board."

Chief Executive Officer, Chief Executive, or CEO

The CEO position is the singular organization-wide, employee position that is primarily responsible to carry out the strategic plans and policies established by the Board of Directors or the owners. The CEO reports to the Board of Directors or owners. Particularly in small or new businesses, the Board members and CEO often seem to work in partnership to oversee and manage operations, even though the Board has the ultimate authority. This Guide uses the phrases Chief Executive Officer (or Chief Executive) and CEO interchangeably.

Leader

This is a role that has significant responsibility for setting direction for oneself, another individual, a group or the entire organization, and ensuring that direction is followed.

Stakeholders

These are people or groups of people who "have a stake," or strong, vested interest in the operations of the organization, for example: Board members, employees, customers, investors, collaborators, suppliers and government agencies. Compare stakeholders with stockholders, the group of people who own stock in the company and thus "own" the company.

Supervisor

This is a position that is responsible for the progress and productivity of people who report directly to the position. The role of supervisor is a leadership role.

The Glossary on page 225 provides definitions of these and other key terms.

Frequent References to Useful Resources

The Guide includes numerous references to useful resources, internal and external to the book. Each reference is marked with a handy symbol for ease of recognition. The following symbols are used.

References to other sections of the Guide that you may want to look at more closely.

References to related content available in external resources, such as other books.

References to related content available on the web, such as tools and sample documents.

1. Numbered lists suggest guidelines and the order in which they should be applied. They also indicate that there are a specific number of items in the list.

   ▪ Bulleted lists provide information that can be considered in any order and may not be all-inclusive.

About the Author

Carter McNamara, MBA, PhD, is a founding partner in Authenticity Consulting, LLC. He has strong real-world experience in leadership and supervision from working his way along the "ladder" from individual contributor to director. He has led and managed in a variety of types of organizations, including startup, large for-profit corporation, nonprofit, public-private, hospital, and university. He has consulted in a wide array of services to for-profit and nonprofit organizations. He is founder and developer of the Authenticity Circles[SM] peer coaching group models, Free Management Library[SM], and Free Micro-eMBA[SM]. He has extensive training and experience in training and coaching, including Action Learning and peer coaching. He is confident of the ability of learners to recognize their own development needs and direct their own learning.

Dr. McNamara holds a BA in Social and Behavioral Sciences, a BS in Computer Science, an MBA from the University of St. Thomas, and a PhD in Human and Organization Development from The Union Institute in Cincinnati, Ohio.

About Authenticity Consulting, LLC

Authenticity Consulting, LLC, publisher of this Guide, is a Minneapolis-based consulting firm specializing in organizational development through customized services, trainings and publications. While many firms specialize in one or a few specific services to organizations, Authenticity brings a highly comprehensive and integrated approach with focus on building the capacity of the entire organization, including its governance, management and staffing, products, marketing, finances and evaluation. We also bring skills in business planning and development. We provide services in:

- Board development and governance

- Strategic planning and strategic management

- Leadership and management development

- Product development and evaluation

- Overall organizational change

We also provide powerful, practical peer learning programs for networking, training, problem solving and support – either freestanding or to enrich other programs – through Authenticity Circles peer coaching group models. Our unique Action Learning-based group coaching process ensures ongoing support and accountability among participants during the organizational change process. Few change models recognize and build in processes to ensure these two critical elements of any change process. We also include ongoing, frequent one-on-one coaching sessions with key leaders in client organizations.

We can be reached at 800.971.2250 or +1.763.971.8890.

You can visit our website at http://www.authenticityconsulting.com .

PART I:

UNDERSTANDING

ORGANIZATIONS

AND

MANAGEMENT

Understanding Business Organizations

In this section, you will learn about the world of organizations in general, and how that understanding can help you as a leader. Then we will expand your learning by looking at what goes on in the world of management, leadership and supervision.

Benefits of A Systems View of Organizations

Management sciences have learned a great deal lately about organizations and how they work. Much of this learning has come from adopting the perspective that organizations are systems, much like people, plants and animals. There are many benefits to leaders who adopt this systems view of their organizations.

1. **More effective problem solving**
   To effectively solve problems in organizations, it is critical to be able to identify the real causes of the problems and how to address those causes. Without a clear understanding of the "big picture" of an organization, leaders tend to focus only on the behaviors and events associated with problems in the workplace, rather than on the systems and structures that caused the problems to occur in the first place.

2. **More effective leadership**
   The most important responsibilities of the role of a leader are to set direction and to influence others to follow that direction. It's difficult to establish direction for an organization and to keep that it on course if you do not understand how the organization works in the first place. Without a clear understanding of the overall nature and needs of an organization, the leader can get lost in the day-to-day activities, never really giving attention to the more important activities, such as planning the overall direction and allocating the organization's resources. As a result, the leader "can't see the forest for the trees." The leader ends up working harder, rather than smarter.

3. **More effective communications**
   One of the most important ingredients for the success of any system, including businesses, is ongoing communications among all the parts of the organization. Some of the first symptoms of an organization in trouble are sporadic and insufficient communications. In these situations, members of the organization often struggle to see beyond their own roles in the organization. Consequently, the organization is much less effective than it could be otherwise. Without a clear understanding of the parts of an organization and how they relate to each other, it is difficult to know what to communicate and to whom.

4. **More effective planning**
   The planning process is basically working one's way backwards through the system of an organization, including identifying desired results (goals and outcomes), what outputs (tangible results) will indicate that those results have been achieved, what processes will produce those outputs, and what inputs are required to conduct those processes in the system.

5. **More effective organizational development**
   The most effective form of organizational development results from the use of various strategies, including strategic planning, management and leadership development, team building, supervisory development, organizational and group and employee performance

management, and principles of organizational change. Any leader would be hard-pressed to employ these various strategies in an effective fashion without a good understanding of the overall systems in their organizations, including its major functions, departments, processes, teams and individual employees. Consequently, having a systems view is critical to accomplishing effective organizational development.

6. **Avoiding Founder's Syndrome**

Founder's Syndrome occurs when an organization operates primarily according to the personality of one of the members of the organization (usually the founder), rather than according to the mission (purpose) of the organization. When first starting their organizations, founders often have to do whatever it takes to get the organizations off the ground, including making seat-of-the-pants decisions in order to deal with frequent crises that suddenly arise in the workplace. As a result, founders often struggle to see the larger picture and to be able to effectively plan in order to make more proactive decisions. Consequently, the organization gets stuck in a highly reactive mode characterized by lack of funds and having to deal with one major crisis after another. The best "cure" for this syndrome is accomplishing a broader understanding of the structures and processes of an organization, including an appreciation for the importance of planning.

More information about Founder's Syndrome is found in Appendix D on page 247.

Understanding "System" of Organizations

Organizations are systems. Simply put, a system is an organized collection of parts that are highly integrated in order to accomplish an overall goal. The system has various inputs, which go through certain processes in order to produce certain outputs, which together, accomplish the overall desired goal for the system. The system continually exchanges feedback among its various parts in order to ensure that they remain closely aligned and focused on achieving the goal of the system. Note that a system is usually made up of many smaller systems. For example, a business is made up of processes, groups and individuals.

Let's look more closely at the important aspects of a system, including your organization.

1. **Inputs**

are items that are used by the various processes in the system in order to achieve the overall goal of the system. Types of inputs are, for example, people, money, equipment, facilities, supplies, people's ideas and people's time. For example, the inputs to a business that provides training to customers might include trained teachers, students, training materials, classrooms, money, paper and pencils. Inputs can also be major forces that influence the organization and its processes. For example, various laws and regulations influence how the training is conducted. Inputs are often identified with the cost to obtain and use them. Simply put, an organization's budget is a listing of the organization's or department's inputs and the costs to obtain and use them.

2. **Processes**

are series of activities conducted by an organization that manipulate the various inputs in order to achieve the overall desired goal of the organization. For example, the major processes used by a business that provides training to customers might include recruitment of students, pre-testing, training, post-testing and certification. Processes can range from putting a piece of paper on a desk to manufacturing a space shuttle. Leaders are usually concerned primarily with the most important, recurring processes in the organization, for example, its plans, products, policies and procedures.

3. **Outputs**
    are the tangible results produced by the organization. Outputs are often described by using numbers, for example, the number of customers who bought a certain product. Outputs are often mistaken with the long-term success of a product, and thus, the likelihood of customers to continue to buy the product. For example, leaders might mistakenly assume that because a large number of customers initially bought a product, then the product will continue to sell very well. That's not a valid assumption. In the long run, the success of a product is often determined, not by the number of customers who bought the product (that number is an output), but by how well the customers benefited from using that product (that benefit is an outcome). The stronger the outcomes, the more likely that customers will keep buying the products.

4. **Outcomes**
    are the benefits that customers gleaned from buying the product. Outcomes are usually specified in terms of changed:

    a. Knowledge, understanding, perceptions, attitudes and behaviors;

    b. Behaviors, especially those that comprise useful skills;

    c. Conditions, such as cleaner homes, increased security, stability and pride.

5. **Feedback**
    is continuously exchanged among the various parts of an organization. Feedback comes from a variety of sources in the organization, including communications among Board members (in the case of corporations), the Chief Executive, other leaders and managers, customers and others in the marketplace. Feedback can also come from an evaluation of the organization and its products and personnel. This ongoing feedback, or communication, is absolutely critical to the success of the organization and its products. That's why, in order to be a highly effective leader, you have to continually be communicating with others in your organization and marketplace.

6. **Goals**
    are the ultimate results that the system wants to accomplish. All systems are goal-directed. For example, plants, animals and people strive to stay alive and to replicate themselves. Organizations and their personnel must have clear goals, as well. That's why it is very important for leaders to establish goals and effectively communicate them throughout the organization. The overall goals of an organization are usually described in terms of its mission, or purpose, and its business and strategic goals. In addition, many organizations often associate a vision, or clear depiction, of what the business will look like when working successfully at some point in the future. The mission, vision and goals are usually determined during business and/or strategic planning. Thus, business and strategic planning are very important responsibilities of the role of leaders.

Table I:1 on the following page depicts the overall system of an organization.

Field Guide to Leadership and Supervision in Business

Table I:1 – Major Parts and Processes in "System" of Organization

Goals	Goals	Goals	Goals

Inputs

Materials and concepts used by the organization, for example:

- Employees
- Ideas
- Time
- Money
- Facilities
- Technologies
- Customers
- Location
- Suppliers
- Etc.

Processes

Practices and other activities conducted with the inputs in order to serve customers, for example:

- Plans, policies and general procedures
- Roles and responsibilities
- Program, product procedures
- Etc.

Outputs

Tangible results from the organization, for example, the amount of:

- Products
- Services
- Sales
- Expenses
- Profit
- Distributors
- Contracts
- Customers
- Etc.

Outcomes

Impacts on customers as a result of the organization's products/services, for example:

- Satisfied customers
- Satisfied employers
- Healthy customers
- Safe customers
- Etc.

Feedback	Feedback	Feedback	Feedback

System Direction: Mission, Goals and Strategies

All systems have a purpose, or mission, in their life. They also have certain methods, or strategies, to work toward that mission. For example, think of people in your life who have complained that they do not feel meaning in their lives. Often, it is because they are not in touch with their purpose or mission. Usually, when people discover their mission in life, they feel much more fulfilled in their lives and work. They may even develop a clear vision for themselves, that is, clear depiction of what they want to be by a certain time in the future. They might identify certain overall priorities, or values, for how they want to work and live.

Some people prefer to set goals along the way while working toward their vision, for example, goals to finish college, have a family and establish a career. They often set about to find ways, or strategies, to achieve their goals, for example, enroll in college, start dating and get career counseling. They may set timelines for achieving their vision and their goals. After they have set timelines, then they think about what resources they will need, such as, money, house and training.

Other systems are very similar, especially organizations. To be an effective leader, you will need to be clear about the mission, or purpose, of your organization. You will also need to establish clear goals along the way while working toward the mission. And, you will need some useful strategies to achieve the goals.

Organizations establish the mission, goals and strategies during the business and strategic planning processes. Many organizations also develop vision statements and values statements. To be effective, the planning processes must include action plans, that is, who will do what and by when in order to implement the plans. The process must also include timelines for completion of goals and a list of resources needed to implement the plans. The list of resources often includes a budget, or list of what money is needed and how it will be spent.

We will review more about the business and strategic planning processes in PART IV: How to Lead – and Change – a Business.

Understanding Culture (Personality) of Your Organization

The nature of how leadership and supervision are carried out in an organization depends to a great extent on the nature, or culture, of the organization because the culture tends to influence how people think and act in the organization. Consequently, it is very important for leaders to have a good understanding of organizational culture, including the culture of their own organization.

Defining Organizational Culture

The nature of how an organizational system works can vary widely. Variations depend on a variety of factors, such as the nature of the people, goals, size and location of the organization. Anthropologists describe culture as the assumptions, values, norms and tangible signs (artifacts) of the organization and its members. Whether you clearly understand this definition or not, you can often get a good sense for the culture of an organization just by, for example, noticing the arrangement of furniture, what people brag about, what people wear, how decisions are made and how people interact. For example, the culture of a large, for-profit corporation is usually depicted by large and well-kept buildings, formal attire among employees, offices or bays that divide individual employees, deference to authority during meetings, discussion mostly about work matters, a sense of urgency to get things done and continued focus on "the bottom line." This is in sharp contrast to the culture of the traditional, small business, which is usually depicted, for example, by modest facilities, casual attire, few bays or offices, and frequent discussion of personal and family matters.

Major Types of Cultures

There are different types of culture just like there are different types of personality. Researcher Jeffrey Sonnenfeld identified the following four major types of cultures.

1. **Academy Culture**
   Employees are highly skilled and tend to stay in the organization, while working their way up the ranks. The organization provides a stable environment in which employees can develop and exercise their skills. Examples are universities, hospitals and large corporations.

2. **Baseball Team Culture**
   Employees are "free agents" who have highly prized skills. They are in high demand and can rather easily get jobs elsewhere. This type of culture exists in fast-paced, high-risk organizations, such as investment banking, advertising and high technology.

   This best defines MSI

3. **Club Culture**
   The most important requirement for employees in this culture is to fit into the group. Usually employees start at the bottom and stay with the organization. The organization promotes from within and highly values seniority. Examples are the military and some law firms.

4. **Fortress Culture**
   Employees do not know if they will be laid off or not. These organizations often undergo massive reorganization. There are many opportunities for those with timely, specialized skills. Examples are savings and loans and large car companies.

Assessing Culture of Your Organization

Quite often, a leader has a very good sense of the culture of their organization. They just have not made that sense conscious to the extent that they can effectively learn from, and lead within, the culture.

Different people in the same organization can have different perceptions of the culture of the organization. This is especially true regarding the different perceptions between the top and bottom levels of the organization. For example, the Chief Executive may view the organization as being highly focused, well organized and even rather formal. On the other hand, the receptionist might view the organization as being confused, disorganized and, sometimes, even rude.

Here are some basic guidelines to help a leader assess the culture of their organization.

1. Understand some of the major types of cultures. There are a number of research efforts that have produced lists of different types of culture. You can start by reviewing the very short list in the previous subsection, Major Types of Cultures.

2. Describe the culture of your organization. Consider what you see and hear, not what you feel and think. Answer the following questions.

   a. Who seems to be accepted and who does not? What is it about those who are accepted as compared to those who are not?

   b. What kinds of behaviors get rewarded? For example, getting along? Getting things done? Other behaviors?

    c. What does management pay the most attention to? For example, problems? Successes? Crises? Other behaviors?

   d. How are decisions made? For example, by one person? Discussion and consensus? Are decisions made at all?

Note that there may not be close alignment between what the organization says it values (for example, creativity, innovation, team-building) as compared to what you are actually seeing (for example, conformity, individualism). This disparity is rather common in organizations. You might explain this disparity to other leaders in the organization. An ideal time to address this disparity is when developing a values statement during the strategic planning process. This Guide includes more information about strategic planning in PART III: How to Lead – and Change – a Business.

Influencing Culture of Your Organization

There are four primary ways to influence the culture of your organization.

1. **Emphasize what's important.**
   This includes widely communicating goals of the organization, posting the mission statement on the wall, talking about accomplishments and repeating what you want to see in the workplace.

2. **Reward employees whose behaviors reflect what's important.**
   This Guide lists numerous ways to reward an employee's behavior, for example, give them compliments in front of other people, say "Thank You" and promote them. See the subsection, Rewarding and Retaining Employees, in PART VI of this Guide.

3. **Discourage behaviors that do not reflect what's important.**
   There is no need to punish or cause prolonged discomfort. Rather, you want to dissuade the employee from continuing unwanted behaviors by giving them constructive feedback, verbal warnings, written warnings, or firing them.

4. **Model the behaviors that you want to see in the workplace.**
   This is perhaps the most powerful way to influence behaviors in the workplace. For example, if you want to see more teamwork among your employees, then involve yourself in teams more often.

Understanding Life Cycles of Organizations

Organizations go through different life cycles just like people do. For example, people go through infancy, childhood and early-teenage phases that are characterized by lots of rapid growth. People in these phases often do whatever it takes just to stay alive, such as eating, seeking shelter and sleeping. These people tend to make impulsive, highly reactive decisions based on whatever is going on around them at the moment.

Start-up organizations and products are like this, too. Often, founders of the organization and its members have to do whatever is necessary just to stay in business. Leaders make highly reactive, seat-of-the-pants decisions. They fear taking the time to slow down and do planning.

In our comparison of organizations to people, we note that as people continue to mature, they begin to understand more about the world and themselves. Over time, they develop a certain kind of wisdom that sees them through many of the challenges in life and work. They learn to plan and use a certain amount of discipline to carry through on those plans. They learn to manage themselves.

To survive well into the future, organizations must be able to do this, as well. Experienced leaders have learned to recognize the particular life cycle that an organization or product is going through. These leaders understand the types of problems faced by the organization or product during the life cycle. That understanding gives them a sense of perspective and helps them decide how to respond to decisions and problems in the workplace.

Table I:2 is summarized from Richard L. Daft's work and book, *Organizational Theory and Design* (West Publishing, St. Paul, Minnesota, 1992), which is based on information from Robert E. Quinn and Kim Cameron's *Organizational Life Cycles and Some Shifting Criteria of Effectiveness,* Management Science, 29, (Institute for Operations Research and the Management Sciences, 1983), pp. 31-51.

Remember that the following information is about life cycles of systems, and systems include organizations, products and even your job. Do you recognize which life cycle your organization is in? What about each of its products? What about your role in the organization?

Founder's Syndrome: Getting Stuck in First Life Cycle

Small- to medium-sized organizations are usually founded by strong and dynamic people who bring clear, consistent visions about what their organizations should be. Unfortunately, visionary founders are not always good at leading and supervising an organization as it grows. In this situation, the organization often continues to struggle around the same set of issues that occur during the first life cycle of an organization. This overall problem is sometimes called "Founder's Syndrome."

Founder's Syndrome occurs when, rather than working toward its overall mission, the organization operates primarily according to the personality of a prominent person in the organization, often the founder. The syndrome is primarily a problem of the organization, not of any one person in the organization.

More information about Founder's Syndrome is found in Appendix D on page 247.

Table I:2 – Life Cycles of Systems

Aspects	Birth	Youth	Midlife	Maturity
Size	Small	Medium	Large	Very large
Bureaucratic	Non-bureaucratic	Pre-bureaucratic	Bureaucratic	Very bureaucratic
Division of labor	Overlapping tasks	Some departments	Many departments	Extensive, with small jobs and many descriptions
Centralization	One-person rule	Two leaders rule	Two department heads	Top-management heavy
Formalization	No written rules	Few rules	Policy and procedures manuals	Extensive
Administrative intensity	Minimal support staff	Increasing clerical and maintenance	Increasing professional and staff support	Large– multiple departments
Internal systems	Nonexistent	Crude budget and information system	Control systems in place: budget, performance, reports, etc.	Extensive – planning, financial and personnel added
Lateral teams for coordination	None	Top leaders only	Some use of task forces	Frequent at lower levels

Using Systems Perspective to Analyze Problems

Experts in systems theories have identified numerous principles about how organizations work and how to solve problems in those organizations. It is not within the scope of this Guide to explain all of those principles. However, a few of the most important principles are listed below. You should keep these principles in mind when reviewing the rest of this Guide and when thinking about how to address challenges in leading your organization.

1. **Structures determine behaviors, which determine events.**
   Typically, when a new supervisor confronts a problem in the workplace, they focus mostly on the major event and the behaviors associated with that event. Let's look at the example of two employees, Tom and Sally, who keep arguing with each other. New supervisors often try to handle the problem by simply telling Tom and Sally not to argue. On the other hand, the wise supervisors would probably consider the structures, or systems, in the organization that might be causing Tom and Sally to argue. For example, Tom and Sally might be not clear on what their roles and responsibilities are in the organization. They may have conflicting roles and responsibilities. They might be lacking the resources required to

effectively carry out their jobs. Rarely is the problem simply that Tom and Sally like to argue with each other.

2. **Problems are usually solved one level above the level where the problem occurs.**
    In our example with Tom and Sally, assuming Tom and Sally are reasonably mature adults, the wise supervisors would probably realize that any long-lasting change in the situation must involve the supervisors of both Tom and Sally, not just Tom and Sally themselves.

3. **Someone who's responsible to address a problem is often a part of the problem.**
    Wise supervisors have learned to first look at themselves before they make conclusions about other peoples' problems or behaviors. These supervisors realize that if they are not effectively leading and managing themselves, then they very likely cannot effectively lead and manage others. A common example of this situation is when supervisors feel tired and overwhelmed, they feel as if everyone else is too. Or they feel as if they are the only ones in the organization who are working hard and everyone else is not working hard enough.

4. **A major problem lies not just in that part, but also in the relationships between parts.**
    For example, if a department in the organization is not getting adequate administrative support but other departments are, then the overall problem is often in the conflicting demands placed on the administrative support staff from all of the various departments. Or, an employee may have had a long-lasting performance problem, but his or her supervisor has not been doing an effective job of supervising the employee so the employee's performance has never improved.

5. **The longest lasting change results from the change of systems and structures.**
    It's not uncommon that new supervisors try to change the performance of their employees merely by preaching at them. This rarely works for the long-term. Wise supervisors have learned that to effect long-lasting change among their employees, they need to establish clear roles and goals for their employees, ensure their employees understand their roles and goals, and then monitor employees' progress toward those goals, as well.

Here are some additional principles that you might find useful. As you read the following principles, keep in mind the perspective of the system, with its major parts and processes. (The following principles are paraphrased from Peter Senge's book, *The Fifth Discipline*, Doubleday, 1990.)

1. **Today's problems are yesterday's solutions.**
    Many times we fail to see the larger ramifications of our favorite, quick fix solutions. Often those quick-fix solutions just make things worse. For example, if we do not know how to manage money wisely in our organization, then it will not do much good to just focus on getting more money from investors. Sooner or later, investors will realize that their money is not being well spent and they will quit investing money in the organization.

2. **The harder you push, the harder the system pushes back.**
    When the parts of a system come together naturally to find their own way of operating, it can be extremely difficult to change that system merely by pushing at the organization to change. For example, it usually does no good to tell a burned-out employee to just "suck it up" and do a better job. Usually, the employee's performance will just get worse. Rather than coming at the employee with warnings and directives, the supervisor should first listen to the employee. With this approach, the supervisor is much more likely to recognize the condition of burnout, what caused the condition, and how it can be addressed.

3.   **Behavior grows better before it grows worse.**
     For example, if your employees often seem confused about what they are doing and why, then it might make them feel good if you keep giving them a short list of things to do. However, it is likely that things will soon get even worse as your employees realize that they are being treated like machines. If you are lucky, you will realize your problem and will take the time required to effectively plan and delegate with your employees.

4.   **The easy way out usually leads back in.**
     Doing what's familiar is easy and comfortable. That's why, when we realize that our organization or product is really struggling, we often resort to doing what we were already doing. We just do it harder. This principle is often hardest for new leaders to learn. When a new supervisor first encounters a problem with the performance of an employee, it is not uncommon for that supervisor to try get rid of the employee, rather than work with the employee to improve their performance. Often, the employee leaves, only to be replaced by another employee who soon has the same problems. Eventually, the supervisor learns that the employee has not received effective training, does not have adequate resources to do the job, or is doing a job that is simply too much for one person to do. Unfortunately, the organization has already spent a great deal of time and money in lost productivity and recruitment of new employees. Perhaps H. L. Mencken said it best, "For every difficult and complex problem, there is an obvious solution that is simple, easy and wrong."

5.   **Faster is slower.**
     For example, if you do not take the time and energy required to effectively develop and implement plans, then it might seem that you have even more time to attend to the day-to-day matters in the organization. However, you will soon realize that you seem to be attending to the same problems over and over again. You will feel that if you do not work even harder, then you will soon be overwhelmed. Hopefully, you will realize that you have to take the time to work smarter, rather than harder. You will begin to plan and to delegate. This principle does not mean that you should never make decisions and act quickly – it means that most of those quick decisions should be guided from plans, policies and practices that are already established in the organization.

6.   **There is no blame.**
     When issues recur in an organization, it is usually the fault of a dysfunctional process or structure in the organization, rather than the fault of the people who are struggling to operate with that dysfunctional process or structure. For example, one of the ways that ineffective leaders try to lead their people is by using fear and blame. They threaten employees that the organization will shut down if the employees do not do a much better job. Then, if the organization does not do much better, they blame the employees even more. Soon the fear and blame just do not motivate employees anymore. Too often, the leaders cannot change their ways and, as a result, the employees leave. These leaders need to recognize that the organizational problem is probably not caused by some amazing coincidence that all of their employees are inept, but rather by larger problems in the organization itself. For example, there may be no demand for the organization's services, prices might be too high, or methods to deliver services might be poorly designed. This overall problem in leadership is common to Founder's Syndrome. Appendix D includes guidelines to recognize this syndrome and how to recover from it.

Organization Charts of Typical Businesses

An organization chart is a handy tool for depicting the various roles in an organization and how those roles relate to each other. They usually convey roles and reporting relationships. They do not always show the relationships that actually support work getting done.

Organization charts for small companies, like the one below, might fit on one page. For larger companies, the organization chart might only include 2-3 reporting levels on each page. For instance there might be one overview page that includes the CEO, vice presidents and directors or managers, with successive pages that show subsets of the organization.

Note that small businesses can be of many designs. The particular design of a small business depends on a variety of factors, such as the complexity of producing and marketing the business's products or services, the size of the market to which the products and services are sold, capabilities of the employees, and the amount of money available to hire employees. More information about organizing employees is provided in PART V of this Guide.

Organization Chart of Typical Small Company

The following organization chart depicts the typical design of a small, start-up company. In this example, the company is privately held and not incorporated. It does not require a Board. If there is a Board, it is contracted or advisory in nature, rather than fiduciary. The owner may or may not be the CEO. Very small companies tend to have a fairly flat hierarchy.

Table I:3 – Organization Chart of Typical Small Company

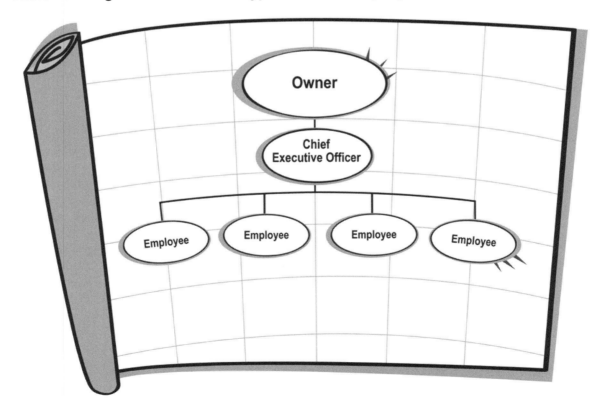

Organization Chart of Typical Small Corporation

In a corporation, the Chief Executive Officer reports to the Board of Directors. The Board reports to the stockholders, or owners. Whether the corporation is publicly or privately held, the stockholders are still the ultimate owners and authority in a corporation.

In a small corporation, the Board might be more of a working Board – attentive to the operational activities of the organization, rather than a policy Board, focused primarily on strategic concerns.

In general, a small corporation looks fairly similar to a small company that is not incorporated from the level of the CEO down through to the individual contributor employees.

Table I:4 – Organization Chart of Typical Small Corporation

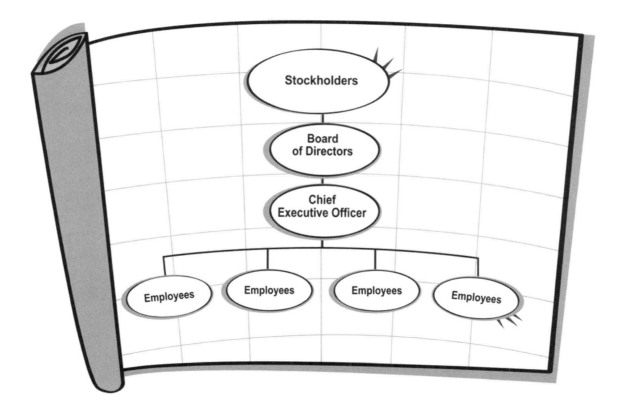

Organization Chart of Typical Medium-Sized Corporation

In a medium-sized corporation, the CEO reports to the Board of Directors. The Board reports to the stockholders or owners. The larger the organization, the more likely that the Board is focused on strategic issues, rather than day-to-day operational activities.

With a larger number of employees, the organization generally forms a hierarchy to allow for more effective management of resources and the increased need for coordination. This example shows a functional organizational design.

Table I:5 – Organization Chart of Typical Medium-Sized Corporation

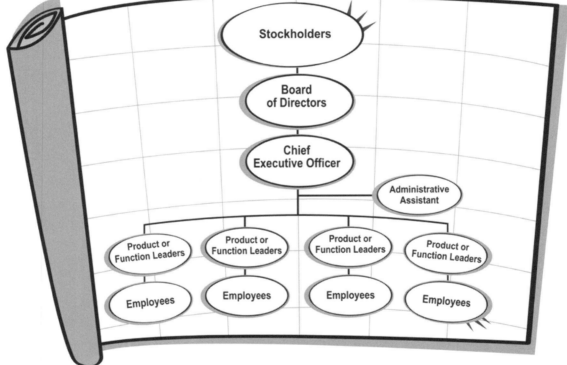

Unique Culture of Traditional Small Businesses

The culture of a small organization tends to be a rather tight-knit group of people who chip in to help wherever and whenever they can. Often, they are like a family. This tends to change as the business goes through various life cycles. The cultural aspects of a small business are reasons why it is so important for leaders to engage and utilize the expertise of Board members. (The following is adapted from an article by, and used with permission of, Sandra Larson, consultant in Minneapolis, Minnesota.)

- **The heart of the matter is leadership and management.**
  At the heart of any successful corporation is an effective Chief Executive Officer (CEO). Ideally, the CEO is wise enough to include his/her Board members in leadership of the organization. These leaders must work almost as a team with vision, skill and sufficient resources to accomplish the organization's mission. Critical management skills must rest with the Chief Executive. However, the Board members must be sufficiently skilled in management to assess the work of the CEO and assist in strategic decision-making.

- **Profit is the bottom line.**
  The bottom line is making a profit and distributing that profit among the owners, or stockholders, and employees. This goal drives decisions about what products are sold and how and where, how priorities are set, how employees are rewarded and what control systems are applicable. Skilled consultants may be needed from time to time to assist in making these decisions.

- **Problems are especially complex for the small business.**
  The majority of small businesses have a small number of employees and small budgets (less than $500,000), which compounds the leadership and management problems they face. Those new to small business may assume that issues in small businesses should be simple in nature. On the contrary, the vast majority of organizations (regardless of size) experience similar issues, for example, challenges in planning, organizing, motivating and guiding. However, when these issues are focused in a small organization, the nature of the organization becomes very dynamic and complex.

- **Sufficient resources to pay and retain employees may be lacking.**
  With lack of sufficient money, attracting and retaining employees also can be problematic. Hard work with little career development opportunity can encourage turnover of employees. This can stall the organization's work. Expertise that is brought in to train and advise leadership may be lost once that leadership leaves.

- **Lack of managerial training is problematic for the small business.**
  Many managers have been promoted primarily out of non-management disciplines and may not have the managerial skills that are needed to run an organization. Training and consultation can do much to help these new leaders and managers to gain the skills they seek and help them up a myriad of learning curves that rainbow out in front of them.

- **Chief Executives wear too many hats.**
  A Chief Executive has to be a current expert in many areas, including planning, marketing, information management, telecommunications, property management, personnel, finance and systems design. Obviously this is not possible, regardless of the size of the organization. A larger organization may be able to hire some internal experts, but this is certainly not the case for the smaller organization. Furthermore, the technology of management progresses

too rapidly today for the non-specialist to keep abreast of new thinking and expertise. Therefore outside expertise is often a must for both the large and small organization.

- **Small business is too small to justify or pay for expensive outside advice.**
  Most small businesses, as well as larger ones, often hesitate to spend money on "overhead" such as training or consultants because this is seen as diverting valuable dollars from the profit margin. Thus, responsibility for many major functions, and all associated problems, is first assumed by leaders in the organization. In small businesses, things might have to get very bad before people even consider getting – and paying for – outside help. That situation is where a diverse group of people – Board members – can be very helpful.

- **One-shot assistance often is not enough.**
  While most consultants want to teach managers "how to fish" rather than give them a "fish," "fishing" – management skills – is not usually something that can be learned in one consultation. Learning comes while grappling with an issue or management problem over a period of time, especially in more technical arenas such as computerization. Building internal management capacity takes more time than a one-shot consultation. Therefore, repeat help is not a sign of failure, but of growth – a new need to know has surfaced.

- **Networks are lacking.**
  People outside the small-business sector might observe, "Why don't Chief Executives get together more, share more ideas, undertake cooperative ventures?" There are many reasons. First of all, running a successful organization is a complex and time-consuming activity, especially when the Chief Executive wears all the management hats. Second, developing networks or researching collaboration is time-consuming, expensive and risky.

- **Small businesses usually have little time and money.**
  Investors do not seem to think research and development activity justifies new expenditures; many are hesitant to invest in what might not succeed. While small businesses may be more entrepreneurial than investors, they have little capital to risk. Collaborative planning can be enhanced by technology, but these investments are also difficult to fund. In some cases, affordable consultants can substitute for expensive, up-front research and development costs, at least at the feasibility level. In many cases, they can carry an organization through the needed planning to actually develop a new system of collaboration, merger, or automation.

- **Small businesses need low-cost management and technical assistance.**
  Small businesses are valuable community assets that must be effectively managed. The need to provide affordable, accessible management and technical assistance to these organizations is clear for all the reasons stated above: the complexity of the task, the lack of Board (in the case of corporations) and internal expertise, the lack of time and money, changing needs, the learning curve, and finally, the importance of the results to the community. What is well done is based on what is well run.

- **Typical nature of planning in small businesses is on current issues.**
  Most small businesses do not have a lot of time, money, or resources for sophisticated, comprehensive business and strategic planning. The focus is usually on the major issues facing the business and quickly addressing them. Typical major challenges for the planning facilitator are: basic training of personnel about planning concepts and processes, helping the business to focus and sustain its limited resources on planning, ensuring strategies are really strategic rather than operational/efficiency measures, and helping design small and focused planning meetings that produce realistic plans that become implemented.

Removing the Mystique from Management, Leadership and Supervision

In the previous major section, you learned about the world of organizations. Now, we will expand your learning by looking at what goes on in the world of management, leadership and supervision.

Whether you are a Chief Executive Officer, department manager or other supervisor in your organization (and these roles overlap), you will benefit from "getting back to the basics" about your understanding of the major functions of management and leadership. This section provides a basic overview of the roles of management, leadership and supervision and breaks through the myths that many have about the role of manager.

Myths about Management

Many people aspire to be a manager, yet when they get to that role, they often find themselves completely overwhelmed and confused. They believed that the role of manager involved making decisions and plans according to a consistent set of rules. They believed that they would be "managing – whatever that means." Here are some of the most common myths about management.

Myth #1: Management is a science, a set of established rules and regulations.
In an ideal world this would be true, but in reality, management is rarely any kind of science. Managers are constantly making new decisions in new situations. They often rely on seat-of-the-pants judgment – which is why it is so important to get a lot of management experience under your belt.

Myth #2: Managers know what their people are doing and are experts at what their people do.
Not necessarily. Many managers do not have the expertise to carry out the roles and responsibilities of the people who work for them. Good managers know how to trust their people and know how to delegate.

Consider "How to Delegate for Growth and Performance of Your Employees" on page 193.

Myth #3: Managers are the "bosses" and are highly respected at all times.
Wrong! In today's rapidly changing world, many times managers cannot make decisions by themselves – and should not. Usually they should include advice and feedback from their employees and their customers. Many times, managers are not liked for the decisions that they make – management is not a popularity contest. It is usually better to be respected than liked.

Myth #4: Employees are adults and should be able to do their jobs on their own.
Watch out! If you treat an employee like a some kind of tool that should just go away and "get the job done," then more than likely the "tool" will go away and not come back! It can be costly to continually have to find and train new employees. Managers need to give a lot of attention to ensuring that their employees have all the resources that they need to get the job done, including occasional guidance and praise about a job well done.

What is "Management"?

What is "Management"?

There are a variety of interpretations of this term. One classic definition is that "Leaders do the right thing and managers do things right." Another common definition is that management is getting things done through other people.

Traditionally, the term "management" refers to the set of activities, and often the group of people, involved in four general functions: planning, organizing, leading and coordinating activities. Note that the four functions recur throughout the organization and are highly integrated.

Some writers, teachers and practitioners assert that the traditional view is rather outmoded and that management needs to focus more on leadership skills, including establishing vision and goals, communicating the vision and goals, and guiding others to accomplish them. Other people assert that this view of leadership really is not a change in the traditional functions of management; rather it is re-emphasizing certain aspects of management.

Yet another view, quite apart from the traditional view, asserts that the job of management is to support the employee's efforts to be fully productive members of the organization.

To most employees, the term "management" probably means the group of people, including executives and other managers, who are primarily responsible for making decisions in the business.

This Guide refers to "management" as the Chief Executive Officer and others who are responsible for a major function or group of people in the organization.

What Do Managers Do?

The traditional view of management is that it includes four major functions, including:

1. **Planning**
    This includes identifying goals, objectives, methods and resources needed to carry out methods, responsibilities and dates for completion of tasks. Examples of planning are strategic planning, business planning, project planning, staffing planning, and advertising and promotions planning.

2. **Organizing**
    Resources are organized to achieve goals in an optimum fashion. Examples are organizing new departments, human resources, office and file systems, and businesses.

3. **Leading**
    Leading includes setting direction for the organization, groups and individuals as well as influencing people to follow that direction. Examples are establishing strategic direction (vision, values, mission and / or goals) and championing methods of organizational performance management to pursue that direction.

4. **Controlling, or coordinating**
    All of the resources have to be coordinated or controlled to effectively and efficiently reach goals and objectives. This includes ongoing monitoring and collection of feedback, with corresponding adjustment of systems, processes and structures. Examples include use of

financial controls, policies and procedures, performance management processes and measures to avoid risks.

Levels of Management

In a traditional sense, large organizations may have different levels of managers, including top managers, middle managers and first-line managers. Top-level, or executive, managers are responsible for overseeing the entire organization or some major function in the organization. These managers engage in more strategic and conceptual matters, with less attention to day-to-day detail. The top executive in an organization is often called the Chief Executive Officer and reports to the Board of Directors. The Board of Directors is the group of people who are legally charged to oversee, or govern, a corporation.

In medium to large organizations, top-level managers often have middle managers working for them. Mid-level managers are in charge of a major function or department. Middle managers may have first-line supervisors working for them. First-line supervisors are usually responsible to manage the day-to-day activities of a group of workers.

Note that you can also have different types of managers across the same levels in the organization. A project manager is in charge of developing a certain project, for example, development of a new building. A functional manager is in charge of a major function, such as a department in the organization, for example, marketing, sales, engineering and finance. A product manager is in charge of a product or service. Similarly, a product line manager is in charge of a group of closely related products.

What is "Leadership"?

The topic of leadership has become dominant in management literature. People have very strong perceptions and feelings about leadership, including widely differing definitions of the concept. In this Guide, leading is establishing direction and influencing others to follow that direction. You can lead yourself, other individuals, groups or the entire organization. Each area of focus might require different skills in leadership.

Some people believe that leading is one of the four major functions of management, along with planning, organizing and controlling resources. Others strongly assert that leading and managing are different. Among the traditional, four major functions of management (planning, organizing, leading, controlling), leading is focused, more than any other function, on conducting activities with other people. Any adult has a lot of experience in working with other people, so most adults also have strong feelings about what comprises good leadership.

The term "leadership" can be used to refer to the top levels of management in an organization. The term can also apply to the nature of activities included in setting direction and influencing others to follow it, whether those activities are conducted by the Chief Executive Officer or an administrative assistant.

No matter what definitions or perceptions that people have about leadership, it is critical for managers and supervisors to have good skills in leadership. This Guide provides guidelines for many areas of leadership, for example: planning, delegating, managing meetings, organizing employees, building teams, setting goals, cultivating motivation among yourself and employees and giving feedback.

What is "Supervision"?

There are several interpretations of the term "supervision," but typically supervision includes the activities carried out by supervisors to oversee the productivity and progress of employees who report directly to the supervisors. For example, first-level supervisors supervise entry-level employees. Depending on the size of the organization, middle managers supervise first-level supervisors and Chief Executive Officers supervise middle managers. Supervision is a management activity and supervisors have a management role in the organization.

The role of supervision is also a leadership role – leading other individuals. Therefore, the roles of supervisors and leaders are very similar and often overlap a great deal.

Supervision of a group of employees often includes:

1.   Utilizing basic management skills (decision making, problem solving, planning, delegation and meeting management).

2.   Organizing department and teams.

3.   Noticing the need for and designing new job roles in the group.

4.   Hiring new employees.

5.   Training employees.

6.   Employee performance management (setting goals, observing and giving feedback, addressing performance issues, firing employees, etc.).

7.   Conforming to personnel policies and other internal regulations.

Important Terms in Supervision

Now that you have a basic sense about organizations and their management, let's briefly look at some key terms that might be valuable as you read the rest of this Guide, especially in PART IV about supervision.

- **Span of control**
  This refers to the number of employees who work for you, or report to you (these are your "direct reports"). You will want enough people in your business or your work group to get the work done. However, you also have to be careful that you do not have so many people that you cannot keep track of (or be helpful to) them all. Supervisors commonly have anywhere from one or two to 10, 15 or even more direct reports. Having up to 15 people can be very difficult to supervise!

- **Authority**
  In your role as a manager, leader or supervisor, you have some formally granted influence to make decisions, pursue goals and get resources to pursue the goals. Note that authority in a managerial role may exist only to the extent that your people agree to grant you this authority or follow your orders! That is why it is so important to effectively work with your direct reports, or the people who report directly to you, so that they understand what you are doing and why.

- **Responsibility**

  Your responsibilities are your obligations when carrying out your assignments or conducting certain activities in your role. Note that you can have lots of responsibilities, but no authority to carry them out! This might happen, for example, if your boss assigns you the responsibility to get a task done, but does not arrange the authority, or influence, that will allow you to succeed at that task.

- **Delegation**

  Good delegation includes giving someone responsibility and also the authority to carry out that responsibility. When delegating to your employees, you should ensure that they understand the "what" of what needs to get done, but, as much as possible, leave it up to them as to the "how" of how it gets done. This Guide includes more information about delegation in PART VI.

- **Chain of command**

  Your chain of command includes all of the employees who eventually report to you, including the employees who report directly to you, employees who report directly to them, etc.

- **Accountability**

  This is having the responsibility for the ultimate outcome of an activity. For example, a Chief Executive can hold a middle manager to be accountable for the success of a project.

PART II:

ROLES OF BOARD,

CHIEF EXECUTIVE

OFFICER

AND EMPLOYEES

Board of Directors – What It Is and How It Works

It is not within the scope of this Guide to provide in-depth descriptions of how to develop and operate a corporate Board. The focus of this section is how a Chief Executive Officer and employees can effectively appreciate and work with the Board. If you are seeking more information about corporate Boards, you are encouraged to read some of the references in the section about Boards in the Bibliography.

You *do not* have to be an expert on Boards of Directors to be a Chief Executive Officer (CEO) or other leader in a corporation. However, because the Board of Directors is ultimately responsible to set the purpose and direction for a corporation, it is critical for a CEO to understand the basic purpose and nature of the Board of Directors. Likewise, it is important that the CEO to have a strong working relationship with the Board. Therefore, this section includes an overview that is sufficient for the Chief Executive Officer and other leaders in the organization to be able to work with their Boards. This Guide does not provide comprehensive information sufficient for complete Board development and operations.

Role of Shareholders

Shareholders are owners of stock in the corporation. Shareholders elect and remove members of the Board (its Directors), develop and amend the corporation's Articles (the legal description of the corporation) and By-Laws (the policies that govern operations of the Board), and approve the sale or dissolution of the corporation. Corporations must hold an annual meeting in which shareholders make their decisions. Many times, shareholders make their decisions by consent resolution, or by signing a document that explains the decision. In small to medium-sized corporations, the shareholders are often Directors and officers (executives) of the corporation.

What is a Board of Directors?

All incorporated organizations must have a Board.
An incorporated organization is an organization that has filed with the appropriate government agency to formally organize as its own official, legal entity (or corporation). This is usually done by filing a legal description – for example, Articles of Incorporation – with the appropriate government agency. (Note that if your business is a sole proprietorship or form of partnership, you are not required to have a Board of Directors. Boards are required if your business is a corporation.)

The Board is legally charged to govern a corporation.
The Board is responsible to the shareholders who own stock in the corporation. A more progressive perspective is that the Board is responsible to stakeholders, that is, to everyone who is interested and/or can be affected by their corporations.

The power of a Board is vested in all Board members, not in its individual Board members.
Individual Board members do not have formal authority. The Board as a body of members must approve the corporation's plans and procedures. Boards have policies and procedures (By-Laws and Board policies) that determine how the Board acts as a body to make plans and procedures.

In theory, the Board establishes top-level policies and employees implement.
Boards are responsible to establish top-level plans and policies that define the purpose and direction for a corporation. The Chief Executive (if the Board chooses to have a CEO in the organization) is

responsible to manage the corporation's resources in an effective and efficient manner according to the plans and policies of the corporation. Employees who work for the Chief Executive are responsible to implement the plans according to the policies of the corporation and the management practices of the CEO. How this all occurs in a business depends very much on the structure of the Board.

Roles and Responsibilities of Board Members

Fiduciary (Legal) Duties

Board members have fiduciary, or legal, duties as established in corporate law. These are the duty of care and duty of loyalty. The nature of the two duties can overlap as described below.

Examples of performing the duty of care include clearly making a reasonable and good faith effort to, for example:

- Be aware of – even drive formation of – the organization's mission, plans and policies.

- Ensure maximum return for shareholders, but do so in the long-term interest of the organization.

- Be sure that all organization activities are in accordance with the mission, plans and policies, in addition to the rules and regulations of the society and community. (Some people refer to these activities as being in accordance with a duty of obedience.)

- Fully participate in Board meetings, deliberations and decisions.

- Read, evaluate and ensure accuracy of all reports, including minutes, financials and evaluations.

- Ensure the organization has sufficient resources, including people, profits, and other assets.

Examples of performing the duty of loyalty include clearly making a reasonable and good faith effort, when acting as a Board or employee, to:

- Always be thinking about, and focusing on, priorities of the organization, and not that of yourself or another organization.

- Share ideas, opinions and advice to forward the progress of the organization.

- Represent the organization in a favorable light.

More clarity will come from considering the following more specific types of activities conducted by Board members.

Governance and Operational Responsibilities

The Board of Directors fulfills its legal duties, usually with the following responsibilities, some of which the Board might choose to fulfill by delegating to the CEO.

1. Establish the organization's mission.

2. Ensure effective strategic and business planning, including approving the Strategic Plan.

3. Select and supervise the Chief Executive Officer, including CEO compensation.

4. Ensure high-quality products and services in accordance with the mission.

5. Ensure that business operations are in conformance with relevant laws and regulations.

6. Ensure that business operations are conducted in a highly ethical manner.

7. Ensure resources are managed efficiently and effectively.

8. Ensure a strong public image for the organization.

9. Ensure high-quality operations of the Board.

Types of Specific Decisions Made by Board Members

The specific types of decisions made by Board members depend on the level of involvement of Board members in the management of the organization. However, there are some decisions that major stakeholders, such as investors, expect Board members to make – and to formally approve – regardless of the level of involvement of the Board.

1. Add or remove Board member(s).

2. Hire and terminate the Chief Executive Officer.

3. Approve the strategic plan – and possibly business plans for each of the major product lines or products.

4. Approve major organizational changes, for example, new product line or a merger.

5. Approve the annual budget.

6. Approve personnel policies.

7. Approve expenditures above a certain limit (the limit is often specified in the By-Laws).

8. Approve contracts with expenditures over a certain limit.

9. Decide issuance of shares and dividends to stockholders, and pay to Board members.

Certainly, there are other decisions that an organization might wish to have Board members attend to, such as modifying compensation and benefits to the Chief Executive and selecting major vendors for certain services.

What Boards Typically Do and When

This section about how Board members do their work includes descriptions of many of the most important activities conducted by a Board of Directors. Board members conduct those activities at certain times of the year. Often, the By-Laws and/or Board policies specify when certain activities will be conducted and when. Activities include, for example, conducting regular Board meetings (every month, two months, etc.), conducting the Board self-evaluation, evaluating the Chief Executive, reviewing and updating Board and personnel policies, conducting strategic planning, recruiting new members, holding an annual meeting, and reviewing and authorizing the yearly budget.

One of the ways that Board members remember to do those activities is by continually referencing a Board Calendar. Therefore, one of the most important Board policies is the calendar of activities. If Board members used only one policy, this is the policy that might produce the most benefit because the calendar would continually remind members to do all of the important activities required in strong governance. Therefore, one of the first policies, in addition to the By-Laws, that Board members should develop and adopt is the Board Calendar.

Table II:1 – Sample Annual Calendar of Board Activities

Yearly Board Activity	Suggested Timing
1. Fiscal year begins (assumes fiscal year beginning January 1)	January (fiscal-year timing is often specified in the By-Laws and fiscal policies)
2. Conduct Board Self-Evaluation (do once a year and in preparation for first Board retreat, might be twice per year)	February-March (do shortly before evaluating Chief Executive)
3. Evaluate Chief Executive (reference his or her progress towards last fiscal year's goals and job description)	March-April (do shortly after completion of last fiscal year)
4. Review and update By-Laws, Board policies, insurances, personnel policies and Board employment policies	March-May (do concurrent to Board and CEO evaluations)
5. Conduct first Board retreat (team building, address Board self-evaluation results, begin strategic planning, etc.)	April
6. Begin recruiting new Board members	April-May (in time for June/July elections)
7. Support strategic planning to produce organizational goals and resources needed to reach goals	May-June-July (start planning in time for setting mission, vision, values, issues, goals, strategies, resource needs, funding needs, and getting funds before start of next fiscal year)
8. Develop slate for potential new Board members	June-July (per By-Laws)
9. Hold annual shareholder's meeting and elect new Board members	July (per By-Laws)
10. Establish Chief Executive's goals for next year (as produced from strategic planning)	August (as organizational goals are realized from planning)
11. Review next year's budget (based on resources needed to reach new strategic goals)	July-August-September
12. Conduct second Board retreat (address Board orientation/training, review Board/employee roles, re-organize or form new committees based on strategic goals, develop committee work plans, update Board operations calendar, review planning status, etc.)	August (in time to orient new Board members soon after they join the Board)

What Does a Healthy Board Look Like?

There has been an extensive amount of research and sharing of opinions about what makes for a highly effective Board. Asking what a healthy Board looks like is akin to asking what a healthy person looks like or how much a car costs. It all depends. Yet most experts on Boards would agree that a healthy Board displays the following features.

- Board members ensure the organization has identified the most appropriate strategic priorities for the organization to thrive, not just survive.

- Board members provide independent opinions – opinions not influenced by members' relationship to the CEO.

- Members diligently identify, understand and address all the current issues of the business.

- Members and the CEO work toward consensus on strategic matters.

- Board members refrain from micro-managing the organization. Micro-managing is when members are so involved in the details of management that they 1) damage operations because employees are continually updating members with trivial information, and 2) do not sufficiently attend to strategic matters of top-level policies and plans.

- Board members ensure that all products and services meet the needs of customers.

- Board members regularly evaluate the quality of their operations, including how they bring in members and train them, how they are organized, how they make decisions, and how they work with the CEO.

- Members ensure that organization is conforming to all relevant laws and regulations.

Others mention overall features of a high-performing Board, for example:

- Governance – Board members employing effective practices to establish the organization's purpose and priorities, and ensuring they are effectively and efficiently addressed for maximum benefit of stakeholders (customers, investors, collaborators, shareholders, etc.).

- Diligence – All Board members consistently attending to their duties of care and loyalty, with full attention, participation and responsibilities in all deliberations, decisions and interactions with stakeholders.

- Transparency – Board members always providing full disclosure and explanation of the organization's governance, finances and effects on communities, and willingly supporting stakeholders' efforts to understand that information.

- Accountability – Board members continually making their organization and themselves responsible to meet the expectations of stakeholders, and continually verifying with those stakeholders that their expectations are indeed being met.

Strategic Questions for Your Board Members to Always Ask

Board members must not be afraid to ask the hard questions of the Chief Executive and each other. That is always better than just "numbing out" and only focusing on whatever is put in front of them during Board meetings. To make strategic impact, Board members and other leaders should always be asking the questions listed in Table II:2. This page could be in front of the Board members during their meetings to encourage strategic questioning.

Table II:2 – Strategic Questions for Board Meetings

Products and Services

1. What are the different products or services?
2. How do we know who really needs our products or services? Have we verified our impressions?
3. Who are our collaborators? Who might be? Have we reached out to them? Should we?
4. Are products and services really meeting the customers' needs? How do we know?

Board Operations and Meetings

1. Do all Board members know their roles? How do we know?
2. Are all Board members participating actively in Board operations?
3. Are the topics on the agenda the ones that we should be addressing? How do we know?
4. Are all pertinent topics being addressed effectively? How do we know?
5. Are all Board members attending meetings?
6. Are all members actively taking part in deliberations and actions?
7. Are meetings effective? How do we know?
8. Are we doing our job to verify that the business is meeting customer needs?

Personnel (Chief Executive Officer and other Employees)

1. Do we have the best people for the jobs? How do we know?
2. Are they doing their jobs well? How do we know?
3. Are all personnel policies up-to-date and adhered to? How do we know?
4. What if the CEO suddenly left the organization? What would we really do?

Promotions and Public Relations

1. What different groups of stakeholders do we have? Customers? Stockholders?
2. What image do we want each to have about our business? Do they have it? Really?
3. Are we clearly conveying the benefits of each of our products or services to customers?

Finances, Rules and Regulations

1. What are the most recent highlights, trends and issues depicted by recent financial reports?
2. Are the financial numbers really accurate? How do we know?
3. Are all taxes being paid? How do we know?
4. Are all rules, regulations and fiscal policies being followed? How do we know?

If Your Gut Tells You "Something Is Not Right," Then SAY SO Now!

What Board Committees Typically Do

When starting your Board, it is useful to have some basic sense about typical Board committees. You will get a good sense for what committees your Board will need after you have done some basic strategic planning. There is more about strategic planning later on in this Guide.

In certain circumstances, corporations are required to have certain committees. For example, those listed on the New York Stock Exchange are required to have Audit, Governance and Compensation Committees. Also, publicly traded companies must adhere to the requirements of the Sarbanes Oxley Act of 2002.

To learn more about the Sarbanes-Oxley Act, go to http://en.wikipedia.org/wiki/Sarbanes%E2%80%93Oxley_Act .

About Committees

The following points are in reference to small, working groups of the overall number of Board members. Whether the Board chooses to call them "committees" or not is up to the Board members.

1. **Committees are useful to take full advantage of Board members' resources.**
   This includes members' expertise, time, commitment and diversity of opinions. These resources are more fully utilized if focused into a small group of members in a committee.

2. **Establish committees when issues are too complex or numerous for quick response.**
   Each of the major functions required to manage an organization requires a complicated range of activities, for example, planning and oversight of financial management and personnel management. All Board members cannot be deeply involved in the planning and oversight of each. Thus, Boards often choose to associate a committee with each function.

3. **Use standing (permanent) and ad hoc (temporary) committees.**
   One of the biggest frustrations of Board members is having a committee for the sake of having a committee. Members of those committees usually struggle to find any purpose in the organization. Have standing committees only for the most important, current priorities; otherwise, terminate the committee. Temporary priorities, such as building a facility or coordinating an event, might need an ad hoc committee.

4. **Committees recommend policy for approval by the entire Board.**
   Be clear that the role of a Board Committee is not to act for the entire Board. Committees should not be making decisions for all Board members. Committees should make recommendations to the full Board for full Board deliberation and approval. (The full Board might delegate to the Executive Committee the ability to make certain types of Board decisions when it is impractical to gather all Board members together. However, all Board members are still responsible for the decisions made by the Executive Committee.)

5. **Frequency of committee meetings depends on urgency and complexity of priorities.**
   The more urgent and complex the issues facing the organization, the more frequent might be the meetings of the committees. For example, an organization that has frequent employee issues (hiring, performing, firing, turnover) might benefit from having a Personnel Committee on the Board and that Committee might meet at least once a month until the employee issues seem resolved.

6. **Minutes should be recorded and approved for all committee meetings.**
   Boards often forget to do this and, as a result, the full Board often is not aware of the activities and results of meetings of the committees. Minutes usually include documentation of the meeting attendance, discussions, decisions and results.

Potential Standing (Permanent) Committees

Table II:3 portrays the various functions often conducted by standing Board committees, or committees that exist year round. This list is not intended to suggest that all of these committees should exist in every corporation; it is ultimately up to the organization to determine which committees should exist and what they should do. Strategic planning often is used to determine the required committees, since it identifies the goals to be achieved by the organization, the methods to achieve the goals and the resources needed to implement the methods. You likely will need only three or four of these standing committees during your first years of operation. The list of standing committees often is specified in the By-Laws.

Table II:3 – Potential Standing Committees

Committee Name	Their Typical Roles
Audit	Ensures accurate tracking, monitoring and accountability for assets and for conformance to laws, rules and regulations, along with priorities to risk management. The role of this committee is increasingly important.
Governance (with Nominations Subcommittee)	Ensure effective Board processes, structures and roles, including retreat planning, committee development, and Board evaluation; sometimes includes role of Nominating Subcommittee, such as keeping list of potential Board members, orientation and training.
Compensation	Conducts analysis to determine and recommend appropriate compensation for employees, particularly the CEO, to the Board for approval.
Ethics	Develops and applies guidelines for ensuring ethical behavior and resolving ethical conflicts during Board and employee operations.
Executive	Oversee operations of the Board; often acts on behalf of the Board during on-demand activities that occur between meetings, and these acts are later presented for full Board review; comprised of Board Chair, other officers and/or committee Chairs (or sometimes just the officers, although this might be too small); sometimes performs evaluation of Chief Executive Officer.

Leadership Role of Your Board Chair

The role of Board Chair is critical to the effectiveness of a Board of Directors. (The other important aspect of Board leadership is the Executive Committee.) Leadership on the Board starts with the role of Board Chair. The CEO, in particular, often works closely with the Board Chair – in too many situations, the CEO and Board Chair are the same person. Therefore, it is important to understand the role and how it is carried out. Here are some observations about what makes for a highly effective Board Chair.

In addition to the following guidelines, you are encouraged to read about the emerging role of the "Lead Director," a position in Boards where the CEO and Board Chair are the same person. The Lead Director is an independent Board member – a member who is not an employee of the organization or a close friend of the CEO. The Lead Director role is meant to be a conduit between the other independent Board members and those who are not independent on the Board. Thus, the Lead Director role is meant to encourage more independent thoughts and participation on those Boards.

For more information about the role of Lead Director, see the Lead Director Network information at http://www.kslaw.com/portal/server.pt?space=KSPublicRedirect&control =KSPublicRedirect&CommunityId=433 .

General Guidelines for Board Chair Effectiveness

The Board Chair should:

1.   Clearly understand the roles and responsibilities of the Board of Directors. (The Board Chair should have this Guide!)

2.   Clearly understand the roles and responsibilities of the Board Chair position.

3.   Maintain clear focus on the organization's plans, particularly its mission, when guiding Board operations. The Chair should be very familiar with the strategic plan.

4.   Focus as much as possible on Board processes and not personalities.

5.   Model strong participation and team building required for a highly effective Board.

6.   Highly value a strong, working relationship with the Chief Executive.

Consider "How Your CEO and Board Can Work Together" on page 38.

7.   Highly value the participation and opinions of Board members.

8.   Possess good decision making and problem solving skills. Have strong facilitation skills during Board meetings, particularly regarding reaching consensus and time management.

For basic guidelines for decision making and problem solving, go to http://www.managementhelp.org/misc/mtgmgmnt.htm .

9.   Not be reluctant to ask for help.

10.   Understand the basic principles of effective delegation.

> For basic guidelines about delegation, go to
> http://www.managementhelp.org/guiding/delegate/basics.htm .

11.   Have basic understanding of parliamentary procedure.

> For basic guidelines about Robert's Rules, go to
> http://www.managementhelp.org/boards/boards.htm#anchor1463640 .

How Your CEO and Board Can Work Together

Role of Typical Chief Executive Officer (CEO)

The Board is responsible to hire and supervise the Chief Executive, though the Board and CEO often work together in a "strategic partnership", as discussed in the next major section. The Chief Executive is the major "player" in the business, the person who often knows the most about the organization's products and services. The first Chief Executive of the organization is commonly the founder of the business. Therefore, the Chief Executive plays a major role in organizing the first Board and helping members do their job as Board members. Here is an overview of the CEO's role.

Consider "How Your Board and CEO Can Work in Strategic Partnership" on page 40.

Board Administration and Support

Theory and law assert that the Board oversees and governs the organization. Some experts assert that it is the CEO who actually facilitates the Board to perform those roles. The CEO often knows much more about the organization than does the members of the Board. Consequently, the CEO must continually update Board members about the organization, often by providing written reports to Board members that are reviewed during Board meetings. An effective Board hires the CEO and regularly evaluates the CEO's performance. The CEO often helps with Board development and administration, often in a Board Development Committee.

Product and Service Delivery

The CEO is an expert on the business' marketplace and the products and services for that marketplace. The CEO oversees development and delivery of products and services to ensure that the organization continually meets the needs of customers in a highly focused and effective fashion. Products and services must be effectively marketed, including researched, tested, priced, positioned, advertised and promoted, sold and serviced for customers.

Financial, Tax, Risk and Facilities Management

The CEO develops the yearly budget. In the case of corporations, the CEO seeks the Board's approval of the yearly budget. The budget should be derived from results of the yearly strategic planning. Once the budget is established, the CEO should operate the business in accordance with the strategic plan, and in a manner that is consistent with various laws and regulations, and also the policies of the Board. This includes ensuring that all relevant taxes are paid. It also includes managing the facilities of the business in an efficient and safe fashion. Progressive CEO's also conduct effective risk management planning, including identifying major risks to the business and how those risks can be addressed effectively.

Human Resource Management

The CEO leads the effort to design organizational roles and responsibilities among employees. These roles and responsibilities should be derived directly from results of yearly strategic planning. The CEO oversees staffing, training and supervision of personnel. These activities must closely conform to up-to-date personnel policies and procedures that are reviewed on a regular basis by an employment law expert and also approved by the Board. The CEO works with the Board in this regard, often in a Personnel Committee.

Community and Public Relations

The CEO often takes the lead in ensuring that the community continues to have a strong positive image about the business and its products and services. It is often most effective if the CEO works from a comprehensive marketing plan. In the case of corporations, some Boards will want to approve the marketing plan.

A good way to depict the role of the CEO is by providing a job description. Take a minute or two to review the following job description. Note that the job description is for the CEO of a corporation.

Table II:4 – Example Job Description of Chief Executive Officer

Title:	Chief Executive Officer
Responsible to:	Board of Directors

Major Functions:

1. Implement the strategic goals and objectives of the organization.

2. With the Chair, to enable the Board to fulfill its governance function.

3. Give direction and leadership toward the achievement of the organization's philosophy, mission, strategy, and its annual goals and objectives.

Major Responsibilities and Accountabilities:

1. Board Administration and Support – Supports operations and administration of the Board by advising and informing Board members, interfacing between Board and employees, and supporting Board's evaluation of Chief Executive Officer.

2. Product and Services Delivery – Oversees design, marketing, promotion, delivery, and quality of products and services.

3. Financial, Tax, Risk and Facilities Management – Recommends yearly budget for Board approval and prudently manages organization's resources within those budget guidelines according to current laws and regulations.

4. Human Resource Management – Effectively manages the human resources of the organization according to authorized personnel policies and procedures that fully conform to current laws and regulations.

5. Community and Public Relations – Assures the organization and its mission, products and services are consistently presented in strong, positive image to relevant stakeholders.

6. Maximizing Return on Investment for Stockholders – Ensures that stockholders continue to receive strong and timely return on investment from their purchase of the company's stock.

Date of Board Approval of Job Description: _____ *Board Chair:* _____

How Your Board and CEO Can Work In Strategic Partnership

Although theory and law assert that the CEO works for the Board, the relationship and mutual support between the Board and CEO is critical to the success of a business. There might be an impression that the traditional structure of Boards, with its conventional job descriptions and committees, is somehow a rigid, top-down hierarchy, but this often is not the case. In many organizations, it is actually the CEO who facilitates and guides the Board members to do their jobs. Many organizations have employees on certain committees. The CEO has strong input to the deliberations and decisions of Board members. Research suggests that a successful working relationship – a "strategic partnership" – between the Board members and CEO is one of the most important criteria for a high-performing organization.

Descriptions of the traditional Board often portray the Board members as the "bosses" of CEOs, handing down directives and then "policing" the CEOs to ensure that those directives are followed. CEOs presented with that perspective often are confounded to understand why they must report to a group of people (Board members), many of whom do not seem to understand much, if anything at all, about the organization and its products and services. Consequently, these CEOs struggle to acknowledge the credibility of, and accept directions from, Board members. New or struggling CEOs can even resent and disrespect Board members, or even ignore them altogether.

Many experts assert that one of the reasons that a Board might struggle to be effective is because the CEO really does not want an effective Board and, therefore, does not help members to realize their roles and does not provide needed information to the Board members. Seasoned CEOs have learned that their jobs can be enhanced considerably with the additional guidance and resources from a highly effective Board of Directors – but the CEOs realize they must help the Board members to be that effective. CEOs can support the development of a Board when they:

- **Help Board members to understand their roles as members of a governing Board.**
  The CEO often has more interest and resources to fully understand the role of a Board and, therefore, can be extremely helpful to Board members learning their roles. The CEO can work with the Board Chair or Chair of a Board Development Committee to design and conduct the first several Board trainings.

- **Suggest people to recruit as Board members.**
  As much as possible, these people should be independent Board members – people who have no other strong, vested interest in the organization, for example, people who are not employees or very close and personal friends of the CEO.

- **Orient Board members about the organization and its products and services.**
  Frequently, members can serve on a Board for years and still not really know what products and services are offered by the organization. CEOs can significantly increase the effectiveness of Board members, and their contributions to the organization, by orienting members about the business, its history, collaborators and successes.

- **Play a strong role in strategic planning discussions and decisions.**
  Boards that view members as attending primarily to top-level policy will sometimes make the mistake of determining mission, vision, values and top-level goals without input from the CEO and senior employees. That is a mistake. The most useful strategic planning sessions often involve information, discussions and suggestions from employees.

■ **Participate in Board committees.**
The CEO can provide great value to committees, especially Finance, Personnel (except when the Board is evaluating the CEO and determining his/her compensation) and Marketing. A trend is for employees to be on some of the Board committees, as well.

■ **Provide useful information to Board members in time for their review before meetings.**
Some CEOs have learned that one of the best ways to incapacitate a Board is by giving them new materials during a Board meeting, so that members are quickly overwhelmed and confused. As a result, members end up listening and agreeing with whatever the CEO suggests. Seasoned and collaborative CEOs share materials well before Board meetings.

Typical Timing of CEO's Tasks

There are certain activities that recur regularly during the calendar year for a Chief Executive Officer. The following sample should be modified according to the nature and needs of the organization.

Table II:5 – Sample Annual Calendar of CEO Tasks

	Yearly Activity	Suggested Timing
1.	Fiscal year begins	January (fiscal-year timing is often specified in the By-Laws)
2.	Participate in evaluation of Chief Executive's performance by referencing his or her progress towards last fiscal year's goals and his or her job description	April-May (do shortly after completion of last fiscal year)
3.	Conduct strategic planning with the Board and senior employees to produce organizational goals and resources needed to reach goals	May-June-July (start early enough to set mission, vision, values, issues, goals, strategies, and resource/funding needs, and to get funds before next fiscal year starts)
4.	Plan and coordinate the annual shareholder's meeting	July (per By-Laws)
5.	Establish CEO's performance goals for next year (as produced from strategic planning); get Board's approval of the goals	August (as organizational goals are realized from planning)
6.	Draft next year's budget (based on resources needed to reach new strategic goals); get Board's approval	July-August-September
7.	With the Board, conduct Board retreat (Board orientation/training, re-organize or form new committees based on strategic plan goals, develop work plans, update Board operations calendar, review planning status, etc.); Board members should take the lead in these activities	August (in time to orient new Board members soon after they join the Board)
8.	Conduct written yearly performance reviews for each employee	Per anniversary date of employees

Sample List of Monthly Activities

The Chief Executive Officer might conduct the following activities on a monthly basis.

1. **Employee-wide meetings**
   This would include meeting with all employees to review the overall condition of the organization and review recent successes. Consider conducting "in service" training about the organization where employees or departments take turns describing their roles to the rest of the employees. For clarity, focus and morale, use agendas and follow up with minutes. Consider bringing in a customer to tell his/her story of how the organization helped them.

2. **Review of financial reports**
   Note that the particular financial statements and their titles depend on the locale of the organization, for example, the following terms are common in the USA. Reports would include:

   a. Cash Flow (to be sure there are sufficient monies to pay the bills)

   b. Income Statement

   c. Balance Sheet

3. **Write CEO's Report to present to the Board, and briefly describe:**

   a. Status of operations

   b. Major accomplishments of the past month

   c. Expected major accomplishments of the coming month

   d. Any highlights, trends and/or issues that Board members should know about

4. **Meet with any Board committees and officers as scheduled by the Board.**

5. **Meet with the Board in the regular (usually monthly) Board meetings.**

6. **Meet face-to-face, one-on-one with each direct report.**

Sample List of Weekly Activities

1. **Collect written weekly status reports from each direct report that include:**

   a. Accomplishments over the past week

   b. Any current highlights, trends and issues

   c. Plans for next week

2. **Meet face-to-face with direct reports together.**
   This further cultivates cohesiveness and communications among employees.

Should CEO Be A Member of Your Board?

There is no clear consensus on this question. Yet, with the recent, major crimes committed by CEOs of very large corporations – corporations in which the Board members arguably could have been more diligent – there is an increasing belief that CEOs should not be members of their Boards. The role of a Board is to provide objective oversight and governance of a corporation, including of the role of the CEO. Many people believe that a Board cannot perform that role if the CEO also is a member of the Board.

How Your Board Members and CEO Can Work Well Together

Basic Practices to Ensure Effective Coordination

1. Board members must know their roles and responsibilities, including how they differ from those of the Chief Executive and other employees. Board training should be conducted at least once a year to ensure all Board members and the Chief Executive clearly understand each other's roles and responsibilities.

2. The Chief Executive and other employees should be aware of the Board's roles and responsibilities, including how they differ from those of the Chief Executive and employees.

3. Board, Chief Executive and employees should engage in yearly strategic planning activities. Board and Chief Executive should be involved primarily in determining the organization's mission, vision, goals and strategies. Chief Executive Officer and employees might be involved primarily in defining action planning, including who will do what and by when in order to implement the strategies. The resulting strategic plan should be provided to everyone in the organization.

4. Board members should have regular Board meetings, usually once a month during the first several years of the organization's life. Thereafter, have Board meetings at least every two or three months, ideally with committee meetings between Board meetings that are every other month.

5. Chief Executive Officer and Board Chair design the agenda for Board meetings, and the agenda is sent to Board members at least one week before the Board meeting.

6. The Chief Executive Officer should provide regular, written reports to Board members, usually on a monthly basis.

7. The Chief Executive Officer and Board Chair should have a strong, ongoing, working relationship.

 Useful pointers are in the next section of this Guide, "How Your Board Chair and CEO Can Work Together" on page 44.

8. The Board should conduct regular, at least annual, formal evaluations of the Chief Executive Officer.

9.   There should be clear Board policies regarding the roles and coordination of Board members and employees, including:

   a.   Employee participation on Board committees.

   b.   Ensuring that the Chief Executive Officer approves Board member contacts to employees (unless a current, major issue suggests the Chief Executive Officer should not be involved).

10.   Board members and employees should meet each other at least once a year in a rather casual environment focused on celebrating the accomplishments of the organization.

11.   Employees should be allowed to make occasional presentations at Board meetings regarding business activities and how they are carried out.

How Your Board Chair and CEO Can Work Well Together

Inherent Struggles Between Both Roles

Many experts assert that one of the most important ingredients to a successful corporation is a high-quality relationship between the Board Chair and the Chief Executive. However, this relationship has several inherent struggles to overcome. The Chief Executive was usually in the organization before the Chair was appointed and will be around after the Chair will be gone. In addition, the Chief Executive is also much closer to the day-to-day activities in the organization. Lastly, the Chief Executive usually knows far more about the organization's customers. Consequently, the Chief Executive may feel that he or she knows much more about the organization than the Board Chair. Yet, the Board Chair is responsible to provide leadership for the Board, to whom the Chief Executive is accountable. The Board Chair leads the Board, which evaluates the performance of the Chief Executive. Maintaining a high-quality relationship between the two roles requires a high level of maturity and understanding from both people filling those roles.

Practices That Can Minimize Destructive Conflict

Conflict is inherent in groups where diverse members are participating in deliberations and decisions about very important matters, in particular when each member is sharing his/her beliefs and opinions. Conflict itself is not bad – conflict becomes destructive when it is prolonged about the same issue or decision, involves members openly making judgments about a member's character or personality, or involves escalating emotions to the extent that some members are shouting or otherwise impeding the group process. The following suggestions are provided to help ensure a high-quality relationship between the Board Chair and the Chief Executive by establishing formal practices and procedures.

1.   **Have clearly written and approved procedures for evaluating the Chief Executive.**
        Ensure the procedures include getting strong input from the Chief Executive.

2.   **Have regular Board training sessions.**
        They should include overviews of the roles of Board Chair and Chief Executive.

3.   **Board Chair and Chief Executive meet to discuss how they can work together.**
        They should share their preferences for how they like to communicate, plan and coordinate.

4. **Board Chair and Chief Executive jointly design Board meeting agendas.**
   This helps to ensure that all-important matters of the Board and employees are included.

5. **Board Chair can consult with the Chief Executive when appointing Committee Chairs.**
   The Chief Executive often has a clearer understanding of who knows what on the Board.

6. **Have clearly written guidelines about the roles of employees.**
   This is especially important when employees provide ongoing support to Board committees.

7. **Get a new person in the Board Chair position at least every few years.**
   This helps to ensure new and fresh perspectives in the role.

8. **Consider developing Board Chairs by having Vice Chairs.**
   The Vice Chair gets a year to "shadow" the Chair to really learn the role.

9. **Have a Board discussion about meetings between the Chief Executive and Board Chair.**
   Get all Board member's ideas about when and why the Board Chair and Chief Executive should meet – do not make the meeting a matter of only those two people.

10. **Avoid frequent meetings that include only the Board Chair and Chief Executive.**
    Involve other Board members or other employees.

11. **Always write and share highlights of meetings of Chief Executive and Board Chair.**
    Otherwise, other Board members forget about these meetings.

12. **Ensure all Board members are trained about the role of the Board.**
    That way, all Board members know what to expect from the Board Chair and CEO roles.

13. **The Chief Executive and Board Chair should never conceal information.**
    CEO and Board Chair information is Board business – all members should know about it.

14. **Celebrate accomplishments.**
    All Board members should recognize and appreciate the hard work of the Chair and CEO.

Personal Practices to Minimize Interpersonal Conflicts

In addition to formal practices to minimize conflicts as listed above, the two people in these roles can follow certain practices themselves.

Consider "How to Understand and Manage Conflict" on page 208.

If Worse Comes to Worst

Obviously, the course of action for a situation such as this depends to a great extent on the nature of the organization and the two people involved. If you are a Board Chair or Chief Executive who continues to feel conflict in working with the other person, then consider the following options:

1. **Approach the other person and ask for five minutes of uninterrupted time.**
    Explain your concern, what you see and hear that leads you to believe there is continued conflicts between both of you, what you would like to see or hear between both of you in the future, and why continued conflict can be so destructive to the organization.

2. **If the other person says there is no conflict, then assert what you want from them.**
    They either will change their behaviors, in which case things should improve, or they will not. In that case, you can escalate the issue up the organization (for example, present the matter to the entire Board), if appropriate, or seek additional assistance about how you plan to handle the problem: avoid it, confront it further or negotiate further.

3. **If the problem persists, ask to have time with the Executive Committee.**
    At this point, it is critical to remember that any "badmouthing" or "conspiring" against the other person will only end up hurting the entire Board and organization. Therefore, talk with a friend or take careful time to reflect about what you want to say and how to say it to the other Board members. Explain the situation in terms of the behaviors in the issue, not the personality or character of the other person. Explain what you have done so far to address the issue. Describe your perception of the results of your efforts with the other person – note that it is your perception. Ask for specific advice to address the issue. At the end of the meeting, echo back what you hear them suggesting. Attempt to follow their advice. Commit to follow up with them about the results of your following their advice.

4. **If the problem persists, you might consider getting outside help.**
    This may be more constructive than posing the problem to the entire Board where it may cause great confusion and unease with little or no clear course of action to resolve the issue.

How Your Board Can Evaluate Your CEO

Many Benefits of Formal Evaluation

Evaluating the Chief Executive Officer is a primary responsibility of the Board. There are several key benefits from this evaluation, including that the process:

1. Ensures the Board is meeting its duty to effectively lead the organization.

2. Ensures organizational goals are being met.

3. Ensures continued development of the Chief Executive to more effectively conduct his or her role.

4. Ensures a formal and documented evaluation process that meets standards of fairness and practicality.

5. Ensures the Chief Executive values his or her role, is benefiting from it and therefore is more likely to stay (finding good Chief Executives seems increasingly difficult).

6. Leaves written record of the Board's impression of the Chief Executive's performance in case this record is needed for future verification, for example, for salary increases, probationary activities or firing.

Table II:6 – Sample Schedule to Evaluate Chief Executive

Activity	Approx. # of months before start of next fiscal year
Evaluate the Chief Executive, by referencing his or her progress towards last fiscal year's organizational goals and the responsibilities list on the CEO's job description	10
Conduct Board self-evaluation	9
Hold Board retreat to address results of Board self-evaluation, conduct any team building and begin strategic planning	7
Conduct strategic planning to produce organizational goals and identify resources needed to accomplish the goals	7
Establish CEO's goals for the next fiscal year, by referencing goals produced from strategic planning	6
Establish next year's financial goals and budget by referencing resources needed to reach strategic goals	6
Conduct operations to generate revenue	6
Fiscal year begins	0

General Guidelines When Evaluating Chief Executive

1. Be sure the process is fully documented in a procedure so the process is well understood and carried out consistently year-to-year. The procedure should be in conformance with up-to-date, Board-approved personnel policies and procedures.

2. If employees are involved in evaluation of the Chief Executive, be sure this procedure is clearly specified and understood by the Chief Executive.

3. A Board committee should manage the evaluation process, not just one Board member, and all Board members should have input to the evaluation feedback to the Chief Executive. Committees might be the Executive Committee, a Personnel Committee or an ad hoc committee.

4. If the Board perceives the Chief Executive to have performance issues, then Board members can initiate an evaluation. However, do not initiate evaluations only when there are perceived issues – this is abusive. Be sure that conclusions about performance issues are based on observed behaviors of the Chief Executive, rather than on interpretations or speculations about the Chief Executive's character or personality.

Sample Form to Evaluate Chief Executive: Guidelines

Table II:7 provides one sample set of guidelines and a form that might be used by the Board to evaluate the Chief Executive. This sample should be customized to the particular culture and purpose of the business by modifying the performance criteria in the left column as appropriate for the organization, updating those criteria in the table, and conducting the evaluation using the updated table.

1. The Board should establish a policy for evaluating the Chief Executive and establish a current or ad hoc committee to carry out the evaluation.

2. The Board, working with the Chief Executive, should establish performance criteria and insert them in the table below. Criteria should come from the Chief Executive's job description and any strategic goals from the most current strategic plan.

3. The Board then assigns specific weighting factors for each of the major categories below. Factors depend on what the Board believes should be priorities for the Chief Executive during the evaluation period. The factors should total 100%. Example weightings might be finances 15%, revenue 20%, human resources 15%, products/services 20%, facilities 10%, planning and governance 20%.

4. Each Board member and the Chief Executive complete the table below about the Chief Executive's performance during the evaluation period. Each criteria is ranked from 1-5, with 1=unsatisfactory, 2 = partially within expectations, 3=meets expectations, 4=exceeds expectations, and 5= far exceeds expectations. This numerical ranking system tends to give clear perspective more than commentary. Rankings with commentary are ideal.

5. Multiply each ranking by the category's weighting factor. Put the answer in the score column.

6. On a separate sheet of paper, provide any commentary that addresses rankings lower than 3. Consider adding commentary for high ratings as well.

7. Provide evaluation sheets and commentary to the Board member who is assigned to collate the sheets (usually the Board Chair).

8. The Board may decide to provide the Chief Executive an average ranking for each category. Similarly, commentary can be summarized or each comment provided to the Chief Executive.

9. The evaluation committee provides the evaluation report to the Chief Executive and schedules a meeting with him or her shortly thereafter.

10. Ensure the meeting ends on a positive note.

11. Ensure plans are made to address ratings below 3, including specific actions by specific dates.

Table II:7 – Sample Form to Evaluate Chief Executive

Name of Preparer	Ratings	Weight Factor	= Score
Planning and support of governance, consider: ■ Provides relevant and meaningful information to support Board plans and policies ■ Establishes appropriate plans and priorities, which are clearly described to employees ■ Ensures implementation of plans in a timely manner Comments:			
Finances, consider: ■ Stays within budgets and/or gets approval for deviations ■ Maintains needed cash flow to pay bills on time ■ Receives a "clean" financial audit ■ No loss of operating funds ■ No prolonged legal difficulties Comments:			
Revenue, consider: ■ Raises enough revenue through sales or fees for services to accomplish significant strategic goals ■ Maintains a financial balance in keeping with organizational policy Comments:			
Products and services, consider: ■ Ensures high-quality operations ■ Verifies that each product or service is meeting the needs of customers Comments:			
Human resources, consider: ■ Maintains or increases productivity of employees ■ No undue employee turnover ■ No ongoing personnel complaints Comments:			

How Your Board Can Ensure Smooth Succession to New CEO When Needed

The Board is responsible to ensure that the organization continually has high-quality operations. It is extremely important that that CEO position be filled reliably with a high-quality person. CEOs leave their jobs on an unplanned or a planned basis. Unplanned termination may occur because of sudden illnesses or death, or poor performance on the part of the CEO. Planned termination usually occurs because the CEO is making a career or life change.

Demographic trends indicate that there are not sufficient numbers of next-generation leaders to replace retiring baby-boomers in organizations. Thus, succession management is an increasingly important priority for Board members. (Various phrases are used to refer to aspects of ensuring a complete and successful transition to a new CEO, for example, succession planning, succession management and transition management.)

- **Do not wait until the CEO will be terminating employment. Start planning now.**
  Succession management is a matter of strong practices in ongoing governance and management, not a matter of sudden crisis management. Start attending to those practices now.

- **Focus on practices, not on personalities.**
  Succession management is re-filling a role, not replacing a certain person. Be sure the CEO position is defined well, and then look to find the best person to fill the position. Do not look for someone who is just like, or a lot different than, the previous CEO.

- **Succession management is a responsibility of the Board and the CEO.**
  The best succession management results from 1) a working partnership of Board members working to understand and define and fill the CEO role, and 2) the CEO ensuring that Board members have the information and resources to refill the role.

- **Succession management is leadership transition, and staffing and risk management.**
  Leadership is ensuring clear direction and creating the environment so that others are motivated to follow that direction – that function must continue during a transition. The CEO is an employee role and, therefore, must be filled by using up-to-date personnel policies to ensure fair, equitable and legally compliant employment practices. Activities must minimize the risks from lapses in poor management and undue fears among stakeholders.

- **Quality in managing succession is often proportionate to the quality of the new CEO.**
  The more thorough and careful that Board members are during succession, the more likely that the organization will get a new CEO who successfully fills the position for the long-term. The best way for Board members to convey their expectations of high quality in the CEO role now, is to have the CEO perceive a high-quality succession management process.

Key Governance and Management Practices in Succession Management

If Board members have already established strong practices in governance and in management, then succession management often is a matter of using current practices, rather than establishing many new ones. Key practices include having:

1.   A strategic plan that clearly conveys the organization's mission and current strategic priorities. Ideally, that plan also includes specific action plans that specify who is going to do what and by when in order to address each priority.

2.   Up-to-date and Board-approved personnel policies about hiring, supervising and firing personnel in a fair and equitable manner that complies with employment laws.

3.   An up-to-date job description for the CEO role that explains the general duties and responsibilities of the position.

4.   Suitable compensation for the CEO role (often this is a major challenge for new organizations because they often have very limited resources).

5.   An annual calendar of the CEO's most important activities, for example, when the CEO: evaluates personnel, does any staffing analysis, updates job descriptions and participates in certain Board committees.

6.   Regular reports from CEO, in particular reports to Board members prior to or during Board meetings. These reports should include the trends, highlights and issues regarding the CEO's activities.

7.   Evaluation of the CEO on an annual basis, including in reference to the CEO's job description and any performance goals established for that role.

8.   Arrangements with the CEO when he/she goes on vacation so Board members and employees have an opportunity to effectively replace the CEO if only for a temporary period of time.

9.   A complete list of major stakeholders. Get a list of investors, including contact information, how each is approached and who does that, in case that information is needed when/if the CEO leaves. Get a complete list of other stakeholders, including collaborators, suppliers, facilities management contacts, etc.

10.   Fiscal policies and procedures to ensure strong Board oversight of finances, including that financial numbers are correct and tracked accurately, and also that there are sufficient funds to pay near-term expenses.

11.   At least annual discussions with the CEO regarding succession management, including how to manage effectively in the CEO's absence. (Be sensitive in raising this topic with the CEO so that he/she is not overly concerned that Board members somehow want a change now). This discussion can be an opportunity to hear about the CEO's career plans and desires, too.

12.   At least annual discussions not only about succession of the CEO role, but of other critical employee positions, for example, supervisors.

Replacing an Outgoing CEO

If the organization has regularly been conducting succession planning with the current CEO, then it could be a straightforward matter to replace the CEO in a relatively low-risk and smooth manner. The following guidelines assume that the CEO has given sufficient notice that he/she is leaving soon. Some of the guidelines in the following section will need to be modified if the CEO is suddenly leaving, for example, was fired, seriously ill or deceased.

CEO's Notification to Board

1. **Typically, the Chief Executive will notify the Board Chair or other Board member.**
   The Chair should immediately notify the rest of the Board members prior to the next Board meeting.

2. **Ask the Chief Executive to document his/her decision in writing to the Board.**
   This documentation makes the decision "official" and is good to have to verify that the official decision had been made.

3. **Attempt to negotiate a four-week-notice period from the Chief Executive.**
   It is not unlikely that there will be a period without a new Chief Executive. This procedure will minimize disruption through that period.

Maintaining Confidentiality During Transition

1. **All Board members should be apprised as soon as possible.**
   Occasionally, members believe that transitions should be handled so cautiously that even some Board members should not hear about the transition. This is the wrong approach. Each Board member is legally responsible for the leadership of the organization, and deserves to know about all matters when they occur.

2. **Discuss how to handle public relations.**
   The community will soon hear or read that the Chief Executive is leaving. Agree on how this message will be conveyed. If the transition is expected to take over a month (they often do), consider sending a letter to the major stakeholders (advisors, suppliers, "peer" organizations, investors, etc.) notifying them of the transition and assuring them that transition planning is being carried out thoroughly. Invite them to contact the Board Chair if they have any concerns or questions.

Board Activities During Transition

1. **Start activities to hire new CEO. Consider appointing an ad hoc Search Committee.**
   The Board might choose to form a Board Search Committee (or task force) now, in which case that Committee could handle the search activities, too. The Committee will manage the transition, including developing a transition plan. This Committee role could be assumed by the current Executive Committee or a Personnel Committee. Committee members should commit to availability over the next four to eight weeks. The Search Committee should focus on:

   a. Identifying desired skills of the new Chief Executive, if not already identified.

   b. Verifying the accuracy of the job description of the Chief Executive.

   c. Conducting the recruiting and selection activities itemized in this section.

2.   **Develop a written transition plan and have the Board approve it.**
      The contents of this section about succession management could comprise much of the transition plan, but responsibilities and deadlines would need to be added to the plan.

3.   **As soon as the transition plan is developed, promptly notify employees of the transition.**
      A Board member should attend the staff meeting where notification is given and the employees should be assured that the transition is being carefully planned and carried out. The plan might be reviewed in the staff meeting. A copy of the transition plan should be shared with all employees.

4.   **Identify any necessary funding for the transition.**
      For example, are any funds needed for a national search, to move the new candidate, for training the new candidate or for consultants on interim basis?

Administrative Activities During Transition Before New CEO Arrives

1.   **Establish an interim staff structure.**
      Consider appointing an acting Chief Executive from among the employees reporting to the current Chief Executive. If this course is followed, ensure the job description is well understood by the acting Chief Executive and the acting arrangement is documented in a letter between the acting Chief Executive and the Board. Send a memo to all employees, describing this interim appointment and how the acting Chief Executive will work with the employees until a permanent Chief Executive is identified. (Be very careful with this type of temporary arrangement as it can lull Board members into believing the transition is complete, which it is not. Also, it can foster the illusion that the Board members will always be delegating directly to employees.)

2.   **Update the administrative calendar for the organization.**
      Ask the outgoing Chief Executive to make a schedule of all major recurring activities during the year, for example, of performance reviews, special events, staff meetings, one-on-one meetings, lease/contract expiration dates and when paychecks come out. Be sure any deadlines for contracts are included in the schedule.

3.   **Get a list of key stakeholders from the outgoing CEO.**
      Have the outgoing Chief Executive make or update a list of all key stakeholders whom the new Chief Executive should know about, for example, investors, advisors (legal, accounting, real estate) and collaborators.

4.   **Review outgoing Chief Executive's office facilities.**
      Ask the outgoing Chief Executive to document the status of his/her office, for example, ensure there are labels on all documents and drawers. Appropriate employees and at least two Board members should meet with the Chief Executive to review where he/she keeps files and major documents. Appropriate employees should retain a key to the office and appropriate Board members should retain keys to the desk drawers and file cabinets.

5.   **Review personnel status with the outgoing CEO.**
      Two or more Board members, ideally from the Personnel Committee, should meet with the outgoing Chief Executive to review personnel files, for example, are there any current personnel issues, for example, some personnel will be leaving/retiring or have performance issues.

6. **Outgoing CEO should complete performance reviews on all personnel.**
This ensures that the outgoing Chief Executive's important feedback to personnel is collected before he/she goes, gives personnel a fair opportunity to reflect their past performance to the new Chief Executive, and gives the new Chief Executive the input he/she deserves about each employee to ensure effective supervision.

Interim Coordination Between Board and Employees During Transition

1. **Offer emergency contact information to employees.**
Employees might be given names and phone numbers of either the acting CEO or at least two Board members who can be contacted if needed. These two members should brief the entire Board on the nature of any emergency calls from employees, if calls were made.

2. **Have weekly meetings with employees until the new CEO arrives.**
Depending on the size of the organization, have weekly meetings of all employees (if the number is small) or all managers (if large) during the transition until a new Chief Executive is hired. Have a Board member attend the meetings. Have an employee (acting Chief Executive, or the current top reports, or rotate among top reports) attend portions of the Board meetings.

3. **Come up to speed on outgoing CEO's current activities in the organization.**
Have the current Chief Executive ask all employees to update a "to do" list of their current major activities over the past month, planned activities over the coming two months and any major issues they are having now. These "to do" lists will serve to coordinate work details during the transition and help the new Chief Executive come up to speed.

4. **Develop any authorization lists.**
Decide who will issue paychecks and sign off on them during the transition. Often, the Board Treasurer and/or Secretary will conduct this sign-off role.

5. **Board members should meet with the outgoing CEO once a week until he/she goes.**
Review status of work activities, any current issues, etc.

How Your Board Can Determine Your CEO's Compensation

Determination of compensation is one of the most important activities of the Board, especially of a Compensation Committee. However, the Board as a body (with at least a quorum) should approve the approach to determining compensation and benefits, and the resulting amount and benefits. The shareholders are usually quite interested in the Board's process to determine compensation; thus, the process should be fair, accurate and in accordance with standard – and justifiable – practices.

The position of CEO is one of the most critical assets in the organization. It is very important that the CEO's compensation be sufficient to attract, keep and help motivate a highly competent CEO. Much of that activity should be done even before a new CEO is hired. Unfortunately, there is no specific procedure that accurately and reliably computes exactly what you should pay your CEO. Instead, the process is one of addressing certain general and specific considerations, referencing some salary surveys to identify suitable pay ranges for the CEO role in the organization and locale, and making a best estimate on what might be a reasonable salary and set of benefits. This section explains major considerations and suggests additional resources for salary and benefits information.

Board members' explanation of how they addressed each consideration can support and justify the CEO compensation and benefits to stakeholders. That explanation might be valuable if, for example, the organization was ever challenged about its compensation to the CEO.

The following information is not offered as legal or tax advice. Organizations would benefit from consulting experts in the related fields to gain the most up-to-date and thorough advice and materials. In addition to considering the information in this section, Board members would benefit from consulting a local specialist who has expertise in benefits and compensation for executives. Final compensation and benefits decisions should be carefully described in updated personnel policies.

Broad Considerations – Societal, Public and Community

1. **Consider the strength of the economy, local and national.**
    For example, a lower unemployment rate might be reason to offer a higher salary in order to be more competitive with other jobs that the CEO might be able to get. A weak economy, for example, a rate of slow spending or low confidence in the economy, might suggest reason to be conservative, offering a lower salary.

2. **Consider public perception.**
    The public already has strong distaste for the seemingly exorbitant salaries of CEOs. A trend is for some very large businesses to pay their CEOs very high salaries in order to attract highly experienced executives, but this can result in negative public perceptions. Consequently, executive compensation is increasingly under public scrutiny.

3. **Consider pay for similar, local positions with similar products or services.**
    This consideration is one of the strongest to address when determining salary. (The end of this section references a list of sources of salary surveys.)

Considerations – Organizational and Personal

1. **Consider the organization's personnel policies.**
    Personnel policies should have up-to-date guidelines about how to hire, manage and fire personnel in a fair, equitable and legally compliant manner. The guidelines should be reviewed annually by an expert on employment laws and then approved by the Board. Guidelines in the policies should be referenced in case they provide any direction about determining salaries.

2. **Consider the CEO's match to the job description.**
    This consideration is probably the strongest when determining the CEO's salary. The job description should specify the duties and responsibilities of the position, along with ideal and minimal requirements for the position. The closer the match between the CEO's expertise and the job description, the higher the salary that you would offer.

3. **Consider the match between the CEO's expertise and current strategic priorities.**
    For example, if the organization has strategic goals to build a firm foundation for further growth by instilling strong management systems, then a CEO with that kind of experience would warrant a higher salary.

4. **Consider the culture and values of the organization.**
    For example, if the culture highly values an inclusive and participatory management style, then a CEO with those values might warrant a higher salary.

Considerations – Some Restrictions and Limitations

1. **Consider expectations of investors.**
    For example, some investors prefer that administrative costs (such as the CEO's salary, facilities costs and general supplies) be under a certain threshold. The higher the CEO's salary, the greater the likelihood that the organization will exceed that threshold.

2. **Address concerns of governmental agencies.**
    For businesses that are subject to governmental oversight, compensation should be "reasonable" and approved by the Board of Directors. Reasonable compensation might be determined by using salary surveys that depict salaries for similar positions in similar types of organizations in the locale. The Board's approach to determining compensation for employees should be explained in the personnel policies, which also should be approved by the Board. Board members' deliberations and decisions about the compensation should be fully described in the minutes of the Board meeting. If a Board member has a conflict of interest in the consideration, then he/she should abstain from that matter.

3. **Consider requirements for fair and ethical treatment.**
    Compensation should not be based on the CEO's personal features, including age, race, gender, sexual orientation or physical disability. Compensation should be based on the person's expertise and match to the job requirements.

Forms of Compensation and Benefits

Payments

1. **Salary**
    This is the most common form of compensation. Executives in the USA usually are classified by the government as "exempt" (rather than "non-exempt"), meaning they usually should be paid a certain amount (a salary), regardless of the hours worked (within reason). Non-exempt personnel usually are paid by the hour (wages). Salary surveys are extremely useful when determining salary. There is more information about surveys at the end of this section.

2. **Incentive-based compensation (bonuses, stock grants and option grants)**
    Bonuses seem to be used increasingly as means to reward CEOs for his/her, or the organization's, performance. Ideally, the performance is measured in reference to pre-established and specific goals that were discussed with the CEO before this form of compensation is determined and issued. Additionally, stock grants and option grants are another means for the Board to correlate the forms of compensation with the CEO's and the organization's short-term and long-term performance.

3. **Salary adjustments**
    These are sometimes used when organizations do not have funds to pay all of a salary payment. Instead, the business might issue a payment near the end of the year in order to make up for the amount that was not afforded and paid earlier. Sometimes these are paid as means to compensate a CEO who wanted other forms of benefits, such as a certain form of insurance, which the organization was not able to provide. These should not be a regular form of payment, but should be used only on rare occasions when funds for the full salary were not available.

Benefits

1. **Insurances**
    The most common forms of insurance in benefits include life insurance, medical insurance, disability insurance and dental insurance. In the USA, costs of insurance have increased dramatically, resulting in organizations dropping forms of insurance from benefits or expecting employees to pay an increasing percentage of the costs of their insurance.

2. **Pensions and individual retirement plans (deferred compensation)**
    Pensions are not as important as they were decades ago when an employee expected to remain with an organization through his/her entire career. There are a variety of individual retirement options for individuals, such as 401(k) and Roth IRA plans, to which organizations can contribute amounts. Sometimes the organizations provide a "matching" amount, meaning they contribute a certain percentage of the amount contributed by the employee on a regular basis.

Other Forms of Reward

1. **Professional development (and/or tuition reimbursements)**
    This is one of the most important forms of providing value to the CEO because it helps him/her not only to enhance competence and credibility, but also to provide more value and performance to the organization. Many would argue that professional development should not be means of compensation and benefits, but rather should be a right for the CEO within an organization.

2. **Flexible time or compensation time**
    This might be particularly valuable to a CEO who has worked a large number of hours in a certain month or who needs a particular flexible schedule for personal needs, such as family responsibilities.

Using Salary Surveys

It is extremely useful to reference salary surveys when determining salaries. The surveys lend tremendous credibility and fairness to the process of determining compensation. Be sure that surveys are somewhat current. Reference them to find the salaries for the job roles that are the closest match to your CEOs. The closer you can match your CEO role to the type of services, locale and job title, the more useful the survey is likely to be to you, especially if the survey was generated in the past five years or less.

Here is a site with lists of different salary surveys:
http://jobstar.org/tools/salary/index.php .

How Your Board Can Use an Employment Contract With Your CEO

Before hiring a new CEO, it is appropriate to consider how to retain the person in that role. Many organizations directly hire the CEO as an employee. However, some organizations are now considering use of an employment contract instead.

Rather than the standard employee-business relationship that is usually entered into when an employee accepts a letter of offer, an employment contract is like hiring a contractor to do the job of CEO. However the organization might still withhold payroll taxes. Consult a tax specialist about this specific matter because the appropriate governmental tax agency (for example, the Internal Revenue Service in the USA) might be particularly concerned about organizations hiring contractors to avoid paying payroll taxes. The terms of the contract supersede standard personnel requirements as specified in personnel policies and any state laws about "at will" employment. Contracts can bring an extra level of specificity, clarity, credibility and focus to the agreement between the CEO and the organization. Contracts might decrease the likelihood of lawsuits about unfair employee termination because contracts can specify specific start and stop dates of service, so Board members can simply choose not to renew the contract as a means to remove the CEO.

An employment contract might include the following (the following is not offered as legal advice):

- Name of the organization
- Name of the CEO
- Date the contract went into effect
- Date service starts and stops
- Duties and responsibilities to be met (for example, those in a job description)
- Performance goals
- Contractor's conformance to mission, vision, values, plans and policies

- Non-compete and confidentiality requirements
- Specification of compensation and benefits
- Specification of termination (with cause, without cause)
- How the contract can be amended
- Terms of mediation, if needed
- Signatures of all parties

 Consider "How to Hire and Work With Consultants" on page 145.

How Your Board and Employees Can Work Together

Organization Chart of Typical Board and Employee Relationships

The drawing in Table II:8 depicts the typical Board structure. The solid lines indicate formal lines of authority – authority that is official to the position. For example, corporate law asserts that the Board of Directors is legally responsible for the corporation. Therefore, the Chief Executive Officer formally reports to the Board of Directors. The official authority of the Chief Executive Officer position is derived from the Board's specification for the position, for example, in the By-Laws and/or Board-approved job description of the CEO.

The power of the Board is vested in the Board as an entirety of all of its members – no one member has the full authority of the Board. Therefore, the Board Chair (a single Board member) formally reports to the full Board. Committees formally report to the Board Chair or the full Board, depending on the official specification in the By-Laws. Employees, other than the Chief Executive Officer, typically report to the CEO, as specified in the By-Laws and/or Board-approved job description of the Chief Executive.

Table II:8 – Organization Chart of Typical Board and Employees Relationships

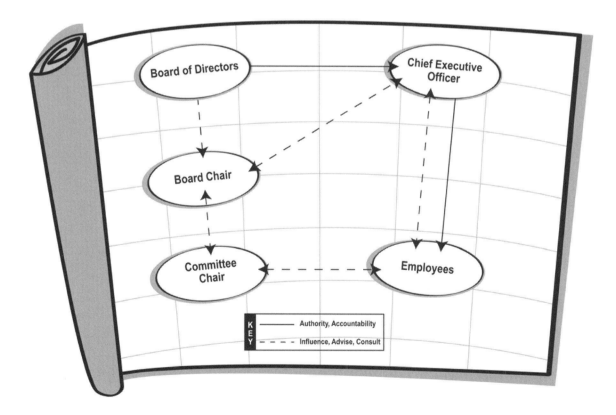

(Adapted with permission of Greater Twin Cities United Way)

Comparing Board and Employee Roles

The following table is adapted from James M. Hardy, *Developing Dynamic Boards* (Essex Press, Erwin, Tennessee, 1990). The nature of the extent of separation between Board and employees, if at all, depends very much on the particular Board model that members prefer.

Table II:9 – Comparison of Board and Employee Roles

Activities	Primary Responsibility
Organizational Planning	
Drive the process of strategic and organizational planning	Board
Provide input to mission and long range goals	Joint
Approve mission and long range, strategic goals	Board
Develop action plans (who does what and when) to achieve long-range goals	Employees
Approve action plans (for example, in an annual Operating Plan)	Board
Implement action plans to achieve long-range goals (Board via committee work plans)	Joint
Follow-up to ensure achievement of major goals and objectives	Board
Board of Directors	
Select new Board members	Board
Orient, train and organize members into committees	Board
Promote attendance at Board/committee meetings	Board
Plan agenda for Board meetings (joint with Board Chair and CEO)	Joint
Take minutes at Board meetings (Board Secretary)	Board
Products and Services	
Assess stakeholder (customers, community, shareholders, etc.) needs	Joint
Suggest customers, outcomes, goals, etc.	Joint
Approve products or services	Board
Ensure evaluation of products or services	Board
Evaluate products or services	Employees
Maintain product and service records; prepare reports	Employees
Financial management	
Prepare preliminary annual budget	Employees
Finalize and approve annual budget	Board
Approve major expenditures outside authorized budget	Board
Ensure annual audit of organization accounts	Board
Ensure that expenditures are within budget during the year	Joint
Personnel Activities	
Employ and supervise Chief Executive Officer	Board
Decision to add general staff roles	Employees
Select / train general staff	Employees
Direct work of the general staff	Employees
Public / Community Relations Activities	
Present / describe organization to community	Joint
Write descriptions of organization (newsletters, web, etc.)	Employees

How Much Should Your Board Be Involved in Management?

Policy-Making Versus Management Activities?

Experts often frame the question in terms of how much Board members should be attending to establishing top-level plans and policies versus how much Board members should be involved in management, that is, in actually implementing those plans and policies.

First, it is helpful to recognize that there are different levels of policies in organizations, as listed below. A policy is a set of guidelines that can guide behaviors in a certain area or practice, including generation of more detailed policies, or procedures.

1.   **Strategic (top-level) policies**
      These affect the entire organization and how it is integrated with other organizations, for example, the organization's mission, vision, values and strategic goals. Strategic policies direct and guide the management activities in the organization.

2.   **Management / functional policies**
      These guide the activities in major functions and operations, for example, Boards, strategic planning, staffing, finances and evaluations.

3.   **Day-to-day policies and procedures**
      These are detailed sets of directions, for example, what to do in case of fire and how to ensure that there is always a sufficient amount of office supplies.

Factors That Influence Focus of Board Members' Involvement

Experts often have strong beliefs and feelings about what should be the extent of involvement of Board members in developing top-level policies versus actually implementing those policies in the day-to-day affairs of the organization. Many experts would assert that Board members should attend primarily to top-level policies. However, various factors influence how involved Board members are in policy making versus "management," that is, in implementing the policies.

- New and small organizations might have hands-on Board members who are somewhat involved in day-to-day activities because the organizations have a very small number of employees.

- Larger, established organizations usually have members who attend primarily to top-level planning and policies because those organizations have adequate resources in staffing to effectively implement top-level policies.

- If Board members have little confidence in the CEO, there have been frequent operational problems, or the CEO is leaving the organization, then Board members often are highly involved in management affairs, at least temporarily.

- Very autocratic cultures usually place strong value on respecting the role of top-level leaders, in which case Board members would be perceived as being on a rather superior level and probably not involved in management affairs.

- Very egalitarian cultures that value equal treatment, value and participation of people might perceive Board members and shareholders to have equal influence in the affairs of the organization, in which case members and others would have similar roles.

- If an organization has been struggling to work toward clear mission and priorities, then Board members (who had previously been focused primarily on the activities of management) should probably focus much more on policy making – thereby ensuring more clear mission and priorities that can be conveyed to all members of the organization.

Regardless of the model chosen by the Board, the organization has to be sure that certain strategic decisions are always made and certain questions are always addressed.

 Consider "Roles and Responsibilities of Board Members" on page 28.

Should Your Employees Be On Your Board?

Many experts assert that employees should not be on the Board because it is an inherent conflict of interest. Board members who are also employees might struggle when trying to govern for the best interests of the organization as a whole. This happens when they encounter the opportunity to make decisions that might benefit themselves personally, such as deliberation over employee salaries. Also, it might be a major challenge for Board members to remain effective when attending to their employee roles.

As with membership of the Chief Executive to the Board (mentioned above), it is probably best if employees are not Board members. This is for some of the same reasons that the Chief Executive eventually should not be a member of the Board. Employees can attend Board meetings (unless the Board is in Executive Session), for example, to make presentations or be acquainted with Board members. Employees, when not attending as official Board members, cannot vote in Board decisions.

How Your Employees Might Participate In Various Board Committees

As with many other aspects of Board design, whether employees are on Board committees or not depends on the nature of the organization. The following diagram depicts what might be a typical arrangement for employees on committees. Terms of whether employees can be on committees should be specified somehow, for example, in the By-Laws and/or in the charter document that describes the purpose of the committee.

Table II:10 – Typical Board Committees with Employee Participation

Employees can provide tremendous value to Board committees because of their strong knowledge of the organization, including its operations. However, the Board Development Committee should be a primary responsibility of the Board members because they should see themselves as primarily responsible for the quality of their own Board operations.

Should Your Employees Attend Your Board Meetings?

It is often a major benefit to have employees attending at least portions of a Board meeting. Remember that the CEO is an employee, as well, and his or her presence in Board meetings is often critical to the success of the Board and the CEO role. Attendance of other employees can be a major benefit as well. For example, presentations by employees to the Board are often very enlightening for Board members. They learn more about employee roles and the benefits employees provide for customers. Employees' attendance to Board meetings should not be discouraged, just coordinated carefully.

There are times (for example, in Executive or in camera Sessions) when Board members should hold meetings that are private amongst themselves. This may be to consider the CEO's performance or deliberate about how to handle a pending lawsuit.

PART III:

CORE SKILLS FOR

LEADING AND

MANAGING

To Lead Others, First Lead Yourself

Skills to lead oneself are often the most neglected skills, yet they are the most important in being an effective leader of others. Therefore, this Guide provides substantial information about leading oneself.

Understand the Typical Experiences of First-Time Leaders

They Rarely Have Adequate Training

Often, the first leadership position for an employee is that of supervisor. They are promoted to supervision because of their strong technical expertise – expertise in building a product or providing a service. Suddenly, the new supervisor is now charged with a whole new range of responsibilities, many of which have little to do with technical expertise.

People are not predictable. They have moods, illnesses, career expectations and crises in their family lives. The supervisor's original field of expertise, especially if somewhat technical, can be useless when it comes to supervising people.

Sometimes Intimidated by Wide Range of Policies and Procedures

The new supervisor is suddenly faced with a wide range of rules and regulations – each of which the supervisor is responsible to enforce. The supervisor is often responsible for signing time cards, authorizing overtime, granting compensation time, dealing with performance problems, developing job descriptions, following hiring procedures, dealing with grievances, conforming to a complicated pay system, and the list goes on. It can be quite difficult to conform to today's wide range of employee laws, rules and regulations – and at the same time, produce a product or service.

New Supervisors Rarely Have Enough Time

No matter how many courses or degrees a new supervisor has completed, they are often surprised that management activities are so hectic and demanding. No matter how thorough the planning, managers rarely get to spend much time on any one activity. The role of most managers, whether new supervisors or executives, is interspersed with frequent interruptions. Any surprises in the work or lives of employees are a sudden demand on supervisors.

New supervisors often expect to have complete knowledge of everything that goes on in their group. They do not want to encounter any surprises. So they spend more time reading, thinking, planning, communicating with employees – new supervisors often spend 60 hours a week on the job. Still, they do not feel they have enough time to do the job right.

New Supervisors Often Feel Very Alone

Each manager has a unique role in the organization. Each organization is unique. Usually there are no standard procedures for dealing with all of the numerous challenges that suddenly face management. Ultimately, it is up to each manager to get through the day. Faced with a great deal of pressure, little time and continuing demands from other people, the new supervisor can feel quite alone.

The supervisor is responsible to be an advocate for the organization and an advocate for the employee. For example, if the organization implements an unpopular new policy, the supervisor is often responsible to communicate and justify that new policy to the employee. In this case, management expects the supervisor to present and support the new policy, and the employee vents his or her frustration to the supervisor. However, if the supervisor wants to promote the employee or present some other reward, he or she is now representing the employee's case to the rest of management. The supervisor is often alone, stuck in the middle.

The new supervisor wants to impress others as having deserved his/her promotion, as being in control of the situation. It is difficult to seek help from others in the organization. Even when there is someone to talk to, it is difficult to fully explain the situation – the new supervisor sometimes does not know how things got so hectic and confusing.

New Supervisors Often Feel Overwhelmed, Stressed Out

The new supervisor is responsible, often for the first time, for the activities of another employee. The supervisor must ensure the employee knows his or her job, has the resources to do the job and does the job as effectively as possible.

Until new supervisors develop a "feeling for the territory," they often deal with the stresses of supervision by working harder, rather than smarter. They miss the comfort and predictability of the previous jobs.

The stress and loneliness in the role of new supervisor can bring out the worst in people. If they deal with stress by retreating, they will retreat to their office and close the door. If they deal with stress as frustration, they will become angry and unreasonable with others. If they are used to getting strong praise and high grades, they will work harder and harder until their jobs become their lives.

Support and Development Are Critical for New Supervisors

Courses in supervision, delegation, time management, stress management, etc., are not enough. New supervisors need ongoing coaching and support. They need someone in whom they can confide. Ideally, they have a mentor in the organization that remembers what it is like to be a first-time supervisor, someone who makes himself or herself available.

If the experience of first-time supervision is successful, then the supervisor goes on to become a progressive, supportive leader and manager of other supervisors.

Understand Your Biases and How They Affect Others

Your biases play a major role in how you perceive others. Your perceptions are your reality, whether they are the reality for someone else or not. Differences in perception between you and others can make the difference between successful leadership and a complete disaster. So know your own biases! For example:

- Do you believe that leaders should "take charge" and lead from the front of the organization? If so, you might encounter frustration and resistance when working with others who believe that leaders should lead from the middle.

- Do you believe that others should just "shut up and listen to you?" If so, they will probably only do what you say – and no more – until their frustration is overwhelming and they leave.

68

- Do you believe that meetings should start and end on time? If so, you will certainly be frustrated with people from cultures that place far less emphasis on time.

- Do you believe that most problems would be solved if people just did "what they were supposed to do"? What if people really do not know what they are supposed to do?

How to Articulate Your Professional Mission and Values

Your professional mission and values serve as your "compass" in life and work. They guide how you make decisions and solve problems, especially during complex and challenging activities. For many of us, our mission and values are implicit – we have not taken the time to clarify them explicitly or to write them down. Without explicitly proclaiming the mission and values from which we want to operate as leaders, we are prone to getting ourselves into situations – and operating in those situations – in a manner that does not match our nature and needs. Your professional mission and values can be communicated to others to help them understand and trust you, which is critical in effective leadership. Therefore, it is important for leaders to carefully consider articulating their own mission and values, ideally into mission statements and values statements.

Developing Your Professional Mission Statement

There are various perspectives on mission statements. Some people believe the statements should describe an overall purpose. Some people believe the mission should also include a description of a vision, or future state. Some people believe the mission should also include a description of overall values. Mission statements can be just a few sentences long.

There are also various perspectives on how to develop a mission statement. The process of producing your own professional mission statement is as important as the mission statement itself. Therefore, it is important for you to carefully think about your own mission before you reference any mission statements produced by others.

When you write your professional mission statement, it should:

1. Succinctly describe the purpose of your career and leadership activities.

2. Mention the particular results (new knowledge, skills and/or conditions) that you work to help your people and you to achieve.

3. Mention any particular strengths and expertise that you have and will use.

4. Be clearly understandable by your people and you.

Developing Your Professional Values Statement

Your professional values statement describes the most important priorities in the nature of how you want to lead others and yourself. Some people might prefer to do a principles statement. Principles are descriptions of values in action and often begin with the phrase, "I will ..." or "I believe ..." Similar to the mission statement, the process of producing the values statement is as important as the values statement itself. The following guidelines will be helpful to you as you develop your own professional values statement.

1.   **When identifying values, think about behaviors produced by those values.**
      Many of us struggle to directly identify desired values. We can get bogged down in words
      that seem too general, idealized – even romanticized – to be useful. Often, it helps first to
      identify desired behaviors and then the values that produce those behaviors.

2.   **Consider relevant employment laws, for example, to protect minorities and disabled.**
      Identify behaviors or values that will help you avoid breaking these laws and follow the
      necessary regulations, for example, not to discriminate against others.

3.   **Consider your own lens, biases, style, response to feedback and conflict.**
      You might identify behaviors and values that will help you to counter any potential
      misperceptions or obstacles that you might develop because of your own particular nature
      and needs.

4.   **Consider any current, major issues in your work.**
      Identify the behaviors needed to resolve these issues and to identify which values would
      generate those preferred behaviors, for example, team building and more productivity.

5.   **Consider any ethical values that might be prized by your people.**
      Consider expectations of customers, suppliers, investors and members of the local
      community, for example, strong reliability, honesty and integrity.

6.   **From the above steps, select the top five to ten values.**
      You cannot be all things to all people, including to yourself. Even if you do include all the
      values on your statement, it is still important for you to carefully think about which values
      are most important to you.

7.   **Associate with each value, two example behaviors which reflect each value.**
      Examples of behaviors for each value make the values much more explicit and understood to
      you and to others, for example, the behaviors of sharing communications and helping fellow
      employees can be associated with the value of developing teamwork.

8.   **Update the statement at least once a year.**
      The most important aspect of the statement is developing it, not the statement itself.
      Continued dialogue and reflection around your values cultivates awareness and sensitivity to
      act in accordance to your values. Therefore, revisit your statement at least once – preferably
      two or three times – a year.

How to Manage Your Motivation

Leaders are like everyone else. They must manage for balance in their lives and their work. If the
leaders do not seem motivated, then other employees will probably not be motivated either.
Therefore, leaders in the organization must give attention to managing their own personal motivation
– and it can be managed.

Guidelines

1.   **Learn to delegate.**
      This is one of the most critical skills for a leader. Delegation involves assigning tasks to
      your employees along with the necessary authority and resources that they can learn to carry
      out the tasks in their own way. Assign the "what" and guide them to figure out the "how."

2. **Even if you do not like goals, set some goals, however small.**
   Without goals, you probably will not know if you are really accomplishing anything. Working hard is not necessarily an end in itself – especially if you expect your employees to do the same thing. Set some small goals. It will be good practice for you if you have not done that before. (If you do not like goals, then you are in for a major challenge in leading a business because, without goals, it is very difficult to give direction and measure success.)

3. **Celebrate accomplishments.**
   Many hard-working people seem to believe that celebrating accomplishments is a form of complacency, that the job should be celebration in itself. Those beliefs can hold true maybe for the first couple years of the leader's job. Then the grind gets old. It is critical for employees to recognize that they are accomplishing something – it is usually not enough to be continually "working for the cause." Take time out to recognize what did get done and celebrate the accomplishments.

4. **Ask for help.**
   It can be quite difficult for leaders to ask for help. Often, they are passionate, hard-working people who want to be able to carry their own load. Thus, they are often reluctant to ask for help from others in the organization. This is a mistake, particularly for the Chief Executive Officer. The quality of the relationship between the Board Chair and Chief Executive Officer is one of the most important determinants of the success of a corporation. This relationship can be built around mutual support, especially if the Chief Executive Officer knows how to ask for – and value – the help from the Board.

5. **Find out what motivates you – it is not the same for everyone.**
   One of the most important learnings for new supervisors is that different things can motivate different people. Consider the following reference.

 Consider "How to Support Your Employee's Self-Motivation" on page 194.

6. **Get some direct contact with your customers.**
   Few things are as motivational as hearing from a customer how he/she benefited from the products or services of your business. Unfortunately, it is too easy for leaders to inadvertently become detached from providing direct service and to get lost in the management activities of the business. At least once a month, have a customer come to an employee-wide meeting and share his/her experiences with the business.

7. **Post the mission of your business on the walls of all the rooms in your facilities.**
   It is amazing how many organizations give careful thought to the wording of their mission statements, and then file them away in file cabinets. Post your mission statement in all the rooms in your facility. Notice it each day. The mission statement depicts the reason that the business even exists.

8. **Follow simple guidelines of time and stress management.**
   With a few simple steps, you can make a lot of difference in managing your stress, often by first addressing how you spend your own time.

Consider "How to Manage Your Time and Stress – Avoiding Burnout" on page 75.

9.   **Watch your diet. Get enough sleep.**
Do not resort to lots of caffeine and sugar to give you a boost. Research shows that the boost is usually followed by a major let down in energy. It is better to get up for a short walk, get some protein and do some stretches. Also, it is interesting how bleak the world looks to people who do not eat right or do not get enough sleep. A little bit of the right kinds of food and more sleep can make the world seem a lot better.

10.   **Get some variety in your job.**
Do not get lost in the "circle of paperwork." Often, the only way that you will get variety in your work is to schedule it. Schedule time to provide direct services to customers. Schedule time to help clean out the storage closet.

11.   **Have personal goals.**
Even if you have a few goals, at least those goals are in regard to your own development. Examples of goals might be to become acquainted with at least three other Chief Executive Officers or managers of organizations in your geographic area, or read a book a week, or even to start a hobby.

12.   **Get some professional development.**
Go to a course. Join a professional networking organization. Read professional journals that relate to your services. Join a Speakers Bureau to share your knowledge.

13.   **Be sure that your job makes sense to you. Have an overall strategic plan.**
One of the best outcomes from a strategic plan is that it helps to make sense of all of the work going on around people. People get some perspective and, thus, some meaning from their jobs.

Consider "How to Set Clear Purpose and Direction for the Business" on page 101.

14.   **Write status reports.**
Status reports can be weekly reports that document what you have accomplished over the past week, any highlights and trends and issues that currently exist, and what you plan to do next week. One of the most important outcomes from this activity is the opportunity to stand back, think about your job, and notice that you are actually getting a lot done.

15.   **Understand Founder's Syndrome.**
This Syndrome can occur with almost anyone in the organization, not just the Founder. It is not unusual that the people who work the hardest in an organization (and are most prone to burnout) are also the people around whom all else seems to revolve. It is hard not to be the "hero" of the workplace, the person who gets everything done. Too often, this hero becomes the unintended villain when the organization succumbs to Founder's Syndrome.

Consider "Founder's Syndrome – How to Detect It, How to Avoid It" on page 247.

16.   **Know when to leave.**
It may be that you and your job just have to part, that you are simply no longer motivated in your work. It is a wise leader who can recognize this and arrange for a healthy transition to a new leader.

How to Appreciate – Critical Ability for Leaders

Why Is the Ability to Appreciate Accomplishments So Important?

Particularly with personnel in small- to medium-size organizations, it is rare that there is not a large amount of work to do. Because time is such a precious commodity in these organizations, it is common that their people cannot provide sustained effort to priorities and projects. Many times, they get put on "hold" for a few weeks as people attend to other sudden demands for their time, for example, developing a major proposal for a new customer, the Chief Executive Officer's leaving for vacation, preparing for their annual meeting, or finishing a large product evaluation. For you and your employees, it can seem that activities have stalled out completely.

For many of us, it can seem like we are stuck in a merry-go-round that never goes anywhere and we cannot seem to get off. By ignoring our accomplishments, we are ignoring vast portions of our lives and our work – our perspective can become skewed and incomplete. That perspective can be a major obstacle to the success of leaders.

How Can You Maintain Appreciation for Appreciation?

As a leader, you can make a big difference in your effectiveness and that of your peoples' accomplishments if all of you have the ability to recognize and appreciate your accomplishments regularly. Consider the following guidelines.

1.   **Convey the importance of appreciation when you start working with others.**
Explain how important it is to recognize accomplishments as well as the tasks yet to be done. Mention it is really important in small- to medium-sized organizations.

2.   **Ask employees for ideas about how to regularly recognize completion of tasks.**
Different cultures have different practices. Some might prefer a simple "Thank you," while others might prefer a ritual of some sort. Therefore, it is important early in your leadership role to get ideas from your people.

3.   **When planning, build in acknowledgement of completion in plans.**
Planning always results in a list of things to do. Too often, the design of the plans does not include means to recognize accomplishments. Planning is one of the best opportunities to regularly build in means to recognize accomplishments.

4.   **Design project tasks so it is clear whether they were finished or not.**
This is often one of the biggest challenges in developing a sense of appreciation. Ideally, goals, objectives and other tasks are designed to be SMART, an acronym for specific, measurable, achievable, relevant and timely.

5. **Regularly acknowledge the completion of the tasks or progress on tasks.**
Always seek to find opportunities to appreciate the work of your people. That practice can be a powerful means to model behaviors that they learn from in their lives and work.

How to Keep It Real – Managing for Realistic Expectations

It is not uncommon that when people have been struggling with a major issue, they urgently search for quick fixes to address those issues. That search can cause a great deal of despair and cynicism. Consequently, one of the most important requirements for successful leadership is for your people and you to share the same relevant and realistic expectations. Consider the following approaches:

1. **Use authentic behavior to verify whether plans are relevant and realistic.**
It is important for your people and you to speak up if you have any confusion and concerns whatsoever about suggestions, recommendations, plans or actions. This is true particularly if plans and expectations seem unrealistic.

2. **Regularly ask your people for their perceptions of how the business is doing.**
It is important that both your people and you frequently discuss the quality and progress of activities. One of the outcomes from those discussions is verification of your mutual expectations, as they may shift over time.

3. **Avoid quick fixes.**
The typical organization is short on time, money and people. There can be tremendous pressure to get a lot done and to do it quickly. However, it takes time to cultivate long-lasting change. You are far better off to take your time and do it right, than to have your people and you lose credibility in your leadership.

4. **Acknowledge both the ups and the downs that often occur in businesses.**
Inexperienced leaders sometimes count on optimism and good wishes to motivate people for change. That approach may work for the short-term, but rarely for the long-term. So, trust and respect your people enough to tell them the whole story.

5. **Use written action plans, specifying who is doing what and by when.**
At the end of each one-on-one and group meeting, always review who is going to do what and by when. Document plans and share them with others involved in the effort.

6. **Conduct coaching sessions around your employee's current issues and goals.**
Coaching sessions can be useful for relevant and realistic action planning to specify who is going to do what and by when, and in particular, whether those plans are realistic. The sessions also collect key learning about plans and actions.

Consider "How to Coach for Deep Problem-Solving and Learning" on page 202.

How to Manage Your Time and Stress – Avoiding Burnout

The two topics of time management and stress management are often addressed together because they are so closely intertwined.

Myths About Stress and Time Management

1. **All stress is bad.**
    No, some stress is good and some is bad. Good stress can include excitement or thrills. The goal is to recognize your personal signs of bad stress and deal with them.

2. **Planning my time just takes more time.**
    Planning helps you work smarter, rather than harder. The attitude that stopping to plan is a problem is itself a symptom of stress and time management problems.

3. **I get more done in more time when I use caffeine, sugar, alcohol or nicotine.**
    Wrong! Research shows that the body always has to "come down." When it does, you will not be effective in your work, which offsets whatever gains you achieved from the boost from these stimulants.

4. **A time problem means there is not enough time to do what I need to do.**
    No, a time management problem is not using your time to your fullest advantage to get done what you want done. You need to know what you really want to do.

5. **The busier I am, the better I am using my time.**
    You may only be doing what seems urgent, and not what is important. Doing what is important often addresses the many matters that later seem to be urgent.

6. **I feel very hurried and busy, so I must have a time management problem.**
    Not necessarily. You should verify that you have a time management problem. This requires knowing what you really want to get done and if it is getting done or not.

7. **I feel OK, so I must not be stressed.**
    In reality, many adults do not even know when they are really stressed out until their bodies tell them so. They miss the early warning signs from their bodies.

Major Causes of Stress

1. **Not knowing what you want or if you are getting it – poor planning.**
    If you ask adults where they are needed, they can give you many answers. If you ask them what they want, they often struggle to answer.

2. **The *feeling* that there is too much to do.**
    One can have this feeling even if there is hardly anything to do at all. Knowing what you want to do often helps address the vague feelings that there is too much to do.

3. **Not enjoying your work.**
    This can be caused by lots of things, such as, not knowing what you want or not eating well.

4.   **Conflicting demands in your work.**
      Unless you have some sense of your priorities, it is likely that you will feel conflicting demands in your work.

5.   **Having insufficient resources to do your work.**
      As a leader, one of your most important resources is usually your time. You will benefit a great deal from finding your own style of time management.

6.   **Not feeling appreciated.**
      This can be a major problem for leaders. You can ask your people to tell you how you are doing. You have to accept and remember their compliments.

Biggest Time Wasters

1.   **Interruptions**
      There will always be interruptions. The interruptions are not the problem. The problem is how they are handled.

2.   **Hopelessness**
      People "give in," "numb out" and "march through the day." This is probably the worst time and stress management problem. Other guidelines in this section can help you to avoid this time waster.

3.   **Poor delegation skills**
      This involves not asking for help and/or sharing work with others. You can ask your people for help, consider working with colleagues or cut back your workload.

Common Symptoms of Poor Stress and Time Management

1.   **Irritability**
      Your family, friends, peers and employees usually notice this before you do. If they have noticed your symptoms, you will have to find a better means to manage your time and stress.

2.   **Fatigue**
      How many adults even notice this? We often work with a vague sense of tiredness. Your body sends the first message of problems, so learn to sense your own fatigue.

3.   **Difficulty concentrating**
      You can often get through the day without concentrating, so this symptom can go unnoticed.

4.   **Forgetfulness**
      If you cannot remember what you did all day, what you ate today or whom you talked to, then you need to address your time and stress problem as soon as possible.

5.   **Loss of sleep**
      This affects everything else! Recognize what you can do to have a full night's sleep, for example, cut back on coffee or do not work late.

6.   **Physical disorders**
      Common symptoms are headaches, rashes, tics or cramps. At worst, consistent withdrawal and depression.

Wise Principles of Good Stress and Time Management

1. **Learn your signs for being overstressed or having a time management problem.**
    Ask your friends about you. Perhaps they can tell you what they see when you are overstressed. Their feedback is often more accurate than your own perceptions.

2. **Most people *feel* that they are stressed and/or have a time problem.**
    Verify that you really have a problem. What do you see, hear or feel that leads you to conclude that you have a time or stress problem?

3. **Do not have the illusion that doing more will make you happier.**
    Is it the quantity of time that you want or the quality? If not quantity or quality, then what?

4. **Stress and time problems usually require more than one technique to fix.**
    You do not need a lot of techniques, but usually more than one. Pick a few that are realistic and practical, get started, notice your successes and give yourself credit.

5. **One of the major benefits of time planning is feeling that you are in control.**
    It might even help at this point to think about what you mean by "control." Does it mean that you control everything in your life or only what is most important in the long run?

6. **Focus on results, not on "busyness."**
    This guideline is the main point about performance – a person can seem busy, but that does not mean that he/she is actually accomplishing what is most important.

7. **The trying counts – at least as much as finishing the perfect technique.**
    As people get older and wiser, they let go of frustrations around not achieving enough quantity of things. Instead, they focus on the quality of the process.

Simple Techniques to Manage Stress

There are many things people can do to cut down on bad stress. Most people probably even know what they could do. It is not the lack of knowing what to do to cut down stress – it is doing what you know you have to do. The following techniques are geared to help you do what you know you have to do.

1. **Talk to someone.**
    You do not have to fix the problem. Similar to addressing resistance and conflicts, it often makes a big difference just to recognize and name the problem.

2. **Notice if any of the muscles in your body are tense.**
    Just noticing that will often relax the muscles. Pay attention to your neck, shoulders, arms and legs. Tightness? Soreness?

3. **Ask your employees if you are doing OK.**
    This simple question can make a lot of difference. Also, it further helps to build trust and openness between you and your employees.

4. **Ask for help.**
    Ask peers. Hire some help. Get a mentor. Get a coach. Join a support or networking group.

5.   **If you take on a technique to manage stress, tell someone else.**
      They can help you be accountable to them and yourself. Otherwise, your attempts to use
      techniques can get lost in the other time and stress problems that you have.

6.   **Cut down on caffeine and sweets.**
      It is difficult to cut down on something without replacing it with something else instead. Do
      isometric exercises. Chew sugarless gum.

7.   **Use basic techniques of planning, problem solving and decision-making.**
      Concise guidelines are in this Guide. It might help to focus on the 2080 Rule, that is, do the
      20% of effort that generates 80% of result. Remember, it is often the trying that counts, not
      just the final results.

8.   **Monitor the number of hours that you work in a week.**
      Tell your family, friends and peers how many hours that you are working per week now and
      how many hours that you intend to work.

9.   **Write status reports.**
      Reports can be drudgery to finish, but they are usually helpful to remind you of what you
      have done. You should be writing reports anyway.

10.   **"Wash the dishes."**
      Do something simple that you can feel good about. Following this guideline, as with others,
      starts with gumption: making that initial effort to move yourself.

Simple Techniques to Manage Time

The goal of time management should not be to find more time. The goal is to spend time on what
you really need and want to be spending time on.

1.   **Start with the simple techniques of stress management above.**
      Many times, techniques of stress management are valuable in managing time, as well.

2.   **Practice.**
      Practice asking yourself throughout the day: "Is this what I want or need to be doing right
      now?" If yes, keep doing it. If not, get help from family and friends.

3.   **Analyze your time.**
      Logging your time for a week in 15-minute intervals is not that hard and does not take up
      that much time. Do it for a week and review your results. This is both realistic and an
      objective way to analyze your time.

4.   **Do a "to do" list for your day at the end of the previous day.**
      Mark items as "A" and "B" in priority. Set aside two hours right away each day to do the
      important "A" items and then do the "B" items in the afternoon. Let your voicemail or
      someone else take your calls during your "A" time.

5.   **At the end of your day, spend five minutes cleaning up your space.**
      Use this time, too, to organize your space, including your desktop. That will give you a
      clean and fresh start for the next day.

6. **Learn the difference between "Where am I needed?" and "What do I want?"**
   The former question is about your employee's time. The latter question is about yours.

7. **Distinguish between "Do I need to do this now?" and "Do I need to do it at all?"**
   Finding the answers might require some careful reflection about what has been important in the past and what is important to you now.

8. **Use a "Do Not Disturb" sign!**
   During the prime part of the day, when you are attending to your important items (your "A" list), hang this sign on the doorknob outside your door.

9. **Sort your mail into categories: "read now," "handle now," "trash" and "read later."**
   You will quickly get a knack for sorting through mail. You will also notice that much of what you think you need to read was not really all that important anyway.

10. **Read your mail at the same time each day.**
    That way, you will likely get to your mail on a regular basis and will not become distracted into any certain piece of mail that ends up taking too much of your time.

11. **Have a place for everything and put everything in its place.**
    That way, you will know where to find it when you need it. Perhaps the most important outcome is that you have a *feeling* of being in control.

12. **Schedule 10 minutes to do nothing.**
    That time can be used to just sit and clear your mind. You will end up thinking more clearly, resulting in more time that is productive in your day. The best outcome of this practice is that it reminds you that you are not a slave to a clock – and that if you take 10 minutes out of your day, your work will not fall apart.

Understand How You Solve Problems and Make Decisions

Different people have quite different preferences and approaches for solving problems and making decisions. Those differences can often cause conflict between people unless they each understand their own particular preferences.

The following preferences represent probably the most common. It is important for you to note that any preference is not necessarily better than others. Certain preferences might work better in certain situations. The important point for you to realize is the diverse ways that people – including you – address problems and decisions. Consider that diversity when leading others.

Rational Versus Organic Approach to Problem Solving

Rational

A person with this preference often prefers using a comprehensive and logical approach similar to the following procedure. The rational approach, described below, is often used when addressing large, complex matters, for example, when conducting strategic planning.

1. Define the problem.

2. Examine all potential causes for the problem.

3.   Identify all alternatives to resolve the problem.

4.   Carefully select an alternative.

5.   Develop an orderly implementation plan to implement that best alternative.

6.   Carefully monitor implementation of the plan.

7.   Verify if the problem has been resolved or not.

A major advantage of this approach is that it gives a strong sense of order in an otherwise chaotic situation and provides a common frame of reference from which people can communicate in the situation. A major disadvantage of this approach is that it can take a long time to finish. Some people might argue, too, that the world is much too chaotic for the rational approach to be useful.

Organic

Some people assert that the dynamics of organizations and people are not nearly so mechanistic as to be improved by solving one problem after another. Often, the quality of an organization or life comes from how one handles being "on the road" itself, rather than "arriving at the destination." The quality comes from the ongoing process of trying, rather than from having fixed a lot of problems. For many people it is an approach to leading organizations. The following quote explains the organic (or holistic) approach to problem solving.

> *"All the greatest and most important problems in life are fundamentally insoluble ...*
> *They can never be solved, but only outgrown. This "outgrowing" proves on further*
> *investigation to require a new level of consciousness. Some higher or wider interest*
> *appeared on the horizon and through this broadening of outlook, the insoluble lost*
> *its urgency. It was not solved logically in its own terms, but faded when confronted*
> *with a new and stronger life urge."*
>
>   From Jung, Carl, *Psychological Types (*Pantheon Books, 1923)

A major advantage of the organic approach is that it is highly adaptable to understanding and explaining the chaotic changes that occur in organizations and everyday life. It also suits the nature of people who shun linear and mechanistic approaches to projects. The major disadvantage is that the approach often provides little clear and consistent frame of reference around which people can communicate, feel comfortable and measure progress toward solutions to problems.

Intuitive Versus Sensing Approaches to Gathering Information

There are a variety of assessment instruments that are often referenced when helping people understand their own unique styles when solving problems and making decisions, for example, the Myers-Briggs Type Indicator® instrument. One of the dimensions of the Myers-Briggs is "Intuitive versus Sensing," which considers how a person gathers information. (Myers-Briggs is a registered trademark of Consulting Psychologists Press, Inc.).

Intuitive

Highly intuitive people often gather information instinctively. They thrive on ideas and possibilities. They might seem oblivious to what is going on around them, yet they often effectively solve problems and make decisions based on surprisingly valid information. Many times, they might not even know how they did it. Some experts on leadership and management assert that highly experienced people often have developed intuition that enables them to make quick, effective decisions. A major advantage of this approach is that it can save a great deal of time. A major challenge can be how to explain their choices to others.

Sensing

These people thrive on facts and information. They are detail-oriented and accuracy is extremely important to them. They are aware of their physical surroundings, of who is saying what. They solve problems and make decisions by considering the "data" around them. One of the major advantages of sensing people is that their actions are often based on valid information. Thus, they are able to explain their reasoning and their actions to others. A major challenge is the time and care required for them to solve problems and make decisions.

Thinking Versus Feeling Approaches to Process Information

Another major dimension of the Myers-Briggs Indicator® instrument is "Thinking versus Feeling," which considers how a person makes decisions about information.

Thinking

A thinking person often uses a highly objective, sometimes rational approach to organizing, analyzing and making decisions about information. At their extreme, he/she might shun consideration of emotions. The thinking person probably prefers the rational approach to problem solving as described above in this subsection. The advantage of this approach is that it often generates valid problem solving and decision-making. A major challenge can be that it might require an extensive amount of time to come to action.

Feeling

The feeling approach is used most often by individuals who are quite sensitive to their values in processing information. When people focus on their values, emotions often come into play. A major advantage of this approach is that it can help to ensure that people are happy and fulfilled in the situation – that their values have been considered during the process and are reflected in the outcome. A major challenge is that there are a variety of short-term factors other than the current major problem or decision that can influence a person's emotions, for example, his/her not having had enough sleep or having eaten right.

Understand How You Respond to Feedback and Conflict

How Do You Respond to Feedback?

One of the best ways to influence your employees is to model the behavior that you want from them. Usually, you want them to be open to receiving feedback, whether the feedback is about the organization and its problems or even about the role that your people play in the problems. Thus, to model that kind of behavior, you want to be open to feedback yourself. Often, that is easier said than done.

In this context, feedback is information about your actions or performance and is information that you act on. This is in contrast to information that is about others or is either too vague or indirect to be useful to you.

Feedback from others might make you feel uncomfortable. However, you can manage your reactions in response to their feedback. Even if you feel threatened, frustrated or angry about the feedback, you can remind yourself that the feedback is not necessarily directed at you personally. Often, the feedback has more to do with another's fear about something than about you as a person.

You can also remind yourself that feedback from others is a valuable gift to you. For example, it is not uncommon that leaders get so highly involved in the organization's problems that they lose the professional objectivity required to be effective. Feedback from others can be valuable forms of learning in these situations.

How Do You Respond to Conflict?

Experienced leaders realize that conflict is a natural outcome from interactions among different people and from changes in an organization. Conflict can have a variety of causes, for example, differences in perceptions among people, feelings of fear or disrespect, power conflicts, poor communication techniques or just plain fatigue during organizational change.

Conflict is not inherently bad. Problems come from how the conflict is addressed. Effective conflict management includes focusing on the issue at the heart of the conflict, rather than on the personalities of the people involved. It includes using effective means of communication, such as effective listening, supportive questioning and noticing non-verbal (non-spoken) communications.

You want your employees to advantageously recognize and manage their conflicts, rather than denying that those conflicts exist or engaging in ongoing destructive arguments with others. You can model successful conflict management by effectively responding to conflict within yourself.

It is not uncommon for people to have strong emotions, especially about major changes in the organization. It will be important for you to carefully respond to those emotions, including recognizing them and allowing people the freedom to express them. How you respond to conflict yourself is often how you respond to the strong emotions of others.

What Is Your Emotional Intelligence?

There are different definitions for emotional intelligence (EI), but it is probably fair to generalize that it is the ability to recognize our emotions and then manage our responses to those emotions in a manner that enhances our health and relationships with others. There are some basic guidelines that might be helpful in enhancing your own EI. Consider the following basic guidelines:

1. Notice how you are feeling and be able to name the emotion, for example, mad, glad, sad or bad. Be careful not to get confused between your thoughts and feelings. Notice the difference between and then use "I feel …" and "I think …" statements.

2. Notice how you judge those emotions, for example, you might believe that "it is scary and bad to feel angry."

3. Notice what situations typically evoke those emotions in you.

4. Notice the difference between your emotions and your outward responses to those emotions – what others would see you do and say. Ask yourself how you choose to feel about something and whether your behavior is aligned with that choice.

5. Realize that it is OK to have strong emotional reactions. It is what you do with those emotions that can be a problem for you and others.

6. Notice how long you retain those emotions. What changes them?

7. Notice what makes you happy and plan for those situations on a regular basis.

8. Notice how you make conclusions about other peoples' feelings. What are they doing or saying?

Understand How You View Organizations

One of the most frequent reasons that experts and leaders argue about the best methods for organizational change is because they often have a different perspective, or lens, through which they view organizations. The impact of these differences is often underestimated. For example, you can have two different people study an organization and then provide very different descriptions of the same organization. Therefore, it is critical that people understand their own perspective and be sensitive to the perspectives of others.

 One of the most useful resources to explain these perspectives is *Reframing Organizations* (Bolman and Deal, Jossey-Bass, 1991). The authors depict four quite different and major organizational perspectives among researchers, writers, educators, consultants and members of organizations.

Table III:1 – Various "Lens" Through Which We View Organizations

Lens	Examples of What is Noticed or Talked About from That Lens
Structural	Goals, objectives, roles, responsibilities, performance, policies and procedures, efficiency, hierarchy and coordination and control
Human Resource	Participation, feelings, fulfillment, communication, needs of people, relationships, motivation, enrichment and commitment
Political	Power, conflict, competition, authority, experts, coalitions, allocation of resources, bargaining and decision making
Symbolic	Rituals, culture, values, stories, different perspectives, language, expressions, myths, commitment and metaphors

Note that these are horizontal lenses regarding what different people notice across the activities in organizations. There are also many vertical lenses through which we view intra-personal dynamics, for example, the many perspectives put forth in the increasing amount of books on personal development.

It is important for you to realize that no lens, or perspective, is better than the others. Experienced leaders have learned that the more perspectives that they can get from their employees about an issue in their organization, often the more accurate and useful are the plans to address that issue. Thus, the more lenses through which you can view organizations, the more useful you will be to your employees and yourself.

How to Manage Your Own Professional Development

Professional development is learning how to be more effective in your current and planned roles in your life, work and career. Leaders, in particular those leading small to medium-sized organizations, often tend to forget professional development – usually because there are not sufficient funds to pay for development. There are many free or low-cost sources of professional development. The key is to use them.

Free, or Low-Cost, Sources of Professional Development

1. **Join an online discussion group.**
    There are numerous free, online groups.

    Numerous groups are listed at
    http://www.managementhelp.org/gen_rsrc/newsgrps/newsgrps.htm .

2. **Attend workshops and seminars.**
    Many cities have local management support organizations. Contact local universities and colleges for courses on business management.

3. **Form a local book study.**
    Pick a book about business management (you are holding one). Call several of your peers. Invite them to get a copy of this Guide, get together once a week or month and discuss certain topics from the Guide.

4. **Regularly reflect on your activities in your job.**
    Your job can be a wonderful source of learning! Schedule even just 15 minutes a week to look back on your week. Ask yourself:

    a. What did I do?

    b. What did I learn from that? (Think of enhanced knowledge, skills or values.)

    c. How can I take that learning forward into my life and work?

5. **Keep in mind that you do not have to know it all in order to be effective at your job.**
    Adults tend to learn best when they actually *apply* new information and materials to current, real-life challenges. Therefore, you will learn what you need when you need it.

6. **Consider forming your own peer group of leaders.**
    In these groups, members help each other to reach goals by exchanging ongoing feedback and support.

Summary Principles for Staying Sane When Leading in Business

Everyone in management has gone through the transition from individual contributor to manager. Each person finds his/her own way to "survive." The following guidelines will help you to keep your perspective and your health.

1. **Monitor your work hours.**
    The first visible, undeniable sign that things are out of hand is that you are working far too many hours. Note how many hours you are working per week. Set a limit and stick to that limit. Ask your peers or boss for help.

2. **Recognize your own signs of stress.**
    Different people show their stress in different ways. Some people have "blow ups." Some people get very forgetful. Some people lose concentration. For many people, they excel at their jobs, but their home life falls apart. Know your signs of stress. Tell someone else what they are. Ask them to check in with you every two weeks to see how you are doing. Every two weeks, write down how you are doing – if only for a minute. Stick in it a file marked "%*#)%&!!#$."

3. **Get a mentor or a coach.**
    Ideally, your supervisor is a very good mentor and coach. Many other people have "been there, done that" and can also serve as great mentors to you.

4. **Learn to delegate.**
    Delegating is giving others the responsibility and authority to carry out tasks. You maintain the accountability to get them done, but you let others decide how they will carry out the tasks themselves. Delegation is a skill to learn. Start learning it.

5. **Communicate as much as you can.**
    Consider the following guidelines:

    a. Have at least one person in your life with whom you are completely honest.

    b. Hold regular meetings with employees – all of them in one meeting at least once a month, and meet at least once every two weeks with each of your direct reports. A common problem among new managers and supervisors (or among experienced, but ineffective ones) is not meeting unless there is something to say. There is always something to communicate, even if to say that things are going well and then share the health of your pets.

    c. Err on the side of too much communication, rather than not enough. New managers and supervisors often assume that their employees know as much as they do. One of the first signs of an organization in trouble is that communications break down.

6. **Distinguish between what is important and what is urgent.**
    One of the major lessons that experienced leaders have learned is to respond to what is important, rather than what is urgent. Phone calls, sick employees, lost paperwork, disagreements between employees all seem to suddenly crop up and demand immediate attention. It can seem like your day is responding to one crisis after another. As you gain experience, you quit responding to the crisis. You get an answering machine or someone

else to answer the phone. You plan for employees being gone for the day – and you accept that people get sick. You develop a filing system to keep track of your paperwork. You learn basic skills in conflict management. Most important, you recognize that management is a process – you never really "finish" your to-do list – your list is there to help you keep track of details. Over time, you learn to relax.

7.   **Recognize accomplishments.**
Our society promotes problem solvers. We solve one problem and quickly move on to the next. The culture of many organizations rewards problem solvers. Once a problem is solved, we quickly move on to the next one to solve. Pretty soon we feel empty. We feel as if we are not making a difference. Our subordinates do, too. So in all your plans, include time to acknowledge accomplishments – if only by having a good laugh by the coffee machine. Do take time to note that something useful was done.

How to Lead Others By First Understanding Them

It is critical that the managers, leaders and supervisors have very good skills in interpersonal communications. Many books have been written about good listening skills, verbal and nonverbal. One need not be an expert at the materials in these books in order to have good interpersonal communications skills.

How to Make Sure Your Employees Really Hear You

Usually, your most frequent form of communication is spoken words. As with non-verbal communication, spoken communication is highly dependent on the particular culture in which you are working. For example, culture can affect how people speak about conflict, use humor, are honest and direct with each other, use silence and use certain wording.

 Consider "How to Lead in Multicultural Organizations" on page 91.

Consider the following general guidelines, which might be appropriate in a wide variety of cultures.

1. **Know the main point that you want to convey.**
    Sometimes, people begin speaking with the hope that if they talk long enough, they are bound to say what they want to say. Before you speak, take the time to think about the main points that you want to convey.

2. **Convey one point at a time.**
    That approach ensures that the listener is more likely to continue to understand you, rather than being overwhelmed with too many ideas delivered at too fast a rate. You might even find that you understand your own thoughts more completely.

3. **Speak too slowly, rather than too quickly.**
    A good way to practice this guideline is to speak along with a news anchor when you are watching television. You will likely find that they speak much more slowly than you realize. They are professionals who have learned an effective rate of speaking.

4. **Vary your voice.**
    Always avoid monotone. A monotone voice might convey to the listener that you are bored or controlled. It is likely to lull you and/or the listener into a stupor. Varying your voice takes practice, but it is well worth the effort.

5. **State your conclusion before describing how you came to that conclusion.**
    Some speakers convey their recommendations or advice by conveying the necessary information to lead the listener to the same conclusions as the speaker's. Instead, it is often more reliable to first state your point and then explain it.

6. **People speak more frequently and completely when they are comfortable.**
    Therefore, get comfortable with the person to whom you are speaking. Skills in authentic expression can be valuable in these situations. For example, if you are uncomfortable or confused, simply say so.

7.   **Ask the listener to repeat the main points of what you just said to them.**
This guideline ensures that the listener is indeed hearing what you wanted to convey. Be tactful when asking the listener to repeat what you said. For example, say "I want to be sure that I made sense to you just now, so I would appreciate if you could tell me what you heard me say."

8.   **Ask others to provide feedback about your spoken communication.**
One of the most powerful ways to learn about yourself is to ask others for feedback. Therefore, ask others about how you might improve your speaking skills.

See "How to Share Useful – and Respectful – Feedback" on page 208.

How to Recognize and Understand Non-Verbal Communications

Interpreting Other's Body Language

Resistance, confusion, distaste and passivity all show up in the body language of others, regardless of what they are saying verbally. Experienced leaders have learned often to trust what they see more than what they hear. Body language is always present. Too many speakers and listeners are unaware of body language.

The nature of a person's body language is highly dependent on the person's nature. For example, some people are intent on sitting or standing upright with their hands at their sides in a stance of attention and respect. Other people might slouch in their chair or extend their legs, in part, to convey that they feel comfortable around others in the room.

It is difficult to make overall conclusions about body language because it is culturally dependent. However, people trust non-verbal communication more than they do verbal (spoken) communication, so learn to notice non-verbal communication, and be aware of your own.

In general, notice:

1.   **Style of voice, for example, loud, soft, frequent, irregular.**

2.   **Movement of the body, for example, gestures, face, eyes.**

3.   **Distance, space and time between speaker and listener.**

Specifically, notice:

1.   **Eye contact.**
In the United States, this often conveys sincerity. In other cultures, though, it might convey aggressiveness or hostility.

2.   **Frequent movements of the body.**
Frequent movements might convey nervousness, poor listening.

3.   **Openness of the body.**
      Arms crossed may mean defensiveness, which impedes communication.

Interpreting Your Own Body Language

Your body language is often the true "compass" about your impression of something. For you to remain authentic, you need to be in touch with your own non-verbal communication. Different people have different physical reactions in different situations. Consider the following:

1.   **Are you moving your arms and legs a lot?**
      If so, maybe you are afraid, frustrated or confused about something.

2.   **Is your mouth dry?**
      Then maybe you are afraid of something.

3.   **Is your body position closed?**
      Are your legs and arms crossed? Perhaps you feel attacked somehow?

4.   **Is your brow furled?**
      Perhaps you are confused – or you are really interested in what the other has to say.

5.   **Are you looking away from the others a lot?**
      Then there is likely something that is bothering you. Or, perhaps your style is to look away so you can think more clearly. If that is the case, realize that others might be seeing you as having poor eye contact.

6.   **Is your heart racing?**
      Perhaps you are afraid of others, or you are excited about a project you are undertaking.

How to Really Listen to Others

Listening is a critical skill for all adults to have, to learn about others. Also, it is one of the most valuable tools for you to establish a strong rapport with employees.

There are many books about effective listening skills. The following common guidelines can help you to accomplish effective listening in the vast majority of situations.

1.   **Be sure you can hear the speaker.**
      It is surprising how often people do not really listen to other people. It is just as surprising how often people do not realize that they cannot even hear other people. So always make this your first guideline in any situation for effective listening.

2.   **Overall, attempt to listen 75% of time – speak 25% of time.**
      This is one of the most powerful guidelines. Use of the guideline depends on your situation. For example, if you are making a presentation, you will speak more. Otherwise, ensure that the other person speaks more than you do – and listen to them.

3.   **Adopt a culturally compatible physical posture to show you are interested.**
      This can be a powerful means to show others that you are interested in hearing them. For example, you might lean forward and maintain eye contact. Whatever physical gestures you make, be sure they are compatible to the culture of the speaker.

Consider "How to Lead in Multicultural Organizations" on page 91.

4.   **Do not think about what to say while you are also trying to listen to the speaker.**
Your brain goes four times faster than a speaker's voice. Thus, your brain can easily leave the speaker behind. Instead, trust that you will know how to respond to the speaker when the speaker is done.

5.   **Notice the other's speaking style.**
Different people have different speaking styles. Do they speak loud or soft? Slow or fast? Are there disconnects between what they say versus what their body language conveys? Some people convey the central idea first and then support it with additional information. Other people provide information to lead the listener to the same conclusion as the speaker.

6.   **Listen for the central ideas, not for all the facts.**
Experienced leaders develop a sense for noticing the most important information conveyed by their people. They hear the main themes and ideas from their employees. If you notice the major ideas, then often the facts "come along" with those ideas.

7.   **Let the speaker finish each major point that he/she wants to make.**
Do not interrupt – offer your response when the speaker is done. If you do have to interrupt, do so to ensure you are hearing the other person. Interrupt tactfully. For example, put up your hand and say, "Might I interrupt to ask you to clarify something?"

8.   **Reflect back and ask if you are hearing accurately.**
This is also one of the most powerful guidelines. Start by asking if you can reflect back, or summarize, to the other person after he/she has spoken. Then progress to where you can ask the person to summarize back to you what you have just said to him/her.

9.   **Regularly share indications that you are listening to them.**
Those indications can be, for example, nodding your head, saying, "Yes" to short points that you agree with.

10.   **Learn the art of supportive questioning.**
Coaching involves the use of powerful questions to understand yours and other's perceptions, assumptions and conclusions. The coach must practice effective questioning skills to really understand others.

Consider "How to Coach for Deep Problem-Solving and Learning" on page 202.

11.   **Ask others to provide you feedback about your communication skills.**
Often, people do not know what they do not know about themselves. One example is the leader who prizes him/herself on strong listening skills, yet regularly interrupts others when they are speaking. Another is the leader who speaks only in conclusions, but does not share how he/she came to those conclusions. Thus, others do not understand the leader's rationale.

How to Put Yourself "in Their Shoes" – Skills in Empathy

What Is Empathy? Why Is It So Important?

Empathy is the ability to accurately put yourself "in someone else's shoes" – to understand the other's situation, perceptions and feelings from their point of view – and to be able to communicate that understanding back to the other person. Empathy is a critical skill for you to have as a leader. It contributes to an accurate understanding of your employees, their perceptions and concerns. It also enhances your communication skills because you can sense what others want to know and if they are getting it from you or not. Ideally, your employees can learn skills in empathy from you, thereby helping them to become more effective leaders, managers and supervisors themselves.

Empathy is sometimes confused with sympathy. Sympathy involves actually being affected by the other person's perceptions, opinions and feelings. For example, if an employee is frustrated and sad, the sympathetic leader would experience the same emotions, resulting in the leader many times struggling with the same issues as the employee. Thus, sympathy can actually get in the way of effective leading.

Guidelines to Develop Empathy

1. **Experience the major differences among people.**
    One of the best examples of strong skills in empathy is people who have traveled or worked in multicultural environments. They have learned that the way they see and experience things is often different from others. People with little or no skills in empathy might have an intellectual awareness of these differences. However, until they actually experience these differences, their skills in empathy will probably remain quite limited.

2. **Learn to identify your own feelings – develop some emotional intelligence.**
    Many of us are so "processed" and "sophisticated" about feelings that we cannot readily identify them in ourselves, much less in others. For example, we might perceive thoughts to be the same as feelings. So when someone asks you how you feel about a project, you might respond, "I think we have a lot to do." Or, we might not distinguish between related emotions, for example, between frustration and irritability or happiness and excitement.

     Consider "What is Your Emotional Intelligence?" on page 82.

3. **Regularly ask others for their perspectives and/or feelings regarding a situation.**
    Silently compare their responses to what you might have thought they would be. This approach not only helps you to sharpen your own empathic skills, but also helps you to learn more about your employees.

How to Lead in Multicultural Organizations

Cultural Diversity Has a Huge Affect on Perceptions of Leadership

In today's highly diverse organizations, the ability to work in diverse cultures is extremely important. An organization's culture is driven by the values throughout that organization.

Employees need to feel that their values are recognized, understood and respected. They need to feel that their ideas and concerns are being heard. Those conditions create strong motivation and momentum for strong performance in their jobs. Also, to help your employees to make meaningful decisions – and to understand decisions that they may have made already – it is extremely important that you have some understanding of the culture and values of the organization.

It can be a major challenge to work in multicultural environments where others have values, beliefs and certain conventions that are distinctly different from yours. Differences between cultures can lead to increased resistance to leadership because others might not understand and trust you. Those differences can hamper the effectiveness of leadership, if not stop it altogether.

For example, Western cultures tend to be highly rational and value things that are very valuable in meeting a current need. They value rugged individualism and competition. Some cultures might value patience, a sense of community and getting along with others, and still others might value direct authority and privacy. Some cultures may be overly deferential to the leader. Some cultures are deeply guarded about private matters.

You and your employees might not even realize that you all have different values. There are no universal laws to ensure conformity in each culture. Because of complexities in continually learning the cultures of your organization, it is critical for you to continually be open to differences and ask for help from your employees.

Although leading in multicultural organizations comes with its own unique challenges, it comes with many benefits, as well. There are few other such powerful experiences in which you can learn so much about people and organizations and also about yourself. The following guidelines are intended to focus on the most practical suggestions for working in multicultural environments.

Basic Guidelines to Culturally-Specific Leadership

The following guidelines might be helpful, especially if you are new to the organization.

1.   **Be aware of your personal biases, style, preferences, lens and focus.**
     This is critically important for successful leadership in any type of culture. You make a major difference in your organization, whether you know it or not, just by exposing it to your own nature and style of working. Thus, you need to understand your nature.

2.   **Realize that each part of an organization probably has a unique culture.**
     For example, the secretarial staff might interact with each other in a manner quite different from that of the marketing staff. In larger organizations, there are often several differences, for example, between senior management and support staff.

3.   **Promptly convey to employees that you want to be sensitive to their culture.**
     You should start in your first interaction with them. State that you recognize that different people might work differently depending on their own personalities and the culture of the overall organization. Ask them how you can understand the nature of their organization.

4.   **Consider getting a mentor, or representative, from the organization.**
     Attempt to get someone from the organization to help you understand their culture and how to work in a manner compatible with the culture of the organization. This request is not a sign of weakness or lack of expertise; rather it is an authentic request that better serves you and your employees.

Become Knowledgeable About Key Cultural Aspects

Consider asking others to help you understand how each of the following aspects might be unique in the culture of the organization. Key cultural aspects that might affect your leadership include:

1. **Assertiveness**
   Are members of your organization comfortable being honest and direct with each other? If not, how can you still be as authentic as possible and help them to be as authentic as possible, as well?

2. **Body language**
   Are there any specific cues that you can notice to help you to sense how others are experiencing you?

3. **Communication styles and direction**
   Is communication fairly direct and specific or more indirect and general? Does information flow mostly "upward" to executives or is it widely disseminated?

4. **Conflict**
   Is conflict considered bad and avoided? Or is conflict accepted as normal and directly addressed when it appears?

5. **Eye contact**
   Are members of the organization comfortable with sustained eye contact during communication or not?

6. **Gestures**
   Are there any specific gestures that can cause members of the organization discomfort or confusion?

7. **Humor**
   Is use of humor in the organization rather widespread? Is there anything about the use of humor about which you should be aware?

8. **Information collection**
   Should you be aware of any potential problems or use any certain precautions when conducting interviews or using assessments?

9. **Physical space**
   For example, are members of your organization quite conscious of having a minimum amount of space around them when they work or speak with others?

10. **Power**
    Are members attuned to certain people of power when solving problems and making decisions? Is power based on authority and/or respect?

11. **Silence**
    Are members uncomfortable with silence during communication? Or is it a common aspect of communicating in their workplace?

12. **Time**
Is time a precious commodity that seems to underlie many activities, or can activities take as long as they need to take to be done effectively?

13. **Wording**
Are there certain words or phrasings that cause discomfort when people from different cultures interact?

Hints for Talking with Others About Management Activities

It is not uncommon for people of any culture to experience confusion or engage in protracted arguments about activities only to realize later on that they have been in agreement all along – they had been using different definitions for the same terms. Therefore, it is important to ensure that all of you are "speaking the same language" about activities. The following guidelines are most important when ensuring people continue to understand each other when talking about management activities.

Recognize Difference Between Terms That Refer to Results Versus Activities to Produce Those Results

It is common for people from different cultures to become confused because different people are talking about results and others about the activities to produce the results. For example, some people refer to the "plan" to be the document, and others refer to the "plan" to be the activity of developing the plan. It is usually most clear to use the term "plan" to refer to the document itself, and use the term "planning" for the activities that produces the plan.

Here is another example. Inexperienced leaders sometimes assert that, because employees do not have a tangible plan/document on the shelf and do not explicitly reference the document on a regular basis, the employees are not doing planning. That assertion can alienate the leaders from employees who believe that they have been doing planning all along (but probably implicitly) and also have a good plan – they just have not been calling their process "planning" and have not produced a written plan document. Therefore, it is important for you to recognize if your employees have their own form of a certain activity and how that form is carried out in the organization.

Be Able to Separate a Term from the Meaning of That Term

If your conversations with others about management seem to get stuck or mired in confusion, it often helps to separate terms from the intent of those terms. For example:

- Rather than talking about "vision" or "goals," talk about "what" the business wants to accomplish overall.

- Rather than talking about "strategies," talk about "how" to accomplish "what" you want to accomplish overall.

- Rather than talking about "action plans," talk about "who is going to do what, and by when."

Hints for Talking with Others About Leadership Activities

The topic of leadership has become so prominent and passionate with so many people that it sometimes causes great confusion. Here are a few tips to help people to "stay on the same page" when talking about leadership.

1.   **Be clear about whether you are talking about leadership roles or traits.**
     When people talk about leadership, they might be talking about traits of leaders, such as being charismatic, influential and ethical. However, when others talk about leadership, they might be talking about roles of leadership, such as the Board Chair or the Chief Executive Officer. Both discussions are about leadership, but both are about quite different aspects.

2.   **Be clear about the domain of leadership about which you are talking.**
     For example, when talking about leading yourself, you might be talking about leadership skills, such as being assertive or having good time and stress management skills. When talking about leading other individuals, you might be talking about skills, such as coaching, delegating or mentoring. When talking about leading groups, you might be talking about skills, such as facilitation or meeting management. When talking about leading organizations, you might be talking about skills, such as strategic planning or business planning. In each of these four cases, the term "leadership" refers to different sets of skills.

How to Deliver Effective Presentations

Leaders make presentations to a wide variety of audiences, for example: Board members, employees, investors, shareholders and groups of customers. Usually there is a lot that can be quickly gained or quickly lost from a presentation. A little bit of guidance goes a long way toward making a highly effective presentation.

Note that meeting management skills are often helpful in designing an effective presentation. Also note that the following guidelines are intended for general presentations, not for training sessions where your presentation is to help learners to gain specific knowledge, skills or attitudes in order to improve their performance on a task or job.

Consider "How to Design Highly Effective Meetings" on page 160.

Basic Guidelines for Designing Your Presentation

1.   **List and prioritize the top three goals that you want to accomplish with your audience.**
     It is not enough just to talk at them. You may think you know what you want to accomplish in your presentation, but if you are not clear with yourself and others, it is very easy – too easy – for your audience to completely miss the point of your presentation. For example, your goals may be for them appreciate the accomplishments of your organization, to understand your need for funding or learn how to use your services. Again, the goals should be in terms of what you want to accomplish with the audience, not with the business.

2.   **Be really clear about who your audience is and what they should learn in the meeting.**
     Members of your audience will want to know right away why they were the ones chosen to be in your presentation. Be sure that your presentation makes this clear to them right away. This will help you clarify your invitation list and design your invitation to them.

3.   **List the major points of information that you want to convey to your audience.**
     When you are done making that list, ask yourself, "If everyone in the audience understands all of those points, then will I have achieved the goal that I set for this meeting?"

4. **Be clear about the tone that you want to set for your presentation.**
    For example, are you conveying hopefulness, celebration, warning or teamwork? Consciously identifying the tone to yourself can help you cultivate that mood to your audience.

5. **Design a brief opening (about 5% of your total presentation time) that:**

    a. Presents your goals for the presentation.

    b. Clarifies the benefits of the presentation to the audience.

    c. Explains the overall layout of your presentation.

6. **Prepare the body of your presentation (about 75% of your presentation time).**

7. **Allocate 10% of the time to summarize the key points from your presentation.**

8. **Allocate 10% of the time to answer any questions from the audience.**

Basic Guidelines About Presentation Materials

You might be handing out supplemental materials, for example, articles and reports along with making your presentation. You might also be handing out copies of your presentation, either as a report or as copies of the slides that you will be referencing during your presentation. You might be using transparency slides or showing slides from a personal computer onto a projection screen.

1. If you plan to project your slides from a computer onto a projection screen, then be sure to check out the computer system before people come into the meeting room, if at all possible.

2. Use a consistent layout, or organization of colors and images, on your materials.

3. If you present from slides, then allocate 3-5 minutes for each slide of your presentation. Include 5-8 lines of bulleted phrases on each slide.

4. If you provide supplemental information during your presentation, then your audience will likely read that information during your presentation, rather than listening to you. Therefore, consider distributing this information after you have completed your presentation. Or, hand it out at the beginning of your presentation and ask them not to read it until you have completed your presentation.

5. If you hand out copies of your slides, be sure that the text on the handouts is large enough that your audience can read the handouts on the table in front of them without having to hold them up to their face. Be sure to leave space on the handouts for the audience to make notes on them.

Basic Guidelines About Your Delivery

1. If you are speaking to a small group (for example, 2-15 people), then try to accomplish eye contact with each person for a few seconds throughout your delivery.

2. Look up from your materials, or notes, every 5-10 seconds, and look into the audience.

3. Speak a little bit louder and a little bit slower than you normally would with a friend. A good way to practice this is to speak along with a news anchor when watching television.

4. Vary the volume and rate of your speech. A monotone voice is absolutely toxic to keeping the attention of an audience.

5. Stand with your feet at shoulder-length apart.

6. Keep your hands relatively still.

Communication Tools to Use With Employees

Effective communication is the "life's blood" of an organization. Organizations that are highly successful have strong systems of communication. One of the first signs that an organization is struggling is that communications have broken down. The following guidelines are basic in nature, but comprise the critical fundamentals for ensuring strong ongoing, internal communications.

1. **Each employee writes a one-page weekly status report to his/her supervisor.**
   These reports may seem a tedious task, but they are precious in ensuring that the employee and supervisor have mutual understanding of what is going on. The reports also come in handy for planning purposes. They make otherwise harried employees stand back and reflect on what they are doing. In the dated report, include a description of:

   a. What tasks were done last week.

   b. What tasks are planned next week.

   c. Any current highlights, trends or issues regarding your activities.

2. **Chief Executive Officer conducts employee-wide meetings.**
   Employees greatly appreciate that the CEO finds time to talk to them, and the opportunity to meet their CEO in person.

   a. For clarity, focus and morale, be sure to use agendas and ensure follow-up minutes.

   b. Mention any significant events for employees, for example, birthdays.

   c. Review the overall condition of the organization.

   d. Consider conducting "in service" training about the organization where employees take turns describing their roles to the rest of the employees.

   e. Consider bringing in a customer to tell his/her story of how the organization helped them.

3. **Each supervisor conducts meetings with all employees together.**
   Have these meetings even if there is not a specific problem to solve – just make them shorter. Holding meetings only when there are problems to solve cultivates a crisis-oriented environment where managers believe their only job is to solve problems.

   a. Prepare for these meetings by reviewing the employee's weekly status report.

   b. For clarity, focus and morale, be sure to use agendas, take minutes and ensure follow-up minutes.

   c. Facilitate the meetings to support exchange of ideas and questions.

   d. Use these meetings for each person to briefly give an overview of what they are doing that week. If the meeting includes 10 people or less, then have each person give a one-minute description of what they did last week and plan to do next week.

   e. Have each person bring his/her calendar to ensure the scheduling of future meetings accommodates everyone's calendar.

3.   **Each supervisor conducts one-on-one, monthly meetings with each employee.**
This ultimately produces more efficient time management and supervision.

   a. Review overall status of work activities.

   b. Hear status from both the supervisor and the employee.

   c. Exchange feedback and answer any questions about current products and services.

   d. Discuss career planning, training plans, performance review plans, etc.

4.   **Use memos.**
It is much more effective if important day-to-day information is written to people rather than said to people. Use of memos, or even e-mail messages, is ideal in these situations. In your memos or e-mail messages, include:

   a. "Subject" line, with a phrase describing the topic of the memo.

   b. "To" and "From" lines.

   c. "Date."

   d. "Summary" describing the highlights in a paragraph near the top of the memo.

   e. "Action" specifying what you want the recipients to do with the information in the memo, for example: to respond, to take note, to starting doing something or to stop doing something.

   f. "Signature" line, that includes the signature of who wrote the memo.

5.   **Every employee gets an Employee Manual.**
The Employee Manual includes all of the up-to-date personnel policies of the organization.

Consider "How to Use An Employee Manual" on page 174.

PART IV:

HOW TO LEAD

– AND CHANGE –

A BUSINESS

How to Set Clear Purpose and Direction for the Business

Leading is setting direction and then motivating oneself, others, groups or an organization to follow that direction. There are many ways to lead, ranging from highly participatory to highly directive. The direction for an organization is usually established during strategic planning. Most organizations do some form of strategic planning – some without knowing it because planning can be done in a very explicit, comprehensive and systematic manner or in a rather implicit, partial and spotted manner. The former is usually the more effective approach to planning.

This section provides guidelines sufficient for you to develop a basic strategic plan from which you can begin or continue to effectively lead the organization. It will be helpful to recruit the involvement of a Planning Committee, comprised of key Board members and employees, to follow the guidelines in this section about strategic planning.

It is not within the scope of this Guide to provide comprehensive guidelines and procedures to carry out a complete, in-depth strategic planning process. Resources about strategic planning are included in the Bibliography on page 255.

All Else Flows From Your Strategic Planning

Strategic planning, when well done, identifies or clarifies:

1. Major trends, rules and regulations, and expectations of stakeholders that influence the organization's purpose, priorities and operations.

2. Specific needs among specific customers, the results (outcomes) that would meet those needs, the products and services that would achieve those outcomes, and the specific customers to be served by the products and services.

3. The organization's purpose (mission), overall goal (its vision), nature of how it wants to operate (its values), and the priorities and accomplishments (goals) to work toward the mission and vision.

4. How the organization and its resources should be structured and organized to best operate according to the mission, vision, values and goals.

5. Milestones, or objectives, that together accomplish each of the goals.

6. Resources (people, money, facilities, etc.) needed to achieve those goals and objectives.

7. How the strategic plan (which documents the mission, vision, values, goals and objectives) will be developed and how its implementation will be monitored.

The most important part of strategic planning is not the strategic plan document itself, but rather the planning process, which, in reality, is always an ongoing process. Good organizational leadership is essentially an ongoing process of good strategic planning and implementation.

Particularly for small organizations, the process of strategic planning should be carried out in a highly practical fashion. During planning, do the 20% of effort that generates 80% of the results. The remaining 20% of a good plan often comes from actually implementing the plan. While the mission, vision and values are certainly important, do not spend most of your planning time and energy on those matters. Strategic planning should always include solid action planning, which specifies who will do what and by when, in order to achieve the goals and associated objectives.

Strategic Planning – How, Who and When

How Should Strategic Planning Be Done?

There are many perspectives on the strategic planning process, including on the various terms and steps in the process. Some experts assert that organizations should start by examining their mission, vision and values statements. Others assert that organizations should start by analyzing what is going on in their external and internal environments, and then use the results of that analysis to update the mission, vision and values statements. Most experts assert that planners should identify major goals, set strategies to achieve the goals, and perform action planning – action planning includes identifying who will be doing what and by when in order to achieve the goals.

Who Should Develop the Plan?

Board members and leaders among employees must be highly involved in clarifying the mission statement. They also should be involved in writing the vision and values statements, if the organization decides to develop vision and values statements. They also should be highly involved in identifying strategic goals. Employees are often involved with the Board in identifying strategic goals and associated objectives to achieve each of the goals. Employees are also highly involved in action planning. However, some organizations prefer that Board members and employees work together in all aspects of strategic planning, especially if the organization is new, small or has members who prefer highly egalitarian and team-oriented approaches to activities.

If you have not done strategic planning before, consider recruiting an experienced facilitator. You should obtain an outside facilitator, someone who is not part of your organization, if any of the following are true:

- The organization has not conducted strategic planning before.

- For a variety of reasons, previous strategic planning was not deemed to be successful.

- There appears to be a wide range of ideas and/or concerns among organization members about strategic planning and current organizational issues to be addressed in the plan.

- There is no one in the organization who feels that he/she has sufficient facilitation skills.

- No one in the organization feels committed to facilitating strategic planning for the business.

- Leaders believe that an inside facilitator will either inhibit participation from others or will not have the opportunity to fully participate in planning themselves.

- Leaders want an objective voice, that is, someone who is not likely to have strong predispositions about the organization's strategic issues and ideas.

When Should Strategic Planning Be Done?

Strategic planning should be done:

- When an organization is just getting started.

- In preparation for a new major venture, for example, developing a new product.

- At least once a year in order to be ready for the coming fiscal year.

It also should be done if:

- There are many new Board members who need to agree on the direction of the organization.

- There are many recurring problems in the organization.

Sample Planning Process for Short-Term Strategic Plan

The length of time for strategic planning depends on whether the organization has done planning before, how many strategic issues and goals the organization faces, whether the culture of the organization prefers short or long meetings, and how much time the organization is willing to commit to strategic planning. However, for small organizations in particular, the planning process might be too long if it drags out over several months. Therefore, it is often much better for small organizations to spend several weeks doing a top-level, short-term strategic plan than to spend several months or longer doing a more detailed, long-term strategic plan.

Here is an example of a basic strategic planning format, which results in a short-term, strategic plan that can be embellished later by employees adding more detailed action plans, if necessary. The plan is focused on the coming six-month period. Some strategic planning experts might complain that the following procedure does not produce a highly "strategic" plan, that is, the procedure does not include getting input from all major stakeholders or enough analysis of external factors. However, the following recommended procedure is likely to "jump start" a highly practical plan from which you can later develop a longer-term plan.

1. **Have a meeting to announce planning process to Board members and key employees.**

    a. The Board Chair and Chief Executive announce to Board members and employees that a strategic planning process will soon be underway. The announcement includes explanation of the purpose and benefits of strategic planning, and the role of Board members and employees in the process. The Chair and/or Chief Executive explain who will be involved in the planning process. Time is allowed for Board members and employees to ask questions in their respective meetings.

    b. All Board and certain employees are asked to think about current challenges that the organization faces and/or goals that they recommend for the organization to achieve over the coming six months. Employees are encouraged to talk to other employees to get ideas, as well.

    c. The next upcoming planning sessions are scheduled.

2.   **In a half-day Board retreat, identify major challenges over the next six months.**
Include Board members and key employees. Activities include:

a.   Introductions by the Board Chair and/or Chief Executive along with their explanations of the organization's benefits from strategic planning, and the organization's commitment to the planning process. Explanations should indicate that the planning process will focus particularly on the next six months.

b.   The facilitator provides an overview of the process. The facilitator might be an external facilitator, that is, someone from outside the organization, or an internal facilitator who has previous experience in strategic planning.

c.   Brief review of the mission (and the vision and values, if applicable) with the bulk of time spent on identifying current, major challenges to address over the next six months. Challenges are clarified and prioritized. Participants may suggest goals to meet the challenges, as well.

d.   Finalize which challenges will be targeted over the next six months.

e.   Finalize which goals will be achieved in order to address each of the challenges.

f.   Before the next meeting, a subcommittee is asked to draft the strategic plan document that describes the major challenges and the goals to address each challenge.

3.   **Finalize action plans for each goal and then draft the strategic plan document.**
The next planning meeting is attended primarily by employees. Some Board members might attend as well, especially Board leadership and any Board members assigned to Board committees whose activities are closely involved in achieving the goals.

a.   Develop an action plan for each of the goals, including objectives needed to achieve each goal, along with who will be doing what by when to achieve each objective.

b.   Ask a subcommittee to update the drafted plan to include the action plans, and to provide the plan to Board members before the next Board meeting.

4.   **In the next Board meeting, Board members authorize the strategic plan document.**
Board members:

a.   Discuss the drafted plan document.

b.   Suggest any changes. If changes are in order, they should be coordinated promptly with employees.

c.   Approve the final draft of the document by signing the document.

In the above example of a planning process, various subcommittees might be charged to gather additional information and distribute it between meetings.

No matter how serious planners are about their strategic planning, they often have concerns about finding the time to attend frequent planning meetings. You can address this concern by ensuring that meetings are well managed, and by having several short meetings rather than one or two long ones.

How to Develop Your Basic Strategic Plan

 For a complete set of worksheets that you can use to fill in the draft of your strategic plan, go to http://www.managementhelp.org/fp_progs/sp_mod/sp_frame.htm .

Draft Your Initial Mission Statement

The description of your mission statement should briefly describe the purpose of your organization, whom it serves and how it serves them. The mission is the compass for the decisions by the Board and other leaders in the organization. Your mission statement is particularly important to product planning because it guides the overall relationship between the activities of your overall organization and your products. There should be strong alignment between the mission of your organization and your products. Therefore, you should give careful thought to the development of your mission statement.

Mission statements vary widely in focus, scope and style, ranging from one sentence to a page. Most important, is that the mission statement clearly articulates the purpose of your business, who it serves, how it serves them, and how your business is different from your competitors.

Example of Simple Mission Statement:

> "Our mission: to inspire and nurture the human spirit – one person, one cup and one neighborhood at a time." – mission statement of Starbucks Coffee.

Draft Your Initial Vision Statement

Your description should depict the overall benefits that your customers will receive from your products or services. It should not just be a picture of your business, but a picture of your customers from having benefited from your products. The vision should help guide Board members' decisions.

Basic Example of Vision Statement:

> From Coca Cola Bottling Company:
> "To achieve sustainable growth, we have established a vision with clear goals.
> Profit: Maximizing return to shareowners while being mindful of our overall responsibilities.
> People: Being a great place to work where people are inspired to be the best they can be.
> Portfolio: Bringing to the world a portfolio of beverage brands that anticipate and satisfy people's desires and needs.
> Partners: Nurturing a winning network of partners and building mutual loyalty.
> Planet: Being a responsible global citizen that makes a difference"

Example of Slogan:

Some companies also adopt a slogan, for example, "It's the real thing" for Coca Cola Bottling Company.

Draft Your Initial Values Statement

The values statement should describe the overall priorities, or principles, that guide how you want the business to operate.

Example of Values Statement:

The following might be a values statement for a company that provides educational products:

> "We believe that
>
> - Employment provides opportunity for adults to develop the community and themselves;
>
> - Every person deserves an opportunity for gainful employment;
>
> - Gainful employment of all citizens is a responsibility of all citizens."

Analyze Outside Environment of the Business Now

Take a wide look around at the world outside the organization and how it might affect the business and its customers. This external analysis looks at societal, technological, political and economic trends affecting the organization. This may include recent or pending legislation, demographic trends, or degree of access to trained labor and competition. In your external analysis, do not forget to consider stakeholders' impressions of the organization including investors, customers and collaborators. If you have limited resources for this external analysis, then be sure to at least consider the needs of current and potential customers, what products might meet those needs and wants, and how your organization stands apart from its competitors.

From this information, try to identify 4-5 opportunities facing the organization now, for example, more customers, useful technologies for more efficiency, and strong relationships with stakeholders.

From this information, try to identify 4-5 threats facing the organization now, for example, decreasing number of customers, less access to customers, little innovation in the technologies used by your products, poor public relations with stakeholders, and changes in laws that might decrease attention to your products or services.

Note that opportunities and threats can seem very similar. What might seem like an opportunity to one person might seem like a threat to another because not enough of the opportunity seems present to that other person. Many times, opportunities and threats can seem like two opposite ways of looking at the same situation. For example, the threat of decreasing funds can be an opportunity to increase efficiencies in operations to reduce expenses. The perspective is up to the planners.

For another comprehensive list of considerations about the external environment, go to
http://www.managementhelp.org/plan_dec/str_plan/drvnforc.htm .

Analyze Inside Environment of the Business Now

Now consider the quality of operations inside your organization, for example, of the Board, employees, marketing, finances, facilities and evaluations. Think about the organization's strengths and weaknesses.

From this information, try to identify 4-5 strengths of the organization, for example, strong expertise among employees, effective Board, strong public image, strong products or services, and strong motivation of Board members and employees.

From this information, try to identify 4-5 weaknesses of the organization, for example, high turnover of Board members and employees, continual financial crises, complaints from customers and poor facilities.

Consider "How to Use Organizational Assessments" on page 237.

Identify Your Most Important 5-7 Issues to Address For Now

Think about your external and internal analyses. Which issues (usually threats and/or weaknesses) seem most important to address for now? Usually, it is best to describe them in terms of a question. How can we establish a new Chief Executive Officer position? How do we strengthen and develop our Board so it can be more effective in helping to set direction? How do we establish overall direction for our business? How do we enhance our management skills? How can we serve more customers? How do we respond to increased competition?

Identify Your Goals to Address Each Issue Now

Consider what must be done (what goals must be achieved) to address each of the issues that you identified from the threats and weaknesses. Consider what strengths you can use and what opportunities you might take advantage of in order to achieve the goals. (Planners refer to this step as a SWOT analysis. SWOT is an acronym for strengths, weaknesses, opportunities and threats. Think about the SWOT information that you can identify so far from doing the external analysis.)

The following sites might have examples of SWOT analyses:
1. http://cbae.nmsu.edu/~dboje/sbc/pages/page3.html .
2. http://www.businessballs.com/swotanalysisfreetemplate.htm .
3. http://www.marketingteacher.com/Lessons/lesson_swot.htm .
4. http://www.consultancymarketing.co.uk/swot.htm .
5. http://erc.msh.org/quality/example/swot.cfm .

Example:

> Issue #1: How do we establish a full-time CEO position?
>
> 1) Goal 1.1: Obtain funds to pay CEO for at least one year.
>
> 2) Goal 1.2: Establish and operate Board Search Committee.
>
> 3) Goal 1.3: Search Committee recommends CEO candidate.
>
> 4) Goal 1.4: Board selects new CEO.

Develop Action Plans for Each Goal

For example, for Goal 1.1 above:

Objectives for Goal 1.1	Date of Completion	Responsibility	Status and Date
1.1.1. Recruit financial manager.	1/1/10	CEO	
1.1.2. Schedule Board and CEO training about finances.	1/1/10	CEO	
1.1.3. Conduct training.	1/21/10	CEO	
1.1.4. Draft short-term financial plan.	2/1/10	CEO	
1.1.5. Board approve plan.	2/8/10	CEO	
1.1.6. Implement plan.	2/8/10	CEO	

How Do You Ensure Implementation of Your Plan?

The following guidelines will help ensure that the strategic plan is implemented.

1. **In planning, involve the people who will be responsible for implementing the plan.**
   Use a cross-functional team (representatives from each of the organization's major teams) in planning in order to ensure that the plan is realistic and collaborative.

2. **Ensure the plan has realistic vision, goals and objectives.**
   During planning, continue to ask planners, "Is this realistic? Can we really do this?" When implementing the plan, adjust deadlines as needed in order to keep the plan relevant.

3. **The Board Chair and Chief Executive should show very visible support.**
   For example, they should clearly convey the purpose of the planning to Board members and employees, and should stress that they will monitor implementation of the plan.

4. **Organize the overall strategic plan into smaller action plans.**
   Be sure that the plan specifies who is going to do what and by when in order to achieve the goals and associated objectives in the plan.

5. **Build in regular reviews of the status of the implementation of the plan.**
   Board and employee meetings are very good opportunities to quickly review status. During reviews, monitor achievement of goals and objectives according to their deadlines.

6. **Translate plan's goals and objectives into job descriptions and performance goals.**
   Unless the plan is integrated into the day-to-day activities in the business, the plan is likely to sit on a shelf, collecting dust.

7. **Be sure one internal person has ultimate responsibility to ensure implementation.**
   Even though one person is responsible to coordinate the plan's activities (often the Chief Executive Officer), Board members are still responsible to monitor the implementation.

8. **Ensure Board members regularly review status reports on the plan's implementation.**
   This is one of the members' most important jobs – to be sure that the organization is meeting its goals by implementing the strategic plan.

For more information on strategic planning, go to
http://www.managementhelp.org/plan_dec/str_plan/str_plan.htm .

How Your Board and Employees Together Can Lead the Organization

Ultimately, Board members have the responsibility and accountability for the direction, purpose and priorities of the business. However, research suggests that the most successful and well-respected businesses are led by a strategic partnership of the Board and Chief Executive. Thus, the guidelines in this section are best addressed by this working partnership.

Consider "How Your Board and CEO Can Work in Strategic Partnership" on page 39. Also, consider "How Much Should Your Board Be Involved in Management" on page 61.

How to Make Sure Your Stakeholders Are Always Heard

Leaders must focus strong attention to listening to their stakeholders. This activity is sometimes called "inbound marketing." This activity is critical to the primary job of Board members and leaders among employees. Far too often organizations focus on aggressive advertising, promotions and media campaigns that go *at* their stakeholders: investors, customers and others. Too many organizations do not really *listen to* their stakeholders.

Guidelines for Effective Leadership of Inbound Marketing

If your Board uses Committees, then a Marketing Committee would be helpful in this area, which involves market research.

1. **Understand laws and regulations that apply to the business.**
   This includes, for example, filings with appropriate government agencies, benefits and limitations of corporate status.

2. **Know who the major groups of stakeholders are for the organization.**
   Consider Board members, employees, customers, suppliers, collaborators, investors, and shareholders.

3. **Establish policies to regularly collect information from stakeholders.**
   Collect information, for example, about impressions of the business, other organizations with similar products or services.

4. **Ensure strategic planning includes feedback from stakeholders.**
   Collect input, for example, from Board members, employees, customers, shareholders and collaborators. Ask, "What does each stakeholder consider to be 'success' for the organization?"

5. **Ensure the mission is centered on providing products that meet the needs of markets.**
   Mission statements should describe at least what products are provided to which markets, and how the organization is different than its competitors.

6.   **Design and conduct Annual Meetings.**
      In the meeting, take time to ask others about what they need from the organization and what would meet that need.

7.   **Ensure means to effectively verify satisfaction among customers.**
      Conduct practical outcomes-based evaluations that collect information from customers to determine whether their expectations are being met or not.

8.   **Ensure Board members represent, or understand, your stockholders.**
      Board members are responsible to represent the stockholders, but also want to consider other constituents as well, such as customers, collaborators, community leaders and suppliers.

How to Ensure That Relevant and Realistic Strategic Planning Takes Place

Strategic planning establishes purpose and overall direction for the organization, including where it should to be at some point in the future and how it is going to get there. In a previous section, this guidebook explained "all else flows from strategic planning." The process has been emphasized so much that a variety of proponents and opponents have voiced their opinions about the process. Some business leaders recoil at hearing the phrase "strategic planning" because it represents to them a long, tedious process, which, far too often, results in a report that sits collecting dust on the shelf. That need not be the case. Leaders can help ensure that the process is carried out in a highly flexible, relevant and realistic fashion.

When deciding how to go forward, the organization might decide to use a process called "strategic planning" or something else. Whatever process the organization chooses to use, leaders have the responsibility to ensure that the process establishes clear direction and alignment for all of the important parts of the business.

Guidelines for Effective Leadership of Strategic Planning

If your Board uses Committees, then an ad hoc Strategic Planning Committee would be helpful in this area.

1.   **Actively participate in strategic planning, whether formal or informal.**
      A major responsibility of Board members is to ensure that the organization has a clear purpose and direction, and has guidelines to work toward both of these. Developing and implementing a strategic plan usually fulfills that responsibility.

2.   **Ensure strategic planning includes feedback from stakeholders.**
      Far too often, strategic planning tends to include only the opinions of those internal to the organization. Consequently, a "beautiful ladder can be built entirely to the wrong roof" – the plan includes wonderfully worded mission and vision statements, but little else that directly applies to stakeholders. Therefore, in planning, include the perspectives of Board members, employees, customers, and the other stakeholders.

3.   **Craft your mission statement to describe who you serve, for what results and how.**
      The mission statement is the key communication to constituents. Mission statements can be in a wide variety of formats. However, the statements should reflect what you are doing for your customers, not just for your organization.

4.   **During planning, always ask, "Is this realistic?"**
Many plans sit on shelves, collecting dust because the vision and goals were completely unrealistic. It is better to have a plan with a few realistic goals than to have a plan with many inspirational goals, most of which are far too ambitious to achieve.

5.   **Be sure that the goals from the strategic plan are integrated throughout the organization.**
The plan specifies what priorities are most important for the business to address. The organization cannot do that if its various functions are not all aligned with addressing those priorities. Functions include Board operations, products or services, marketing, staffing, and finances.

6.   **Regularly monitor status reports regarding implementation of the plan.**
Top-level information about mission, vision and values and lofty goals have no foundation if there is no specification of who needs to do what and by when in order to work towards those top-level priorities.

Consider the free, online self-directed, learning module about planning at http://www.managementhelp.org/fp_progs/sp_mod/str_plan.htm .

See the topic, "Strategic Planning," in the Free Management Library^{SM} at http://www.managementhelp.org/plan_dec/str_plan/str_plan.htm .

How to Make Sure Your Board's Operations Are Always High-Quality

Guidelines for Effective Leadership of Board Development

Like the physician who has an unhealthy lifestyle, but takes very good care of his/her patients, the Board rarely gives attention as to how it is doing overall. Board development helps ensure that the Board is working smarter rather than harder. The following guidelines are directly in regard to ensuring that activities within the Board are always high quality. Note that it often is the Chief Executive who supports the Board to be doing its job.

If your Board uses Committees, then a Board Development Committee would be helpful in this area.

1.   **Clarify what skills are needed among Board members to effectively govern.**
The approach that you use to recruit Board members depends on whether you are staffing the Board (getting and developing Board members) to get expertise to achieve strategic goals and/or representing the voices of diverse stakeholders. If you are staffing primarily according to passion for mission, then be sure that the members do more than have passionate meetings.

2.   **Orient Board members about the unique aspects of the organization.**
Ensure members know about the organization's history, products or services, successes and other Board members. Be sure to review Board policies, specifically Board calendar,

comparison of Board and employee roles, Board attendance, conflict-of-interest, Board self-evaluation, CEO's job description, committees and ethics policy.

3. **Train members to be effective Board members.**
Train Board members about the roles and responsibilities of a governing Board of Directors. Review the fiduciary duties and associated responsibilities, job descriptions and the major types of decisions made by Board members.

4. **Effectively organize Board expertise and resources to achieve goals.**
You might use committees or task forces to organize members around important strategic priorities. The extent of involvement of Board members depends on the factors listed above.

5. **Use a Board calendar of important events to ensure all those events are conducted.**
To ensure that all-important Board activities are conducted, reference an annual calendar of when the Board, for example, does a self-evaluation, evaluates the CEO, does strategic planning, produces a budget and approves updated policies and procedures.

6. **Evaluate the Board to maximize performance.**
Board self-evaluation might need just 30 minutes a year from each member in order to complete a questionnaire about the quality of operations of the Board. Results of that self-evaluation are usually extremely valuable to the Board.

Consider the free, online, self-directed, learning module about Boards at http://www.managementhelp.org/fp_progs/brd_mod/boards.htm.

See the topic, "Boards of Directors," in the Free Management Library[SM] at http://www.managementhelp.org/boards/boards.htm .

How to Verify Your Products Always Meet Needs of Customers

Business leaders – and even Board members – must have strong knowledge of the organization's products, especially as to whether they are indeed meeting the needs of customers.

Guidelines for Effective Leadership of Products and Services

If your Board uses Committees, then a Products Committee would be helpful in this area.

1. **Know what the products are – many leaders often do not.**
It is amazing how long Board members can serve on a Board, but when asked what the products are, members are not able to identify them. Ask the Chief Executive to describe the organization's products and the markets for those products.

2. **Understand each product, including the markets for each product.**
This requires that customers provide continual feedback about purchase and use of the

product. It also requires that the organization set goals for the development, sales and quality management of the product.

3.   **Ensure products are consistent with the mission of the organization.**
It's important that an organization stay focused on its core competencies – on what it does better than other organizations. Organizations often struggle when they try adding numerous new product lines and services, which go way beyond what they have done well in the past.

4.   **Ensure product development and delivery are sufficiently resourced.**
Major resources include people, expertise, funding and facilities. Resources also can include time and attention from the leaders and experts in the industry.

5.   **Ensure products continue to meet the needs of customers.**
This requires ongoing customer satisfaction surveys that ask customers for opinions about how they learned about the product, how they purchased it, their use of the product and their opinions about its features and benefits.

6.   **Ensure all products are highly integrated in purpose and operations.**
A tight integration of products – including their development, delivery and ongoing support – means maximum savings and efficiency from every product line.

Consider the free, online, self-directed, learning module about marketing at http://www.managementhelp.org/fp_progs/mkt_mod/market.htm .

How to Ensure Fair Management of Your Employees

The human resources (employees) are the organization's most important assets. It is critical that all employees (including the Chief Executive) be recruited, trained and supervised according to up-to-date personnel policies and procedures that are approved by the Board.

Guidelines for Effective Leadership of Human Resources

If your Board uses Committees, then a Personnel Committee would be helpful in this area.

1.   **Ensure the business has up-to-date written personnel policies and procedures.**
Employee laws today are so numerous and complex that organizations have to have written policies and procedures in order to ensure compliance to laws, rules and regulations. An expert on employment laws should review policies on a regular basis. All employees should have copies of the policies and procedures in the form of an employee handbook. The Chief Executive and other management staff, in particular, should be trained to ensure compliance. The Board should formally approve the personnel policies.

2.   **Ensure employees are retained according to expertise, not personalities.**
Employees should not be hired or recruited primarily because they know someone in the organization or because they are likeable. Focus on the requirements of the job and ensure that a job description accurately describes those requirements. Then reference the job description to fill the position.

3.   **Ensure all employees are fully resourced to do their jobs.**
It is very important to give them a brief orientation of the products and services, other employees, and resources available to help them (for example, job training, computers, procedures and internal experts). Sometimes they might seem like they are poor performers when instead they just need better training and resources.

4.   **Ensure all employees receive regular written evaluations.**
Too often, leaders assume that people are doing fine because they keep showing up for work each day. High-performing people usually want to know how they are doing and how they can improve. The best way to convey that information is to provide written evaluations. Those evaluations also serve as a valid benchmark, or indicator, if leaders need to take some form of performance-related action later on.

5.   **Ensure all employees receive fair and equitable benefits and compensation.**
There are many online salary surveys that suggest pay ranges for various positions. Even if a business cannot pay compensation that is well within these ranges, the Board still should approve a formal policy to not only determine how much employees should be paid, but also to ensure that they are treated fairly when compensation is determined.

Consider the free, online, self-directed, learning module about staffing at http://www.managementhelp.org/fp_progs/sup_mod/staff.htm .

How to Effectively Promote the Business to Others

First, it helps to understand what we are talking about. Advertising and promotions are aimed at bringing products and services to the attention of potential and current customers. Successful advertising and promotions depend on knowing what groups of customers your products or services target, what features and benefits you want to convey to the customers, and what methods of communication will be most effective in reaching those customers. Sales is a "partnership" between the business and the customer, geared to explore the customer's needs and assess if there is a suitable match or not. If there is a match, the salesperson helps the customer to take advantage of the products or services. Public relations might be viewed as advertising and promotions, not of a specific product or service, but of the entire organization.

One of the Board's major responsibilities is to represent the organization to the community. Ideally, the Board is comprised of representatives from the various major stakeholders. Thus, Board members are poised to be very effective in advertising, promotions, sales and public relations for the organization. (This activity is sometimes called "outbound marketing.")

Guidelines for Effective Leadership of Outbound Marketing

If your Board uses Committees, then a Marketing Committee would be helpful in this area.

1.   **Be sure that all Board members and leaders understand the products.**
As mentioned above, the Board members and other leaders often do not know the organization's products. They should know each major product, its markets and the performance of each product.

2. **Define an overall desired image for the organization – how should people view it?**
   For example, should the organization be known primarily for its products or services?
   Should the organization adopt a slogan, or a concise phrase, that helps to convey an image?
   Should the organization standardize on a graphic, or logo, to convey its unique identity?

3. **Develop an overall Marketing (or Promotions) Plan – ideally for each product or service.**
   In the Plan, for each different, specific group of customers, specify:

   a. The specific benefits that each different group will achieve from the different products and services.

   b. The different messages that will be conveyed to each different group. (When selecting the messages, consider the different needs and wants for each of the different groups.)

   c. How each group prefers to get its messages, for example, some prefer television, some prefer the radio and some prefer newspapers.

   d. Who will convey the messages by using the preferred communications approaches with each group.

   e. When those messages will be conveyed.

   f. How implementation of the Promotions Plan will be tracked.

4. **Develop a Public Relations Plan about the entire organization.**
   Whereas a Marketing Plan ideally is about marketing each product or service, a Public Relations Plan is about marketing the entire organization. Develop a Plan that specifies:

   a. The unique identity, or branding, of the organization, along with the mission and any slogan.

   b. The major stakeholders of the organization, for example, customers, investors, collaborators and suppliers.

   c. What the organization wants each group of stakeholders to believe or feel about the business.

   d. The communication channels that might be preferred by each group of stakeholders.

   e. The messages to convey to each group via its preferred channel(s).

   f. Who will convey the messages and by when.

5. **Ensure leaders work from a public relations or media kit with a set of talking points.**
   Each Board member and employee is a representative of the organization in the community. They deserve a short training about how to effectively describe each product or service and the entire organization to the community.

6. **Carefully monitor implementation of the Promotions and Public Relations Plans.**
   Are the Plans being implemented? Are you getting the results that you desired? If not, what

should be done? Put more priority on implementation? Get more resources? Extend deadlines in the Plans?

Consider the free, online, self-directed, learning module about marketing at http://www.managementhelp.org/fp_progs/mkt_mod/market.htm .

How to Ensure Sound Management of Finances and Taxes

The reality of how well, or how poor, an organization is doing is reflected in the organization's finances (if the financial numbers are anywhere near accurate). When investors consider whether to provide funds to an organization, they usually consider how well the finances are tracked and managed. Overseeing financial management also means overseeing management of assets, such as facilities, major equipment and personnel.

Guidelines for Effective Leadership of Financial Management

If your Board uses Committees, then a Finance Committee would be helpful in this area.

1. **Develop up-to-date fiscal policies and procedures and have them Board-approved.**
    These policies specify how finances and monies will be collected, managed, reported and dispersed in a highly accurate and controlled fashion that conforms to laws and regulations and minimizes the likelihood of loss, fraud or malfeasance. New organizations might obtain sample policies and modify them according to the organization's nature and needs.

Sample financial policies at http://www.toolkit.com/tools/index.aspx .

2. **Approve an annual operating budget.**
    Usually, the budget is developed and approved near the end of the strategic planning activities when planners have identified what resources will need to be obtained and supported in order to achieve the goals in the strategic plan.

3. **Establish internal controls for the handling of cash and the approval of expenditures.**
    Fiscal policies and procedures usually specify how cash should be managed, for example, that the person who tracks incoming invoices is not the same person who writes checks to pay the invoices, thereby minimizing any likelihood that one person could steal funds without getting caught.

4. **Ensure all federal and state/provincial payroll taxes are paid.**
    Payroll taxes must be paid from wages and salaries. In the USA, taxes are for Social Security and Medicare. Be sure these taxes are being paid.

5. **Report and review the trends, issues and highlights regarding the finances.**
    Instead of leaders reviewing columns of numbers, have the Board Treasurer and/or Chief Executive provide a summary report, in addition to the numbers. The report explains:

a. Highlights to notice about the numbers, for example, an account that is significantly overspent or underspent.

b. Trends to notice about the numbers, for example, significant tendencies in certain accounts that might result in overspending or underspending, which might result in an issue later on.

c. Issues, for example, an account that is so overspent or underspent that Board members need to take action on that item now.

6. **Review financial reports, especially cash flow and budget-versus-actual reports.**
For new or small organizations, a cash-flow statement is extremely important to review because it shows whether the organization has the funds to pay its near-term bills or not. The Statement of Financial Activities (an income statement) should be reviewed at least quarterly and more often if the organization is struggling financially. A Statement of Financial Condition (balance sheet) should be reviewed at least quarterly, as well.

7. **Ensure the organization has adequate insurance coverage.**
For example, the organization might need general liability insurance to cover situations where someone is hurt on the premises, workers compensation if an employee is hurt on the job, property insurance if a major asset is damaged or destroyed or lost, or Directors and Officers (D&O) Insurance for Board members if someone sues the Board for its actions or lack of actions.

8. **Consider financial audits and/or reviews by external auditors.**
There are different types of audits and reviews. Typically, an audit is verification by an outside expert of the organization's financial management practices and its financial numbers in terms of accuracy and completeness. There are requirements for organizations to have an audit under different circumstances, depending on the state in the USA. Audits are a good way to verify that the numbers on the financial reports are accurate – that is always a strong reassurance to Board members. A review is an analysis by an outside expert on some aspect of financial management, usually of the financial numbers, to report on the quality of that aspect.

9. **Be sure that Board members are trained to analyze and decide on finances.**
Far too often, only one Board member – the Treasurer – really understands the finances. Some members even pride themselves that they refuse to try to understand finances – it is "just not their thing." Having that stance is irresponsible. Board members' responsibilities for the organization cannot be delegated to anyone else, especially to only one Board member. There should be at least one other Board member who knows the details of the finances, and who probably is on the Finance Committee. All Board members should be trained about how to analyze financial reports, detect where attention is needed, and make necessary decisions to address any issues.

Consider the free, online, self-directed, learning module about finance at http://www.managementhelp.org/fp_progs/fnc_mod/fnance.htm .

How to Track Performance of Business, Board and Employees

Performance is effectively achieving goals and objectives in a timely manner – goals that are directly aligned with the mission and strategic priorities of the organization. A primary responsibility of an organization's leaders is to ensure that the organization remains a high-performing business. Without specific goals to achieve – or at least monitoring for "best practices" – for the organization and management, leaders have little or no reliable means by which to measure performance.

Guidelines for Effective Leadership of Performance Management

If your Board uses Committees, then an Executive Committee would be helpful in this area, especially if the Executive Committee is comprised of Chairs of each of the other committees.

1.   **Specify goals – what will be achieved, how much, who will achieve them and by when.**
     Specifying goals in plans often is as important as – or more important than – extensive attention to the wording used in mission, vision and values statements. Specify goals in strategic plans, and especially in plans for Board development and finances. Do not worry about the specification of goals having to be perfect the first time, just do your best for now. The specifications can always be changed.

2.   **Monitor status toward achieving specific goals – and then adjust accordingly.**
     On a regular basis, monitor whether the goals are being achieved or not. If goals are not being achieved, then increase priority on achieving the goals, allocate more resources to achieve them, or extend the deadlines to reach the goals.

3.   **Monitor for "best practices" in different governance and management functions.**
     As mentioned in this guide, there can be wide disagreement about what constitutes "best practices." However, particularly for new or struggling businesses, they are much more likely to benefit from at least monitoring if the best practices are being followed than if those businesses ignore the best practices altogether.

 See "How to Use Organizational Assessments" on page 237. That section includes an example of a comprehensive assessment.

4.   **Invite each Board member to evaluate his/her performance on the Board.**
     This can include each member privately using a basic self-assessment tool that asks the member questions about the quality of his/her participation on the Board. Members could be invited to share the results of their self-evaluations in order to get help to improve their participation.

5.   **Ensure all Board members formally evaluate the entire Board, at least annually.**
     This includes all members privately completing an assessment tool that asks questions about the quality of the overall Board operations. These Board evaluations often can be done quickly and conveniently.

6.   **Ensure annual, formal evaluation of the Chief Executive.**
     Board members should ensure the CEO has certain responsibilities to carry out, as specified

in the CEO's job description. Also, the CEO should have certain annual goals to achieve (performance goals) and these goals should closely align with those in the strategic plan.

Consider "How Your Board Can Evaluate Your CEO" on page 46.

7. **Ensure evaluation of employees, according to procedures in personnel policies.**
   All employees, including the CEO, deserve feedback about the quality of their performance. That feedback, including in the form of performance evaluations, should be done according to guidelines in up-to-date personnel policies.

8. **Most importantly, evaluate products to verify they are meeting customer needs.**
   This means regularly hearing customers' opinions about your products.

How to Identify and Avoid Risks to the Business

The organization's leaders are responsible to ensure the reliable, ongoing and effective operations of their business. That includes ensuring that the most critical assets and functions are protected from sudden loss or significant damage. It also includes ensuring the means to quickly recover from those unfortunate situations. Most businesses have limited resources, so damage or loss to any of them means a significant – even traumatic – loss to operations. Therefore, risk management is an extremely important topic for Board members to address.

Guidelines for Effective Leadership of Risk Management

If your Board uses Committees, then a Finance Committee or Audit Committee would be helpful in this area.

Avoiding Sudden Loss or Damage

1. **Compensate the CEO commensurate to his/her capabilities and responsibilities.**

2. **Undertake ongoing CEO succession planning.**
   If the CEO suddenly left that position because of illness, death, firing or other reasons, it would be traumatic for the organization. Board members are responsible to minimize that effect on the organization, as much as possible.

Consider "How Your Board Can Ensure Smooth Succession to New CEO When Needed" on page 50.

3. **Ensure up-to-date job descriptions for all Board roles and critical employee roles.**
   In case any of their positions needs to be filled soon, at least there will be general descriptions so that others can more quickly understand the positions in order to help fill them as soon as possible.

4. **Ensure protected and stable facilities.**
   Computers and peripherals should have consistent levels of electrical protection, so that electrical surges do not damage them. Facilities should have adequate fire protection,

including water sprinklers that would not damage critical electrical components. All important information and materials should be locked, including password protection on computer files.

Avoiding Damaging Acts

1. **Have up-to-date, Board-approved personnel policies for employees.**
    Personnel policies specify how personnel should be hired, supervised and fired in accordance with employment laws that ensure fair, equitable and legally compliant treatment of others. Personnel, particularly those who supervise others, should be trained on the policies.

2. **Conduct background checks on potential new hires.**
    Background checks can detect if a person has committed crimes, major or minor in nature, which might suggest tendencies for how the person will act in the workplace.

3. **Conduct Board orientations once a year for members.**
    Board orientations make members aware of the unique aspects of the Board and the organization, including the Board's policies, for example, about ethics, conflict-of-interest, whistleblowers and document retention/destruction.

4. **Establish a Whistleblower Policy.**
    The policy should specify how Board members, employees and others could safely report that an alleged or actual organizational behavior or practice is illegal, unethical or inappropriate, without retaliation to the whistleblower.

5. **Establish a Board Ethics Policy.**
    The policy should specify the types of behaviors to conduct and/or to avoid in order to ensure that Board members conduct themselves in a manner that treats others fairly, equitably and that is legally compliant.

6. **Ensure accurate and Board-approved meeting minutes.**
    The minutes formally document Board members' deliberations, decisions and actions and, thus, serve as an accurate record to explain or justify to others the intentions, participation and actions of Board members.

7. **Establish up-to-date, Board-approved fiscal policies and procedures.**
    These procedures ensure that the activities in financial management are conducted in a highly thorough, accurate and useful manner that also minimizes the likelihood of malfeasance, including theft, fraud or misappropriation of funds.

8. **Annually conduct a financial audit and/or review.**
    The audit or review verifies the usefulness and accuracy of some or all aspects of financial management and, thus, greatly increases the likelihood that financial numbers and reports are indeed accurate.

Recovering from Loss

1. **All major functions should have written plans that specify current goals and priorities.**
    Organizations can more quickly recover if plans are documented so that personnel can quickly reference them to continue addressing important priorities. These should include the strategic plan, staffing plans, and marketing plan.

2. **Establish written procedures for routine tasks in the workplace.**
   These procedures can be referenced by personnel to quickly restore and resume the practices, thereby reducing adverse impact on operations as a result of a major interruption in operations. Procedures might be in regards to, for example, ordering supplies, operating facilities, delivering products and evaluating services.

3. **Have suitable insurance coverage.**
   Consider general liability insurance in case someone sues because of workplace injury. Consider property insurance in case property is damaged or lost. Consider professional liability insurance in case someone sues as a result of what he/she perceives as malpractice. Consider Directors and Officers Insurance to pay any lawsuits lost by Board members when someone sued the Board, alleging damage because of members' actions or inactions. Consider workers' compensation insurance in case someone is injured on the job.

4. **Establish a Document Retention/Destruction Policy.**
   The policy should specify which documents are retained for how long before they can be destroyed. It also should specify how the organization will completely cooperate if any documents are required by agencies investigating the organization or its affiliates.

Sample policies are in the Board topic in the Free Management Library at http://www.managementhelp.org/boards/boards.htm#anchor1322914 (they mention nonprofits, but the policies are the same).

5. **Keep contact lists of personnel and major stakeholders.**
   Document their names, the role that the personnel have with the organization, and contact information so they can be contacted, especially to help restore operations.

There are many resources about risk management at http://managementhelp.org/risk_mng/risk_mng.htm .

How to Ensure Sustainability of the Organization, People and Money

Sustainability often is misunderstood. It is more than generating enough money to keep paying the bills. True long-term, organizational sustainability for an organization involves four dimensions: strategic, products, personnel and finances. If sufficient attention is given to the first three dimensions of sustainability, then financial sustainability is much more likely to occur – and much easier to accomplish. The following guidelines help leaders ensure sustainability in each dimension.

Guidelines for Effective Leadership of Practices for Sustainability

If your Board uses Committees, then an Executive Committee would be helpful in this area, especially if it is comprised of Chairs of other committees, because that form of Executive Committee is more likely to have representatives from each of the four dimensions of sustainability.

Strategic Dimension of Sustainability

1.   **Ensure realistic vision and strategic goals for the organization.**
      If these are not realistic, then the organization will be trying to do too much. As a result, it will very likely run out of resources, including money and people.

2.   **Ensure realistic strategies to achieve the vision and goals.**
      Even if the vision and goals are realistic, if the efforts to achieve them are unrealistic, then the organization will have the same problems as mentioned above.

3.   **Modify the vision, goals and strategies to remain realistic when implementing plans.**
      One of the most important parts of a plan is often forgotten – procedures for how to change the plans. Consider extending deadlines to achieve goals or dropping them altogether if that is what it takes to ensure long-term sustainability.

Product Dimension of Sustainability

1.   **Verify what customers truly need, versus what they only want – or products will fail.**
      Customers will buy products based on what they want, and they will keep buying them based on what they need. If products are meeting the true needs of customers, then the products will continue to sell.

2.   **Change methods of product development and delivery, if needed, to improve quality.**
      Product development and delivery should undergo continuous improvement to remain effective. Listen to the opinions of customers and make changes accordingly.

Personnel Dimension of Sustainability

1.   **Ensure employees have sufficient expertise, training and resources.**
      Even if the products are designed well, the employees still have to have the capabilities and resources to develop and delivery those products. One of the best ways to know what employees need is to ask them.

2.   **Ensure employees are maximizing their performance.**
      This is a matter of effective supervision. Ensure there is effective delegation to employees (setting goals, sharing feedback, adjusting performance) and evaluation of employees such that members are always doing their best.

3.   **Ensuring redundancy and succession planning for employees in case people leave.**
      In a typical organization, operations would be damaged significantly if involved employees suddenly were no longer available. Ensure that all key employee roles have suitable "backup" personnel who also can do much of their jobs, and that guidelines and procedures exist for jobs, as much as possible.

Financial Dimension of Sustainability

1.   **Identify how much funding is needed to offset expenses.**
      Develop an annual budget and identify any deficits to know how much funding is needed, so that sales and spending targets can be adjusted accordingly to rid those deficits.

2.   **Allocate sufficient funding to administration and departments.**
      Know how much money each department needs. To do that, develop functional budgets. Those budgets identify the expected revenues and expenses associated with each product or

service, along with a percentage allocation of overhead (expenses common to all budget, for example, the salary of the Chief Executive, facilities and costs) to each.

3. **Track expenditures and revenues to promptly address financial priorities and issues.**
    Two reports are useful in particular, a budget-versus-actual report and cash-flow reports.

4. **Ensure adequate reserves and contingencies of funding if revenues are very low.**
    Establish a policy to set aside some percentage of your revenue, for example, 10% to be available in case of emergency. When budgeting, plan a couple of scenarios, one where all expected revenue arrives and another where, for example, only 70% of revenue arrives. Then, if there is a shortage of revenue, the business can reference the latter scenario to more quickly respond.

How to Ensure Transparency and Accountability in Governance and Operations

Board transparency means Board members always providing full disclosure and explanation of the organization's governance, finances and effects on communities, and also willingly supporting stakeholders' efforts to understand that information. Board accountability means members continually making the organization and themselves responsible to meet the expectations of stakeholders, and verifying with those stakeholders that their expectations are indeed being met.

The Sarbanes-Oxley Act of 2002 in the USA (commonly referred to as SOX) instituted certain requirements to make publicly traded companies more legally and ethically compliant, especially in financial practices, by increasing transparency and accountability of governance. For example, some requirements include establishing a skilled and independent Board Audit Committee (a Board committee comprised of independent Board members); the CEO and financial officers certifying accuracy of financial statements; and instituting policies for avoiding conflict of interest, having whistleblower protection and for retention/destruction of documents.

There is more information about *Sarbanes-Oxley* at
http://en.wikipedia.org/wiki/Sarbanes%E2%80%93Oxley_Act .

Guidelines for Effective Leadership to Ensure Transparency and Accountability

If your Board uses Committees, then a Finance Committee or Audit Committee would be helpful in this area.

1. **Recruit independent Board members.**
    These are Board members who are not employees, have no other business affiliation with the business, and are not close and personal friends of any executives in the business. Independent Board members are much more likely to challenge opinions and decisions offered by the CEO and other Board members.

2. **Establish a Board Conflict-of-Interest Policy.**
    The policy should explain conflict of interest, give examples, and specify what Board members can do to report and avoid apparent or real conflict-of-interest situations.

3. **Establish a Whistleblower Policy.**
The policy should specify how Board members, employees and others (the Whistleblower) could readily report apparent or actual events of illegal, unethical or inappropriate behaviors and practices, without retribution to the Whistleblower.

4. **Establish a Document Retention/Destruction Policy.**
The policy should specify which documents (hardcopy and computer-based) are retained and for how long, how documents are protected, and how documents are made readily available in the event of potential or actual criminal proceedings that might involve those documents.

5. **Establish a Board ethics policy.**
The policy should suggest behaviors for Board members to follow and/or avoid in order to ensure legally compliant, fair and equitable dealings when acting as members of the Board.

 Sample policies are in the Board topic in the Free Management Library at
http://www.managementhelp.org/boards/boards.htm#anchor1322914 .

6. **Utilize financial audits and/or reviews.**
The reporting of accurate financial information to the public is a strong requirement for achieving transparency and accountability. One approach to verifying financial accuracy is through reviews and/or audits. There are different types of financial analysis and services related to audits and reviews, ranging from a basic review of financial practices to the auditing for financial practices and their resulting financial data. A significant benefit of a review, especially an audit, is having an outsider's objective conclusions and recommendations regarding financial practices and/or information.

7. **Board review and approval of the annual filing to appropriate tax agency.**
Board members formally approve tax forms, thereby indicating that each member asserts that the information is accurate.

8. **Train Board members and managers how to analyze and decide about finances.**
Frequently, Boards have one member – the Treasurer – who is comfortable dealing with "the numbers." Each and every Board member is responsible to ensure that the numbers are accurate and that the organization is making the best decisions about those numbers. Therefore, all Board members should receive relevant, up-to-date and accurate financial information, and all should be trained how to understand and respond to that information.

9. **Make publicly available information about finances, governance and operations.**
For example, on the organization's website, provide: most recent strategic plan, annual report, list of Board members, Board policies, recent audited financial reports, and list of shareholders.

10. **Finally, be accountable to verify that the organization is meeting customer needs.**
Accountability is about more than efforts to avoid losing lawsuits – it is about Board members doing their primary job to verify that their business is indeed meeting the needs of its customers.

How to Lead Organizational Change and Capacity Building

The workforce is more diverse than it has ever been, so leadership and management styles must accommodate this diversity. Stakeholders and the public are expecting more accountability and results. Organizations are undergoing significant changes like never before. As a result, one of the most important applications of leadership is change in the organization.

Why Change and Capacity Building Can Be Difficult to Accomplish

Change can be difficult for you to accomplish for a variety of reasons.

- **People are afraid of the unknown.**
  They communicate their fear through direct means, such as complaining about the plans for change. Or, they communicate their fear indirectly, for example, by not attending meetings to plan the change.

- **People think things are just fine.**
  This might occur if the leaders have not adequately communicated the need for the change.

- **Many people are inherently cynical about change.**
  This cynicism often occurs if earlier attempts at change were unsuccessful, and not explained to employees.

- **Many doubt there are effective means to accomplish successful change.**
  They may have read publications in which writers assert that most organizational change efforts fail.

- **There may be conflicting goals in the organizational change effort.**
  Conflicting goals might be, for example, to significantly increase resources to accomplish change, yet substantially cut costs to remain viable. That conflict can occur, especially if employees were not involved in plans for the change.

- **Change often goes against values held dear by members in the organization.**
  The change may go against how members believe things should be done.

- **The original reason for the change, changes.**
  This situation is not uncommon, particularly in businesses with customers whose needs are rapidly changing, or in rapidly changing environments.

- **People get burnout during the change effort.**
  Organizational change usually takes longer to achieve than most people expect. Some experts assert that successful change can take from several months to several years.

- **Leaders of the change end up leaving the organization.**
  Especially in smaller organizations or organizations with very limited resources, leaders might not believe they are receiving sufficient value for what they are investing in the

126

organization. They might conclude that it is better to just leave. Or, the change may not be going as expected, and the leaders are asked to leave.

- **Participants do not understand the nature of planned change.**
  Frequently, participants expect the change to be according to a well-designed, well-organized effort that has few surprises. When surprises do occur, they lose faith in the change effort and seek to abandon it.

Requirements for Successful Organizational Change

There is not one standard procedure for accomplishing successful, significant change in all types of organizations. However, there has been a substantial amount of research lately about what seems to be common among projects for change that are deemed to be successful by the leaders in the organizations. So rather than looking for a procedure, perhaps it is most reasonable to consider a set of guidelines based on that research. Cummings and Worley (1995) describe a comprehensive, five-phase, general process for managing change, including: 1) motivating change, 2) creating vision, 3) developing political support, 4) managing the transition and 5) sustaining momentum. As you read the following paragraphs, think about how the guidelines might apply in your organization.

Phase 1: Motivating Change

This phase includes creating a readiness for change in the organization and developing approaches to overcome resistance to change. General guidelines for managing this phase include enlightening members of the organization about the need for change, expressing the current status of the organization and where it needs to be in the future, and developing realistic approaches about how change might be accomplished. Next, organization leaders need to recognize that people in the organization are likely to resist making major changes for a variety of reasons, including fear of the unknown, inadequacy to deal with the change and whether the change will result in an adverse effect on their jobs. People need to feel that their concerns are being heard. Leaders must widely communicate the need for the change and how the change can be accomplished successfully. Leaders must listen to the employees – people need to feel that the approach to change will include their strong input and ongoing involvement.

Phase 2: Creating Vision

Leaders in the organization must articulate a clear vision that describes what the change effort is striving to accomplish. Ideally, people in the organization have strong input to the creation of the vision and how it can be achieved. The vision should clearly depict how the achievement of the vision will improve the organization. It is critically important that people believe that the vision is relevant and realistic. Research indicates that cynicism is increasing in organizations in regard to change efforts. People do not want to hear the need for the latest "silver bullet" that will completely turn the organization around and make things better for everyone all the time. They want to feel respected enough by leaders to be involved and to work toward a vision that is realistic, yet promising in the long run.

Often the vision is described in terms of overall outcomes (or changes) to be achieved by all or parts of the organization, including associated goals and objectives to achieve the outcomes. Sometimes, an overall purpose, or mission, is associated with the effort to achieve the vision, as well.

Phase 3: Developing Political Support

This phase of change management is often overlooked, yet it is the phase that often stops successful change from occurring. Politics in organizations is about power. Power is important among members of the organization when striving for the resources and influence necessary to successfully carry out their jobs. Power is also important when striving to maintain jobs and job security. Power usually comes from credibility, whether from strong expertise or integrity. Power also comes from the authority of one's position in the organization.

Some people have a strong negative reaction when talking about power because power often is associated with negative applications, for example, manipulation, abuse or harassment. However, power, like conflict, exists in all human interactions and is not always bad. It is how power and conflict are used and managed that determine how power and conflict should be perceived.

Matters of power and politics are critically important to recognize and manage during organizational change activities. Change often means shifts in power across management levels, functions, and groups. To be successful, the change effort must recruit the support of all key power players, for example, senior management, subject matter experts and others who are recognized as having strong expertise and integrity.

A strong mechanism for ensuring alignment of power with the change effort is to develop a network of power-players who interact and count on each other to support and guide the change effort. Means to manage power can include ensuring that all power-players are involved in recognizing the need for change, developing the vision and methods to achieve the vision, and organization-wide communication about the status of change. Any recommendations or concerns expressed by those in power must be promptly recognized and worked through.

Phase 4: Managing Transition

This phase occurs when the organization works to make the actual transition from the current state to the future state. In consultations, this phase usually is called implementation of the action plans. The plans can include a wide variety of "interventions," or activities designed to make a change in the organization, for example, creating and/or modifying major structures and processes in the organization. These changes might require ongoing coaching, training and enforcement of new policies and procedures. In addition, means of effective change management must continue, including strong, clear, ongoing communication about the need for the change, status of the change, and solicitation of organization members' continuing input to the change effort.

Ideally, the various actions are integrated into one overall Change Management Plan (or an overall Strategic Plan) that includes specific objectives, or milestones, that must be accomplished by various deadlines, along with responsibilities for achieving each objective. Rarely are these plans implemented exactly as planned. Thus, as important as developing the plan is making the many ongoing adjustments to the plan with key members of the organization, while keeping other members up-to-date about the changes and the reasons for them.

Phase 5: Sustaining Momentum

Often, the most difficult phase in managing change is this phase when leaders work to sustain the momentum of the implementation and adjustment of plans. Change efforts can encounter a wide variety of obstacles, for example, strong resistance from members of the organization, sudden departure of a key leader in the organization, or a dramatic cut in funding. Strong, visible, ongoing support from top leadership is critically important to show overall credibility and accountabilities in the change effort. Those participating in the change effort often require ongoing support, often in the form of provision of resources, along with training and coaching. The role of support cannot be minimized – despite its importance during organizational change, the role of support is often forgotten. Employee performance management systems play a critical role in this phase of organizational change, including in setting goals, sharing feedback about accomplishment of goals, rewarding behaviors that successfully achieve goals and accomplish change, and addressing performance issues.

Major Roles During Change and Capacity Building

The process of organizational change can include a variety of key roles. Various individuals or groups can fill these roles at various times during the change process. Sometimes, individuals or groups can fill more than one role.

Change Initiator

It is conventional wisdom among experts in organizational change that successful change is often provoked by a deep "hurt" or crisis in the organization, for example, loss of a key leader in the organization, warnings from a major investor, or even actions of a key competitor. It is not uncommon then that someone inside the organization reacts to that deep hurt and suggests the need for a major change effort. Often the person who initiates the change is not the person who becomes the primary change agent.

Change Agent

The change agent is the person responsible for organizing and coordinating the overall change effort. Different people can fill the change agent role at different times during the project. For example, an outside consultant might be the first change agent. After the project plan has been developed and begins implementation, the change agent might be an implementation team comprised of people from the organization. If the change effort stalls out, the change agent might be a top leader in the organization who intercedes to ensure the change process continues in a timely fashion.

Champion for Change

Change efforts often require a person or group who continues to build and sustain strong enthusiasm about the change. This includes reminding everyone of why the change is occurring in the first place, and the many benefits that have come and will come from the change process. The champion might be the same person as the change agent at various times in the project.

Sponsor of Change

Usually, there is one key internal person or department that is officially the "sponsor," or official role responsible for coordinating the change process. In large organizations, that sponsor often is a department, such as Human Resources, Strategic Planning or Information Technology. In smaller organizations, the sponsor might be a team of senior leaders working to ensure that the change effort stays on schedule and is sustained by ongoing provision of resources and training.

Leadership, Supervision and Delegation

In this Guide, leadership is defined as setting direction and influencing people to follow that direction. A person can lead themselves, other individuals, other groups or an entire organization. Supervision is guiding the development and productivity of people in the organization. Effective supervisors are able to achieve goals by guiding the work of other people – by delegating.

Note that supervisors exist throughout an organization, depending on the particular structure of the Board members and employees. For example, the Board of Directors supervises the Chief Executive Officer (CEO), the CEO supervises managers or executive assistants, and managers supervise other employees.

The topic of leadership has become one of the most prominent topics in all of management literature today. It is almost impossible to find a general management book that does not include frequent mention of the topic of leadership. There are a variety of reasons for this, one of the most important being that successful organizational change requires strong, ongoing and visible leadership in support of that change. Leaders must model the type of behaviors that they want to see in their organization. Other reasons include:

- Leaders who work with others in the organization to clarify those desired results define the vision and goals, or desired results, for change.

- Leaders in the organization must "walk their talk" – they must behave according to the same values and behaviors that are to be accomplished by the change effort.

- Leaders must ensure the ongoing accountabilities, resources and support to ensure that actions are taken to accomplish the overall change effort.

There simply is no substitute for the role that leadership and supervision play in accomplishing successful organizational change. Thus, it is extremely important that leaders and supervisors in the organization have a strong understanding of basic principles of successful change in organizations.

How to Regularly Measure Overall Health of the Business

One of the biggest questions that lurk – consciously or unconsciously – at the back of leaders' minds is "How's our business really doing?" Despite the importance of this question, leaders rarely pursue means to measure the overall health of their business, even though there are a variety of free, easy-to-use tools available. The tools are usually comprehensive questionnaires that ask about the occurrence of certain "best practices" in the organization or the tools suggest standards of excellence for the organization to pursue in their operations. The tools might ask questions or suggest standards for operations, including: Boards, strategic planning, employees, finances, facilities and evaluations.

Use of the tools, especially questionnaires, can take as little as 30 minutes from each Board member and manager, and the analyses and reporting of results can take 2-3 hours – this is time well spent for the health of the organization.

Guidelines for Measuring Health of the Business

If your Board uses Committees, then a Planning Committee would be helpful, for example, if the assessment is being done as part of the strategic planning process.

1. **Annually, do the quick assessment near the beginning or middle of the fiscal year.**
    This timing is intended to produce results of the assessment that can be considered during strategic planning (strategic planning often is best to do in the middle of the fiscal year in time to produce an approved budget for the next fiscal year).

2. **Or do the assessment whenever the business seems to have many chronic struggles.**
    For example, an assessment is useful if the business continues to have financial shortfalls, high turnover, or frequent conflicts among Board members and employees. The assessment is a great way to identify the "root causes" of issues, rather than focusing only on symptoms.

3. **Be careful not to consider the tools as if they portray the "perfect" business.**
    The practical purpose of these tools is to identify the most important functions or practices that need to be improved in the business for now, not to identify each and every little issue. Answers to the questions should be informed by your own understanding of the business.

4. **Appoint a group of Board members and employees to oversee assessment activity.**
    The group would identify which tool to use, notify others about the purpose of the tool and how to use it, and coordinate the analysis and reporting of results. They might be a project team that works closely with an outside consultant to administer the assessment.

5. **If it is the organization's first time to do an organizational assessment, consider help.**
    You might hire a consultant to work with the group, including to recommend a tool, guide the planning and communication about use of the tool, analyze and report the results, and generate recommendations to address any issues found in the results.

6. **Include recommendations from the assessment in the strategic and Board plans.**
    Be sure that the recommendations somehow are captured in other plans, which greatly increases the likelihood that the recommendations will be followed. The best plans (strategic plans, Board development plans, marketing plans, etc.), include specification of who will do what and by when and also a means to track implementation.

Consider "How to Use Organizational Assessments" on page 237.

How to Focus on Real Causes of Problems, Not Just Symptoms

Leaders are charged to make very important decisions about their organizations. In their roles, they often hear about major, ongoing problems. Often, they do not fully understand the situations and so they end up making the wrong decisions. Employees also do not understand how to identify the true causes of problems. So everyone ends up focusing on the symptoms of the problems, rather than solving the problems. Here are some common examples:

-   The business keeps running out of money. Board members and employees continue to believe that the solution to their problems is to keep maximizing profits – but the cash crises continue to occur. So the Chief Executive blames the Board for not supporting strategies to maximize profits even more.

- Products or services have poor sales. Board members continue to tell the Chief Executive that he/she must do a better job of marketing, but increased advertising is not making any difference. So the Board blames the Chief Executive.

- Leaders continue to notice increasing conflicts and high turnover among Board members and employees. Board members tell the Chief Executive to get some leadership training. The Chief Executive does and later tells the Board that the problem is also caused by poor strategic planning. Board members disagree and lose confidence in their Chief Executive.

In these examples, the Board and Chief Executive are dealing with the symptoms of the problem, rather than the real causes. Wise leaders can see beyond the symptoms to get at the real solutions. Table IV:1 and the rest of this section describe one way to understand the inner workings of organizations and how to be more successful at resolving problems for the long-term. Notice how the functions in a business seem to occur in a cycle, from top to bottom and back to the top again. As you read the rest of this section, notice how problems often show up as symptoms in functions near the bottom of the table, but are resolved by addressing functions at the top.

Table IV:1 includes the roles and integration of standard management functions, including the planning, implementation and evaluation of products or services, staffing, marketing, finances, and facilities. The relationships between these functions and common symptoms are described here.

Planning

1. **Poor strategic planning causes symptoms throughout the organization.**
   During strategic planning, members of the Board and employees determine the overall purpose (mission) and direction (vision and goals) for the organization, as well as the methods (values, strategies and objectives) for the organization to work toward the purpose and direction. The strategic planning process provides direction and efficiency to all other major functions in the organization. Thus, if strategic planning is not done well, symptoms of the problem can show up in Board operations, staffing, and finances. To address these symptoms, strategic planning must be improved.

2. **Poor product planning causes symptoms, especially in sales and finances.**
   During product planning, the marketing research (or "inbound marketing") activities are conducted to identify: what needs and wants exist in which markets, what product will meet those needs and wants, who the competitors are, how the product will be different than its competitors, how the product should be priced and how it should be delivered to the market. If product planning is not done well, products and services will not be meeting the needs of customers. This will result in decreased revenues. Many problems commonly associated with financial shortfalls are really the result of poor planning. Until planning is improved, attempts to improve financial management are likely to be ineffective.

3. **Poor resource planning causes symptoms, especially in staffing and funding.**
   During resource planning, planners identify what resources (for example, the best Board members and employees, money, trainings and facilities) are needed to most effectively work toward the mission. Thus, if resource planning is not done well, the Board members and employees might not be the best for the business, and funding might be inadequate. Facilities might be insufficient, as well. This can cause related symptoms, such as conflicts and burnout among Board members and employees. Many problems commonly associated with Boards, staffing and finances are really the result of poor resource planning, which, in turn, needs good strategic and business planning.

Table IV:1 – Cycle of Important Functions in Business

Inputs: Input from stakeholders, revenue, laws and regulations, etc.		
System Loop	**Major Functions**	**Comments**
Planning	Strategic planning for organization – establish: (mission? vision? values? goals?)	▪ All activities are integrated with each other.

▪ Driving force behind all activities is leadership among Board and employees.

▪ Leadership sets direction, guides resources toward the direction, and makes adjustments to keep resources on track.

▪ Strategic goals set direction for organization and suggest performance goals for Board and employees.

▪ Communicating about these goals is key to achieving them. |
	Planning for each product/service – determine: (customers? marketing? costs?)	
	Resource planning – need what: (people? revenue? technologies? other?)	
Developing	Revenue development (for major activities)	
	Board and employee development (recruiting, training, organizing)	
	Development of other resources (facilities, supplies, policies, procedures, etc.)	
Operating	Supervision and teamwork	
	Operations	
	Advertising and promotions	
	Facilities management	
	Financial management	
	Administration	
Evaluating	Board	
	Individuals	
	Products or Services	
	Processes	
	Organization	
Outputs: Customer needs that were verified to have been met by your products, for example, by conducting customer surveys and interviews.		

Developing

4. **Board and employee development need good strategic planning.**
   Board and staff development begins with identifying what expertise is needed to achieve the goals in the strategic plan. Then the best members are recruited, trained and organized in a manner that best achieves the goals in the strategic plan. If that plan is not done well, then ongoing confusion, conflicts and inefficiencies can occur, resulting in high turnover and poor performance of the Board and employees. Administrative operations can suffer. Problems with Board members and employees can be symptoms of poor overall planning and resource development, including recruitment, selection, organization and development of members.

5. **Successful operations require clarification of roles, and some policies and procedures.**
   There are a variety of types of resources (other than money and people) that need to be obtained and developed, for example, facilities, equipment, roles, policies and procedures. Perhaps most important among these resources are roles, policies and procedures. They form the "glue" that aligns and integrates the resources of money and people. If they are not established, they can cause significant symptoms, such as increasing inefficiencies, conflicts and turnover. The best solution to these conflicts might be to clarify roles, policies and procedures, rather than chastising people to make them get along better with each other.

Operating

By now, you understand that problems that show up in the day-to-day activities (for example, in supervision, operations, financial management and advertising) are often symptoms of larger problems in planning and resource development. Thus, to address those symptoms for the long-term, Board members and employees must ensure that planning and resource development were done well. Without that understanding among Board members and employees, they will likely continue to focus primarily on the symptoms, making things much worse in the long term.

Below are descriptions of other major functions in organizations and how they are integrated and related to each other.

6. **Supervision and teamwork**
   A supervisor is someone who oversees the progress and productivity of people who report directly to the supervisor. Thus, a Board supervises the Chief Executive Officer, and a CEO supervises, for example, department staff. Teamwork is about how people work together to coordinate goals, roles, leadership and communication. The activities of supervision and teamwork are critical to the success of a business because those activities ensure that goals are established in accordance with strategic goals, progress toward the goals is monitored, and adjustments are made among individuals to more effectively achieve the goals. Many times, recurring problems in other types of operating activities are really symptoms of poor teamwork.

7. **Product development and delivery**
   This includes the ongoing activities that provide products directly to the customers. The nature of these activities depends on the types of products and markets. For example, health-related products often require highly trained employees and technologies. In contrast, delivery services need personnel with strong skills in driving vehicles. The success of products depends a great deal on the effectiveness of strategic and product planning and of teamwork in the organization.

8. **Advertising and promotions**
   These "outbound" marketing activities are geared to inform stakeholders (customers, investors and suppliers) about products and services, and also to keep those products and services in the

minds of stakeholders. Many times, problems in advertising and promotions are the result of poor planning, such as unclear identification of what specific groups of customers should be served, the needs of each group, and how the products or services meet each need.

9. **Facilities management**
   This includes identifying what major facilities will be needed and managed, such as buildings, equipment and computer systems. The need for major facilities is identified during resource planning. Thus, problems caused by lack of facilities often are a result of poor resource planning. Ineffective use of facilities might be a symptom of poor employee development.

10. **Financial management**
    Activities of financial management include documenting financial transactions (bookkeeping), generating and analyzing financial statements, and making adjustments to budgets based on the various analyses. This is usually done according to Board-approved fiscal policies and procedures. Many times, people report problems with finances when they really mean problems with inadequate funding. Ineffective planning, resource development and/or financial management often cause those problems. Problems that are truly about financial management often can be addressed by training personnel about bookkeeping, and about generating and analyzing financial statements.

11. **Administrative activities**
    This includes the extensive range of detailed activities that must be coordinated and conducted on a daily basis to ensure the efficient operations of the business. Many people think of these activities as clerical, or "paperwork." Problems with administrative tasks often are the result of poor resource planning and staff development, or lack of appreciation for policies and procedures.

Evaluating

12. **Board self-evaluation**
    Members of the Board of Directors should regularly evaluate the quality of their activities on a regular basis. Activities might include staffing the Board with new members, developing the members into well-trained and resourced members, discussing and debating topics to make wise decisions, and supervising the CEO. Probably the biggest problem with Board self-evaluation is that it does not occur frequently enough. As a result, Board members have no clear impression of how they are performing as members of a governing Board. Poor Board operations, when undetected, can adversely affect the entire organization.

13. **Employee (individual) performance evaluation**
    Most of us are familiar with employee performance appraisals, which evaluate the quality of an individual's performance in their position in the organization. Ideally, those appraisals reference the individual's written job description and performance goals to assess the quality of the individual's progress toward achieving the desired results described in those documents. Continued problems in individual performance often are the results of poor strategic planning, staff development and communications. If overall planning is not done effectively, individuals can experience continued frustration, stress and low morale, resulting in their poor overall performance. If goals that result from planning are not clearly communicated, the individual may not understand how to succeed or perform effectively. Experienced leaders have learned that continued problems in performance are not always the result of a poor work ethic – the recurring problems may be the result of larger, more systemic problems in the organizations.

14. **Product evaluation**

Product evaluations have become much more common, particularly as organizations realize the importance of getting customers' opinions. Product evaluations are typically focused on the quality of the product's design, development, delivery and service. An ineffective product evaluation often is the result of poor product planning – products should be designed so they can be evaluated. It can also be the result of improper training about evaluation – evaluations do not have to be large, scientifically conducted projects. The focus should be on accuracy, but also on practicality, for example, with brief surveys and interviews. When product evaluations are not performed well, or at all, there is little feedback to the strategic and product planning activities. When strategic and product planning are done poorly, the entire organization is adversely effected.

15. **Evaluation of cross-functional processes**

Cross-functional processes are those that span several systems, such as operations, functions and projects. Common examples of major processes include information technology systems and quality management of services. Because these cross-functional processes span so many areas of the organization, problems in these processes can be the result of any type of ineffective planning, development and operating activities.

16. **Organizational evaluation**

Ongoing evaluations of the entire organization are a major responsibility of all leaders in the organization. Leaders sometimes do not recognize that the ongoing activities of management actually include organizational evaluations – but they do. The activities of organizational evaluation occur every day. However, those evaluations usually are not done systematically. As a result, useful evaluation information is not provided to the strategic planning processes. Consequently, both processes can be ineffective because they do not focus on improving the quality of operations in the workplace.

How to Make Sure Your Board Participates in Change

Especially in projects for change in small- to medium-sized organizations, the Board can be the leverage point – the point in the project that can make the biggest difference – for success in the projects because the Board is the ultimate authority in the organization. To ensure that Board members have strong participation in major projects for change, consider the following guidelines.

Benefits of Board Involvement in the Project

1. **The Board ensures the project is fully resourced and shows political support.**
   Board members have full authority for allocation of resources for the business. Consequently, Board members can ensure that the project has all necessary resources, including people, money and time. Their allocation shows strong political support for change, which can sustain ongoing motivation and momentum for change.

2. **The Board ensures that project plans are developed and implemented.**
   The Board supervises the Chief Executive Officer, having full authority over the CEO. Although employees (including the CEO) usually develop and implement many of the action plans in the project for change, the Board can ensure that those plans are fully developed and completely implemented.

3.   **Board members provide a wide range of valuable expertise.**
Board members often have a wide range of useful skills for governing the organization, such as planning, leadership, management, supervision and problem solving. They may also have technical knowledge of the organization or the industry. Those skills can be useful during a project for change.

4.   **The Board provides time and energy to help implement plans for change.**
Employees often are already overloaded. Giving them yet more work to do (during your project) can completely overload them such that they collapse altogether, which could significantly damage the organization. Although the Board is responsible to govern the organization by establishing broad plans and policies, Board members still can help with implementation of various plans by helping to develop and oversee development of plans. Plans might be to address issues in strategic planning, marketing, staffing, or financial management.

5.   **The Board can provide objective assessments on project issues and results.**
Board members usually are not involved a great deal in the day-to-day activities of a project. Consequently, they often retain an objective perspective on the activities and results of the project. Their perspective can be valuable when addressing issues in the project and evaluating results of the project.

6.   **Involvement of Board members is a powerful means of Board development.**
One of the best ways to get or keep good Board members is to give them something to do. One of the best ways to get rid of Board members is to give them something to do. Your project can be useful means to give Board members something to do – and, thus, to develop the Board. If a Board member is not prepared to act, it creates the opportunity for the Board member to leave and for the organization to get a new Board member that is willing to do something.

Ensuring the Board Is Highly Involved in the Project

1.   **The Board should be involved in the first meetings about the project for change.**
In projects that are intended to accomplish significant change in an organization, members of the Board certainly should be aware of – and have approved – the project. That often includes approving a budget to obtain and support resources used in the project.

2.   **Educate Board members about successful organizational change.**
Members of the Board almost always have full-time jobs and are quite busy. Still, you should briefly educate them about what it takes to accomplish successful organizational change. You might provide them a short article, or brief presentation.

 Consider "Requirements for Successful Organizational Change" on page 127.

3.   **Involve at least one Board member in a Project Team.**
In projects for change, you should try to form a Project Team comprised of key personnel from the organization. The Team oversees development of a change management plan. Ensure that at least one Board member, ideally the Board Chair, is included on the Team.

4. **Board members should be highly involved in activities that affect the Board.**
Board members should participate in various aspects of the project, depending on its scope. For example, if the project includes Board development and development of the CEO position, Board members should be highly involved in setting and achieving project goals.

5. **Include Board development in the project if many issues exist in the organization.**
If the organization has many problems, then it is likely that the Board has major problems, as well. Otherwise, the Board would have been effectively governing and the many organizational issues would not have existed. Also, one of the most powerful approaches to addressing problems among employees is to build up the Board to help you to address those problems. Therefore, the Change Management Plan should have a goal to develop the Board.

6. **If there are CEO and/or employee issues, form a Board Personnel Committee.**
A Board Personnel Committee is responsible to ensure that staffing (including the CEO) is carefully planned and fully utilized. That includes providing ongoing coaching to the CEO to ensure that his/her role is competently filled. A Board Personnel Committee can be of tremendous value to coach the CEO through the struggles of making major changes.

7. **All Board members should be copied on project reports.**
All Board members have a responsibility to govern the organization. All Board members should always be able to access any information inside the organization. Consequently, they should be copied on reports about the status of your project.

8. **The Board should formally approve the Change Management Plan.**
Formal approval of the Plan by the Board helps to ensure that Board members have seen and will support the Plan. It also gives the Plan much more credibility to all members of the organization.

9. **The Board Executive Committee should "police" implementation of action plans.**
Ensure that the Board Executive Committee regularly reviews the implementation status of the Change Management Plan. If the organization has many issues, if often helps if the Executive Committee is comprised of Chairs of all Board committees. That design helps the Executive Committee to always be aware of what the other committees are doing.

10. **Board members should be highly involved in reviewing evaluation results.**
Finally, Board members should ensure that the project actually addresses the most prominent issues in the organization. They should regularly review results of evaluations of project activities as those activities occur. Also, they should review results of evaluations of the quality of final results from the project.

How to Structure the Business and Its People

One of the most common ways that organizations make sure that the results of a change effort are maintained for the long term is by way of restructuring all or parts of the organization. There is an increasingly used phrase that states, "Structures determine behaviors, which determine events." That phrase reminds us that, many times when we notice undesirable behaviors or events (for example, poor performance, conflicts or high turnover among employees), the cause is not the people involved; rather the cause is the poorly designed structures in which employees must work. In the context of organizations, structures are the organization's designs, plans, policies and procedures. There also is a common phrase, "form follows function," which means (again, in the context of organizations) that the structures should be designed to best maximize the effectiveness and efficiencies of the functions in the organization. Therefore, when undertaking organizational change to solve problems or to make things even better, organizational structures should get a lot of attention during projects for change.

How to Organize or Re-Organize People

Important Terms in Organizing People

- **Span of control**
  This is depicted by the number of employees who work for you, or report to you. (These are your "direct reports.") You want enough people in the organization or your group to get the work done. However, you also have to be careful that you do not have so many people that you cannot keep track of (or be helpful to) them all. It is common that supervisors have, for example, anywhere from one or two to even 10 or 15 people. Fifteen people can be very difficult for one person to supervise!

- **Authority**
  In your role as a leader, you have some formally granted authority to make decisions, pursue goals and to get the resources to pursue the goals. Authority in a managerial role may exist only to the extent that your people agree to grant you this authority or follow your orders. That is why it is so important to effectively work with your direct reports, so that they understand what you are doing and why.

- **Responsibility**
  Your responsibilities are your obligations when carrying out your assignments or conducting certain activities in your role. It is very important that a person who has responsibility for a certain activity is also given the appropriate authority to get and use the resources needed to do that activity.

- **Delegation**
  Delegation includes giving someone the responsibility to achieve a desired result and the authority to achieve those results. When delegation is done well, the person is assigned the results, but is given the freedom to choose how to achieve the results.

- **Accountability**
  This is having the responsibility for achieving desired results and for proving that those results were achieved. For example, a Chief Executive Officer can hold a product manager accountable for a product to achieve its intended uses for the customers.

- **Chain of command**
  Your chain of command includes all of the employees who eventually report to you, including your direct reports and all others who report to them, etc.

- **Job (or position)**
  A job is a collection of tasks and responsibilities that an employee is responsible to conduct. Jobs, or positions, have titles, such as Chief Executive Officer.

- **Task**
  A task is a unit of work, that is, a set of activities needed to produce some result, for example, vacuuming a carpet, writing a memo and sorting the mail. Jobs often are comprised of numerous tasks.

- **Job description**
  A job description is a list of the general tasks, or functions, and responsibilities of a position. Typically, they also include to whom the position reports, qualifications needed by the person in the job in order to perform the job well, and the salary range for the position. Job descriptions are usually developed by conducting a *job analysis*, which includes examining the tasks and sequences of tasks necessary to perform the job.

- **Role**
  A role is the set of responsibilities or expected results associated with a job. A job usually includes several roles.

Primary Considerations When Organizing People

In the past, organizations were designed primarily by working from such abstract concepts as differentiation and integration of activities. Applications of those concepts too often were vague, confusing and frustrating. Now we have access on the Web to a vast range of examples of organizational designs and job descriptions that we can reference. However, organizations should never just adopt the design or descriptions that they find elsewhere. They should always modify them to suit the nature and needs of their own organization. The following guidelines will be helpful.

1. **Realize that there is no one "perfect" way to organize people in your organization.**
   There are a variety of ways that you might organize the furniture in your house in order to optimize your comfort and activities around the house. There probably is no one perfect design that works for everyone all the time. Organizing people is similar. You do the best you can to organize it in the best design for now, and then keep changing it as you need to.

2. **Consider how people are organized in organizations with similar missions, size and age.**
   For example, if yours is a new retail business, then consider similar businesses in your locale or elsewhere. New and small- to medium-sized organizations often have very similar designs, or ways of organizing people.

 Refer to "Organization Charts of Typical Small/Medium-Sized Businesses" on page 14.

3.   **Differentiate between major functions.**
        Different job functions usually require different capabilities and interests among employees. For example, an employee working to design and develop a product would likely have very different skills than an employee who is successful in selling that product. Employee productivity rests in large part on the commitment of employees. Employees who are not organized into jobs that they enjoy and not able to affiliate with like-minded employees, are less likely to perform well and may even leave the organization.

4.   **Differentiate between product lines.**
        Different product lines may target different markets or require different priorities, rhythms and scale. For example, employees delivering directly to consumers would probably have very different requirements and quotas than employees delivering to production facilities. Employee commitment is influenced by the sense of shared goals and priorities.

5.   **When identifying jobs, review job descriptions in similar organizations.**
        Examples of job descriptions can give you a basic impression of how duties and responsibilities might be grouped together into one job. Now with the Web, people can view examples of a wide range of job descriptions for many different roles in many different types of organizations. As mentioned above, you should never merely adopt another job description exactly as it is. You should always modify descriptions according to the nature and needs of your organization by following guidelines in this section.

Examples of many job descriptions are available on the Web at http://www.job-descriptions.org/ .

6.   **Who should the person in each job, or position, report to?**
        Notice which positions must closely rely on each other in order to do all of their jobs. Those positions might best be organized under the same supervisor. Be careful, though, that the supervisor does not end up having too many direct reports to manage well. Discuss the situation with the supervisor and then closely watch if he/she is indeed able to keep track of all his/her direct reports. Also consider who has the most capability to do the job, has the most control of the resources needed to do the job, or has the most experience in supervising people. The person who most closely meets these qualifications might be the best person to supervise the person in the job. The person might report to a group of people. However, it usually is most effective if the person ultimately reports to one person, or one supervisor.

7.   **How can communication and coordination best be coordinated between positions?**
        Again notice which positions must closely rely on each other in order to do all of their jobs. Make sure that these positions regularly share information, for example, in staff meetings or status reports.

8.   **Communicate the new organization and closely monitor to see if changes are needed.**
        The best way to communicate the new organization is by using organization charts (see the following section). Closely listen to the opinions and recommendations of your people to discern if any changes should be made to the new organization.

Consider "How to Develop New Employee Positions" on page 143.

How to Design Organization Charts

When you are done organizing people, one of the most straightforward means to describe the new organization to others is by providing them an organization chart. The organization chart is a clear depiction of the positions in the organization and how they relate to each other.

 Refer to "Organization Charts of Typical Small/Medium-Sized Businesses" on page 14.

Important considerations in the design of an organization chart are:

1. **Depict the chain of command from the top to the bottom of the chart.**
   The Board of Directors is ultimately responsible to ensure that the business is governed in an effective way in order to serve the needs of the public.

2. **Depict positions, rather than only names of people in the positions.**
   The chain of command is based on the relationships of the positions in the organization, not on the people in the positions. Therefore, always label the positions with their titles, for example, "Chief Executive Officer" or "Product Manager." Optionally, you can include the names of the people in those positions under the titles.

3. **Depict the chain of command between the positions.**
   Draw solid, or continuous, lines between boxes (or positions) where the person in the upper box is the supervisor, or the person with direct authority, over the people in the boxes immediately underneath. If people in various positions have strong influence on each other's jobs (for example, by providing strong expertise or significant resources), but do not have direct authority over each other, then connect the boxes with dotted, or broken, lines to depict that influence, but lack of authority.

4. **Be sure to indicate authorization of the organization chart.**
   The chart should depict that it is official and formally used in the organization. A signature line at the bottom of the page will serve this function. The chart usually is signed by someone in a position depicted near the top of the page.

5. **Be sure to put a date on the chart.**
   The designs of organizations can change rapidly. It is healthy to change the design of an organization if its major priorities, plans and policies have changed. Therefore, be sure to put a date on each version of the chart, so you can refer to a specific version of the chart.

6. **Issue the new organization chart and the reason for it, and invite input from others.**
   Always describe the reasons for the current design. If you are re-organizing an established group, then mention that it is healthy for organizations to re-organize. Be clear that you are open to the opinions of others and how they can provide them to you. Finally, ask for the patience of those involved as the new organization design is further refined.

How to Identify When New Employee Roles are Needed

Formal Method – Reference Strategic Plan

This is much is easier if the organization has been conducting planning, especially strategic planning. When determining staffing needs, consider the following guidelines.

The strategic plan should specify strategic goals and the objectives to achieve each goal. The plan should include an action plan that specifies who will do what and by when in order to achieve the goals. The plan should include a listing of the resources needed to implement the action plan. These resources should include, for example, funding, facilities and expertise (people). When analyzing your staffing needs, reference the action planning and the associated list of what expertise is required from people.

Consider "How to Set Clear Purpose and Direction for the Business" on page 101.

Informal Method – Grow/Change Based on Current Feedback

Often, leaders realize the need for a new organizational position when employees continue to report being short-handed and they mention that certain tasks are not being done. This issue can point to the need for new people. (This issue can also point to other causes, for example, inadequate supervision or training.)

How to Develop New Employee Positions

Activities to develop new positions should be in accordance with the most current, Board-approved personnel policies and procedures. Be sure to understand the role of those policies.

Consider "How to Develop and Update Your Personnel Policies" on page 171.

1. **Draft a job description.**
   Management should draft a job description which specifies the general responsibilities of the new position along with some of the specific duties of the job, the title for the position, and also any special skills, training or credentials required to do the job.

   a. Do not merely seek job descriptions from other organizations and adopt those as is. Your open position is unique and job descriptions are very important so you should develop your own – the process of completing the job description is usually quite enlightening.

   b. Note which job activities are essential and which are non-essential.

   c. Add whom the position reports to and whether the position is full-time or part-time.

d. Consider if the position requires any special physical skills. This may be important when considering accommodations to candidates with physical disabilities and effects. Various government agencies have employment laws in this regard, for example, the Americans with Disabilities Act in the USA.

e. If an employee must fill the position (see the next sections to consider if a consultant is more appropriate), determine whether the position should be salaried or hourly. Usually, highly skilled and/or professional jobs are salaried, while entry-level positions are hourly.

f. Invite employees to review and edit the drafted job description.

g. Consider including a six-month probationary period for the new position and if you do so, be sure to update your personnel policies to describe your organization's use of the probationary conditions. A probationary period allows you to fire an employee during the first six months if you have concerns and greatly decreases the chances you will be sued for wrongful termination.

Examples of many job descriptions are available on the Web at http://www.job-descriptions.org/ .

3. **Would a consultant (independent contractor) be most appropriate?**
At this point, consider if a consultant might fill the new position. For example, it is common for small- to medium-sized organizations to hire accountants as consultants. Generally, if the activities associated with your new role require any of the following, then consider hiring a consultant:

a. Highly skilled personnel for a fixed and limited duration

b. A unique set of resources or tools that are not commonly available and would come with a professional (for example, a graphics designer)

Note that the consideration whether to hire an employee or an independent contractor is a very serious one. If the wrong choice is made, then you may be assessed strong fees and penalties.

See "How to Hire and Work With Consultants" on page 145.

4. **Determine the approximate cost of the new role.**
You should develop a compensation program, with policies that outline the procedure for determination of salary and benefits.

Consider "Basics of Benefits and Compensation" on page 175.

a. Estimate the salary range for the new position. Set this range by talking to other organizations with similar products or services, or by scanning classified sections of newspapers with ads for similar roles. You can also reference various salary surveys.

There's a long list of different salary surveys at http://jobstar.org/tools/salary/index.php .

b. Finalize how much the position will cost the organization by adding "fringe" to the salary. Fringe includes costs of benefits planned for the new role, including health and dental and life insurance, and retirement benefits, along with Workers Compensation and any pension plans. Depending on the state in which you live, you may be required to pay certain employment taxes for part-time people, usually if they are at or over half-time. For planning purposes, fringe might be estimated at 40% of the salary.

c. Additional costs of the position result from, for example, training, equipment, rental of space, postage and copying.

5. **For major, new employee positions, get feedback and authorization from the Board.** In small organizations where addition of an employee is very significant or if the new position is a management position, then the Chief Executive Officer may want to work with the Board Chair to prepare for communication of the new job to the Board. Propose the new position to the Board by attaching a proposal letter to the drafted job description along with description of how the position will be funded and sending it to all Board members for their review before the next Board meeting. At the next Board meeting, invite open discussion and questions about the new role. Seek the Board's authorization for the new position.

6. **Finalize the job description.** Update the job description with relevant feedback from the Board. It is important that the job description be as accurate as possible because it is the basis for determining compensation, conveying the role to the new employee and conducting regular performance appraisals. Be sure to note the version of the job description by including the date on the bottom. The job description should be reviewed and updated annually, usually by the employee and the person's supervisor during the performance review cycle.

How to Hire and Work With Consultants

Good Reasons to Hire an External Consultant

There are many reasons to consider hiring a consultant rather than a permanent employee.

- The organization has limited or no expertise in the area of need, for example, to develop a communications link between current products and a related product from another company.

- The time of need is short-term, for example, less than a year, so it may not be worth hiring a full-time, permanent employee.

2.   **Management consultants**
      They help leaders and managers to be more productive at planning, organizing, leading and coordinating resources in the organization. Applications for their services might include leadership, management and supervisory development. The types of services provided by these consultants might be referred to as either technical assistance or organizational development activities (see the next paragraph).

3.   **Organizational development consultants**
      This type of consultant helps organizations improve performance, often by focusing on changing a significant portion of the organization or the entire organization itself. These consultants often use a wide variety of approaches, tools and techniques to affect various systems and functions across the organization, for example, technical assistance, coaching, facilitation and training.

Generalists and Specialists

Some people refer to specialists and generalists as overall, major types of consultants. They might refer to technical consultants as specialists. Many people would consider organizational development consultants to be generalists.

Whether management consultants are generalists or specialists depends on the nature of their services. The more specific the nature of their services, the more likely they would be referred to as specialists.

Functional or Focused Services

Recently, the terms "functional" and "focused" have been used to refer to servicing a specific system, function or process, for example, marketing systems, financial systems or information technology. Functional and focused activities are similar to or the same as technical assistance.

Types of Consulting Can Overlap

The distinctions among the types of consultants can be blurry. For example, a management consultant or technical consultant might operate as an organizational development consultant if he/she works in a manner that affects a significant portion or all of the organization.

Also, each type of consultant might be needed at various times in a project. For example, an organizational development consultant might work with a client to identify the most important problems in an organization. Later on, a management consultant might be needed to train and coach various leaders and managers during the change effort. You might also bring in various product and technical consultants to contribute their specific expertise to the change effort.

Where to Get Consultants

1.   Contact professional associations, for example, networks of organization development practitioners, facilitators, trainers, accountants, lawyers and computer users.

2.   Consult the local telephone company's Yellow Pages under the category "Consultant. "

3.   Call a local university or college and speak to someone in the college of Human Resources, Training and Development, or Business Administration.

4.   Ask other organizations for ideas, particularly those that have similar services and head-count size, for contacts and references.

How You Can Make Consultancies as Productive as Possible

1.   Know what you want before you get a consultant. Imagine what you would have if the consultancy worked out perfect. Keep that vision when you start to look for a consultant.

2.   For critical projects, get Board agreement on the hiring of the consultant. Ideally, (if your Board uses committees) appoint a committee such as the Personnel Committee or Project Committee to oversee the consultant progress.

3.   Do not become dependent on a consultant. Be sure that the project has a start and stop point.

4.   If possible, do not limit the consultant to recommending action. Get the consultant involved in implementing recommendations.

5.   Fix causes, not symptoms. Do assessments, look closely at what you see and hear, then figure out the cause. It is often not what you see or hear that is the root cause of problems, rather it is the organization's strategies, structures, roles and plans that cause the problems.

Consider "How to Regularly Measure Overall Health of the Business" on page 130 and "How to Focus on Real Causes of Problems, Not Just Symptoms" on page 131.

Getting and Hiring the Best Consultant

(This section includes advice graciously provided by Barbara Davis, Consultant, St. Paul, Minnesota.)

1.   Give interested people the information they need to understand your needs by using a "request for proposal" (RFP) or "request for quotation" (RFQ); direct conversation may work as well.

2.   Get a written proposal from every interested party. Do not just talk to one consultant.

3.   Get a bid on the fee and reimbursable expenses.

4.   Look at more than one proposal and examine them all carefully.

5.   Interview the best prospects and check their references. Consider their extent of expertise, listening skills, ability to adapt to the nature of your organization, and ability to coach to ensure the organization can address the problem in the future.

6.   Do not pick someone based only on price.

7.   Be sure there is no conflict of interest with the consultant that you want to hire. The consultant should not be faced with conflicting roles if working for your organization. For example, the consultant should not also be on your Board of Directors or be an employee.

8.   Write a good contract including:

   a.   Start and stop date of the agreement.

   b.   List of specific, tangible "deliverables" that will be produced by the consultant.

   c.   Checkpoints at which you can evaluate projects, for example, have specific phases.

   d.   Project completion date, including date for deliverables.

   e.   Payment schedule (consider making partial payments based on provision of each deliverable or project phase).

   f.   Agreement on reimbursable expenses.

   g.   Specification of the roles and responsibilities of the consultant and of your organization.

   h.   Name of person in your agency who has the authority to agree to expenditures or approve work.

   i.   A clear understanding of who will do the actual consulting.

   j.   "Bail-out" clause, ideally that you can immediately bail out by providing notice in writing.

   k.   Confidentiality about sharing any information regarding your organization and its activities.

   l.   Ownership of any materials used and/or produced during the project.

   m. Scope of the agreement: that it supersedes any other agreements that you have with the consultant regarding that project.

Additional Advice

Help Consultants Understand Your Organization

A few basic techniques can greatly help the consultant to understand your organization, particularly if brought in to work organization-wide on non-technical issues.

1.   **Help the consultant to understand your products or services, markets and stakeholders.**
Provide them with copies of your strategic plans, budgets, policies, most recent annual report, organization charts and advertising/promotions/sales literature. If there is a full range of these types of documents, your organization probably values careful documentation when making important decisions, and will likely prefer the same from the consulting project. If these documents appear to be very comprehensive and include a great deal of graphs, figures and numbers, then your organization probably highly values careful research, analysis and conclusions, and will prefer the same in the consultation project.

2.   **Give the consultant a sense for the overall nature of your organization.**
For example, are employees highly independent and work alone or do they prefer to work in

teams? Do you aim for consensus during decision-making, even if it takes a long time to get, or do you resort to using the authority of management? Are there strong traditions you require based on the diversity of your workforce? How do employees feel about using consultants?

3.   **Give them a sense for the overall priorities of your organization.**
        You might attempt to identify the general life stage of the business, such as start-up, developing/building, stabilizing and declining. The stage will indicate your overall priorities as well, for example, getting any help you can get, grabbing more market share and/or more customers and/or more revenue, developing a wide range of careful documentation, and divesting resources while ensuring customer needs are met.

Include Frequent Evaluations, Including Project Follow-Up

The extent of the consultant's and client's participation in evaluating the project is often an indicator of how much they really see themselves responsible for the overall, long-term quality of the consulting project.

1.   **The consulting project should be evaluated regularly.**
        For example, include a brief evaluation at the end of each meeting (about the process used in that meeting), at mid-point in the planning effort and at its end. Specify in the contract that certain deliverables (tangible products, such as reports, presentations, project reviews, etc.) be delivered during the project. Ideally, the project is evaluated at three months and six months after completion. Be sure to focus on whether the consultant's recommendations were implemented or not and whether the project's goals were reached or not.

2.   **Establish criteria early on, from which the consulting effort will be evaluated.**
        Together with the consultant, specify what constitutes a successful consulting project and process. Be as detailed as possible in descriptions of success, so that it will be easier to evaluate the project's success in the future.

3.   **Do not base evaluations mostly on feelings.**
        Avoid this mistake by specifying, as much as possible, behaviors that will reflect a successful consulting project.

Be Sure You Have "Independent Contractor" Relationship

A major, recent issue with some government agencies is the distinction between independent contractors and employees. Some organizations hire what they consider to be "independent contractors," but what the agencies conclude are really "employees." In these cases, the agencies demand that the organizations pay employees' taxes and also pay certain penalties. Consequently, a business must be careful when entering into a relationship with a consultant in order to ensure that government agencies will not deem the relationship to be an "employee" relationship.

For example, in the USA, the Internal Revenue Service (IRS) is diligent about this matter and has issued guidelines about how to discern if a relationship is really more of an employee relationship than an independent contractor relationship. The IRS guidelines are similar to guidelines in Canada. Whether someone is deemed by the IRS to be an employee or an independent contractor depends primarily on the extent of control the business has over the person: the less control in the relationship, the less likely the IRS will deem the person to be an employee. Consider the following actions when attempting to define the relationship with an independent contractor:

1. Carefully specify your relationship with the person in a written contract.

2. The terms of the relationship (specific services, fees, project start and stop dates, etc.) should all be specified in the contract.

3. Attempt to arrange fees to be based on results or tasks, rather than on time.

4. In the contract, specify the relationship to be with an "independent contractor" who is responsible to pay his or her own taxes.

5. The person doing the work should have all or considerable discretion in how services are carried out, including the process and scheduling.

6. The person doing the work should be responsible to obtain and pay for his or her own training to carry out the services.

7. The person should not be required to carry out his or her services at the offices of the client.

8. The person should have or be making obvious efforts to advertise and retain business with other clients.

9. The person should have his or her own place of business.

The more a person appears as a manager in the organization (for example, makes operating decisions, supervises people and is responsible for resource allocations), the more likely that a government agency will deem the service provider an employee, and not an independent contractor.

Currently, the Internal Revenue Service in the USA uses a set of questions to help determine which status (employee or independent contractors) best fits the role. To see these questions, go to http://www.irs.gov/govt/fslg/article/0,,id=110344,00.html .

PART V:

HOW TO

LEAD TEAMS

How to Organize Highly Effective Teams

Most successful projects, changes and learning occur in teams in the workplace. Therefore, it is very important for leaders to know how to design, develop and lead highly effective teams.

Types of Teams You Could Use

There are many types of teams you could use in the workplace. The type you choose depends on the nature of the results that the team is to accomplish.

1. **Formal and informal teams**

   These are usually small groups of employees who come together to address some specific goal or need. Management appoints formal teams, that is, teams that are intentionally organized and resourced to address a specific and important goal or need. Informal teams are usually loosely organized groups of people who come together to address a non-critical, short-term purpose.

2. **Committees**

   Committees are organized to address, major ongoing functions or tasks in an organization, and the membership of the committees often is based on the official position of each of the members, for example, committees in Boards of Directors.

3. **Problem-solving teams**

   These teams are formed to address a particular, major problem currently faced by the organization. Often, their overall goal is to provide a written report that includes recommendations for solving the problem. Membership often is comprised of people who perceive and/or experience the problem, as well as those who can do something about it.

4. **Self-directed and self-managed teams**

   These types of teams are increasingly used where a) team members are working to address a complex challenge in a rapidly changing environment, and b) the strong ownership and participation of members are extremely important. These types provide great latitude in how members achieve the overall results to be achieved by the teams. The role of leader in a team might change during the team activities depending on where the team is in its stage of development (see below) and/or achieving is results.

Understand How Teams Grow (Life Stages of Teams)

When developing a team, it helps a great deal to have some basic sense of the stages that a typical team moves through when evolving into a high-performing team. Awareness of each stage helps leaders to understand the reasons for members' behavior during that stage, and to guide members to behavior required to evolve the team into the next stage.

1. **Forming**

   Members first get together during this stage. Individually, they are considering questions like, "What am I here for?", "Who else is here?" and "Who am I comfortable with?" It is important for members to get involved with each other, including introducing themselves to each other. Clear and strong leadership is required from the team leader during this stage to ensure the group members feel the clarity and comfort required to evolve to the next stage.

2. **Storming**

   During this stage, members are beginning to voice their individual differences, join with others who share the same beliefs, and jockey for position in the group. Therefore, it is important for members to continue to be highly involved with each other, including to voice any concerns in order to feel represented and understood. The team leader should help members to voice their views, and to achieve consensus (or commonality of views) about their purpose and priorities.

3. **Norming**

   In this stage, members are beginning to share a common commitment to the purpose of the group, including to its overall goals and how each of the goals can be achieved. The team leader should focus on continuing to clarify the roles of each member, and a clear and workable structure and process for the group to achieve its goals.

4. **Performing**

   In this stage, the team is working effectively and efficiently toward achieving its goals. During this stage, the style of leadership becomes more indirect as members take on stronger participation and involvement in the group process. Ideally, the style includes helping members to reflect on their experiences and to learn from them.

5. **Closing and Celebration**

   At this stage, it is clear to members and their organization that the team has achieved its goals (or a major milestone along the way toward the goal). It is critical to acknowledge this point in the life of the team, lest members feel unfulfilled and skeptical about future team efforts.

How to Build Highly Effective Teams

Too often, teams are formed merely by gathering some people together and then hoping that those people somehow find a way to work together. Teams are most effective when carefully designed. To design, develop and support a highly effective team, use the following guidelines:

1. **Set clear goals for the results to be produced by the team.**

   The goals should be designed to be "SMART." This is an acronym for:

   - Specific,

   - Measurable,

   - Achievable,

   - Relevant and

   - Time-bound.

   As much as possible, include input from other members of the organization when designing and wording these goals. Goals might be, for example, "to produce a project report that includes a project plan, schedule and budget to develop and test a complete employee performance management system within the next year." Write these goals down for eventual communication to and discussion with all team members.

2. **Set clear objectives for measuring the ongoing effectiveness of the team.**
    The objectives, that together achieve the overall goals, should also be designed to be "SMART." Objectives might be, for example, to a) to produce a draft of a project report during the first four weeks of team activities, and b) achieve Board-approval of the proposed performance management system during the next four weeks. Also, write these objectives down for eventual communication to and discussion with all team members.

3. **Define a mechanism for clear and consistent communications among team members.**
    New leaders often assume that all group members know what the leaders know. Consistent communication is the most important trait of a successful group. Without communication, none of the other traits can occur. Successful groups even over-communicate, such that:

    a. All members regularly receive and understand similar information about the group, for example, about the group's purpose, membership, status and accomplishments.

    b. These communications might be delivered through regular newsletters, status reports, meetings, emails and collaboration tools.

4. **Define a procedure for members to make decisions and solve problems.**
    Successful groups regularly encounter situations where they must make decisions and solve problems in a highly effective manner. Too often, the group resorts to extended discussion until members become tired and frustrated and eventually just opt for any action at all, or they count on the same person who seems to voice the strongest opinions. Instead, successful groups:

    a. Document a procedure whereby the group can make decisions and ensure that all members are aware of the procedure.

    b. The procedure might specify that decisions are made, first by aiming for consensus within a certain time frame and if consensus is not achieved, then the group resorts to a majority vote.

5. **Develop staffing procedures (recruiting, training, organizing, replacing).**
    Too often, group members are asked to join the group and somehow to "chip in." Unfortunately, that approach creates "chips," rather than valuable group members. Instead, if group members go through a somewhat organized, systematic process, then new members often believe that the group is well organized and that their role in the group is valuable. Successful groups:

    a. Identify what roles and expertise are needed on the group in order to achieve the group's purpose and plans – they staff according to plans, not personalities.

    b. New group members go through a systematic process to join the group – they understand the group's purpose, their role, their next steps and where to get help.

6. **Determine the membership of the group.**
    Consider the extent of expertise needed to achieve the goals, including areas of knowledge and skills. Include at least one person who has skills in facilitation and meeting management. Attempt to include sufficient diversity of values and perspectives to ensure robust ideas and discussion. A critical consideration is availability – members should have the time to attend every meeting and perform required tasks between meetings.

7. **Determine time frames for starting and terminating the team, if applicable.**
   Now consider the expertise needed to achieve the goals of the team, and how long it might take to recruit and organize those resources. Write these times down for eventual communication to and discussion with all team members.

8. **Determine the membership of the team.**
   What expertise might the team need to achieve the goals of the group? For example, an official authority to gather and allocate resources, or an expert in a certain technology. Always consider if the members will have the time and energy to actively participate in the team.

9. **Assign the role of leader – to ensure systems and practices are followed.**
   The leader focuses on the systems and practices in the team, not on personalities of its members. For example, the leader makes sure that all team members: a) are successfully staffed, b) understand the purpose of the group and their role in it, c) are active toward meeting that purpose and role, and d) utilize procedures for making decisions and solving problems. (Note that the leader does not always have to be a strong, charismatic personality – while that type of personality can often be successful at developing teams, it often can create passivity or frustration in other members over time, thereby crippling the group.)

10. **Assign role of communicator – communication is the life's blood of teams!**
    Communication is the most important trait of a successful team. It cannot be left to chance. Someone should be designated to ensure that all members receive regular communications about purpose, membership, roles and status. Communications should also be with people outside the team, especially those who make decisions or determine if the team is successful or not.

11. **Identify needs for resources (training, materials, supplies, etc.).**
    Start from analysis of the purpose and goals. What is needed to achieve them? For example, members might benefit from a training that provides a brief overview of the typical stages of team development and includes packets of materials about the team's goals, structure and process to make decisions. Consider costs, such as trainers, consultants, room rental and office supplies. How will those funds be obtained and maintained?

12. **Identify the costs to provide necessary resources for the team.**
    Consider costs, such as paying employees to attend the meeting, trainers, consultants, room rental and office supplies. Develop a budget that itemizes the costs associated with obtaining and supporting each of the resources. Get management approval of the budget.

13. **Contact each team member.**
    Before the first meeting, invite each potential team member to be a part of the team. First, send him or her a memo, and then meet with each person individually. Communicate the goals of the project, why the person was selected, the benefit of the goals to the organization, the time frame for the team effort, and who will lead the team (at least initially). Invite the team member to the first meeting.

14. **Early on, plan team building activities to support trust and working relationships.**
    Team building activities can include, for example, a retreat in which members introduce themselves, exercises in which members help each other solve a short problem or meet a specific and achievable goal, or an extended period in which members can voice their concerns and frustrations about their team assignments.

15. **Carefully plan the first team meeting.**
In the first meeting, review the goals of the team, why each member was selected, the benefit of the goals to the organization, the time frame for the team effort, who will lead the team (at least, initially), when the team might meet and where, and any changes that have occurred since the individual meetings. Have this information written down to hand out to each member. At the end of the meeting, ask each person to make a public commitment to the team effort.

16. **Regularly monitor and report on status of team members toward achieving the goal.**
It is amazing how often a team starts out with a carefully designed plan, but then abandons the plan once the initial implementation of the plan is underway. Sometimes if the plan is behind schedule, team members conclude that the project is not successful. Plans can change – just change them systematically with new dates and approval of the changes.

17. **Support team meetings and the members' processes in the team.**
At this point, it is critical that supervisors of team members remain available to provide support and resources as needed. The supervisor should regularly monitor team members' progress on achieving their goals. Provide ongoing encouragement and visibility to members. One of the most important forms of support a supervisor can provide is coordination with other supervisors to ensure that team members are freed up enough to attend meetings.

18. **Regularly celebrate team members' accomplishments!**
One of the best ways to avoid burnout is to regularly celebrate accomplishments. Otherwise, members can feel as if they are on treadmill that has no end. Keep your eye on small and recurring successes, not just the gold at the end of the rainbow.

How to Lead Highly Effective Teams

How to Design Highly Effective Meetings

Meeting design and management tends to be a set of skills often overlooked by leaders. The following guidelines ensure that meetings are highly focused and results-oriented.

1.   **Always first identify the purpose or intended outcome from the meeting.**
     One of the most frustrating experiences for people in the workplace is to attend meetings that seem to have no clear purpose. Always know what you want from a meeting and how to measure whether that result was attained or not. Communicate that to participants.

2.   **Design the agenda with the topics, decisions and/or assignments to achieve the purpose.**
     Consider the meeting to be a strategy, a tool, to achieve the intended outcome, for example, to get consensus among participants or to make necessary assignments. Do not consider the meeting to occur for the sake of having a meeting.

3.   **If possible, design the agenda with some of the people who will be attending.**
     The person who designs the meeting might not be aware of what is needed to achieve its purpose and who should participate in the meeting. It is helpful to involve others in the design of the agenda – those other participants might end up helping to facilitate.

4.   **Include introductions or some type of "check in" for members early in the meeting.**
     If members do not have an opportunity to speak up early in the meeting, they tend to detach from its proceedings. Therefore, always include some brief activity in which each member can speak up briefly, for example, to introduce themselves or report on status of tasks.

5.   **Dedicate time to reviewing the status of actions assigned in previous meetings.**
     If the status of previously assigned actions is not reviewed, then members might feel that it is not really important to make any assignments of new actions if those new actions are not going to be monitored and reviewed either.

6.   **Allow time for brief evaluations, or "satisfaction checks," among the members.**
     If the meeting will be more than 1.5 hours, be sure to include a few minutes to ask members what they think of the meeting so far. Otherwise, if the meeting is not useful to them, they might show it by not speaking up or by not doing tasks assigned to them in the meeting.

7.   **Next to each agenda topic, specify the action needed and by when in the meeting.**
     For example, the agenda might include a topic to "Decide team schedule" and allocate 10 minutes in the meeting to decide that schedule. If the decision is not made within that time, then decide whether to extend the time or delegate the decision to a few members to recommend to the entire set of members in the next meeting.

8.   **Review the agenda, including the meeting's purpose, at the beginning of each meeting.**
     Always make sure that participants clearly understand the purpose of that particular meeting and the reason for the topics and timing on the agenda. Otherwise, members might not feel strong understanding, ownership and commitment to the activities of the meeting.

9.   **Ask participants if they will commit to the agenda.**
     This simple gesture often results in the strong participation needed from each member in

order to ensure a highly successful meeting. It also provides brief time for members to assert their questions or concerns about the agenda.

10. **Keep the agenda visible to all members during the meeting.**
As you address each topic on the agenda, check off that topic on the posted agenda so all members clearly understand where the meeting is at on the agenda and so members feel a sense of progress during the meeting.

11. **Identify someone to document the decisions and actions assigned from the meeting.**
Although meeting minutes may seem the most perfunctory duty from a meeting, the minutes can end up being the most useful part of the meeting by helping people remember all of the actions to be completed. This person should issue meeting minutes shortly after the meeting.

12. **Always issue the minutes (documentation of the meeting) shortly after the meeting.**
This is one of the most important activities to ensuring ongoing, successful meetings. The minutes remind members of the strong value of the meeting and its many accomplishments. It also reminds members that others will monitor their assignments in the meeting.

How to Facilitate for Highly Effective Meetings

How to Prepare to Facilitate Meetings

As a leader of the meeting, it is always important for you to be personally prepared for facilitating the meeting. Depending on the goals of your meeting and the nature of its participants, the experience of facilitation can range from fun and fulfilling to challenging and lonely. The following guidelines will help you to personally prepare for facilitation in any situation.

1. **Always know the goals, structures and membership of the group.**
This is probably the most important activity to successfully prepare for the meeting. Know the purpose of the meeting, the roles of its participants, the methods used to make decisions and solve problems, and the proposed agenda for the meeting.

Consider "How to Build Highly Effective Teams" on page 156.

2. **Know what "centers" you – what calms you down before a meeting.**
Different people "get centered" by different means. For example, do you meditate, take a walk, or memorize an opening to the meeting? Think about successful meetings that you have facilitated in the past. What worked to keep you centered?

3. **Remember how you successfully deal with feedback and conflict.**
Remember your typical reactions to feedback and conflict and how you have learned to successfully manage those reactions.

Consider "Understand How You Respond to Feedback and Conflict" on page 81.

4. **Use your emotional intelligence (EI).**
   Remember how you recognize and name uncomfortable feelings and how you have learned to successfully manage those emotions.

 Consider "What is Your Emotional Intelligence?" on page 82.

5. **Have an opening – something to say when you start the group meeting.**
   Always know what you are going to say for the first minute of the meeting. Your sense of purpose and direction will be contagious to group members. For example, memorize a certain opening to the meeting or tell a joke.

How to Open Meetings

1. **Start the meeting on time.**
   This approach shows strong respect for those who bothered to show up on time and it reminds any latecomers that the meeting and its scheduling are serious. Also, meetings that start late are meetings that usually are rushed to end on time.

2. **Ask if anyone is missing who should be present.**
   If there is anyone who should be there and is not, visit the reason for the absence and address how to get him or her involved. Decide how those not present will be updated about the highlights and actions from the meeting.

3. **Ask if introductions would be useful.**
   Do not assume that everyone knows everyone else in the meeting. Even though members of the group might all be from the same organization, some members still might not know each other. Introductions are a great opportunity for members to begin speaking at the beginning of the meeting and to quickly feel involved.

4. **Review the agenda, including the topics and timing of each topic for the meeting.**
   This ensures that all members fully understand the agenda and the timing with each topic. When you have finished reviewing the agenda, always ask the group if they will work according to the agenda. This gets their implied commitment to focus during the meeting.

5. **Model the kind of energy and focus needed by the meeting's participants.**
   One of the most powerful means to ensure that all members actively participate and focus on the current topic in the meeting is for the facilitator to show the same kinds of energy and focus. A seemingly detached and disinterested facilitator can be toxic to a meeting.

6. **Clarify your roles for that meeting – when you will be facilitating, training or directing.**
   It is very important for participants to understand how they should be participating in a meeting, for example, whether they should be participative (in which case you might be facilitating), listening to expert information (you are a trainer) or capturing actions to do (you are the supervisor directing your workers).

How to Establish Ground Rules for Meetings

The ground rules establish the overall "personality" of the meeting, so they are important to establish early on when working with a group. Ground rules can be identified before the group meeting and then proposed to the group members for their review, modification and/or approval. Or, members of the group in a meeting can develop the ground rules. Common ground rules are:

1.   Meetings start and stop on time.

2.   Focus on priorities, not on personalities.

3.   Everyone participates.

4.   All opinions are honored.

5.   No interruptions.

6.   No sidebars (or conversations not involving the main group).

7.   Celebrate accomplishments.

How to Manage Time in Meetings

One of the most difficult facilitation tasks is time management. In a highly energized meeting, time seems to run out before tasks are finished. Therefore, the biggest challenge is keeping the process moving.

1.   **Start the meeting on time.**
        As mentioned above, it is very important to start meetings on time in order to respect the effort of those who bothered to come on time. If you do not start on time, then you are sending the strong message that timing is not really that important in the meeting.

2.   **Be sure the agenda allocates certain times to address each topic on the agenda.**
        This is one of the most powerful means to ensure strong time management. If the time allotted for a topic has expired, then ask the group if they want to allocate more time, make a decision about the topic now, or assign an action to a subgroup to get more information in order to make a more timely decision the next time that you meet.

3.   **Ask the group for a volunteer to help monitor and remind the group about the time.**
        If you will be leading the group as a facilitator, trainer or work director, then it is very useful to ask someone to help you manage the time. That is perhaps the most valuable form of help to you in a meeting. It affords you complete focus on leading the meeting.

4.   **Adjourn a meeting when scheduled – rarely deter from this guideline.**
        It is far better to adjourn a meeting even if members feel work is incomplete than to drag a meeting on and on with the illusion that everyone should leave the meeting with a strong sense of closure. Adjourning a meeting on time ensures that all members feel their time is respected and they can continue to count on sound meeting management.

How to Guide Members to Evaluate the Meeting

Leave 5-10 minutes (depending on the number of participants in the meeting) near the end of the meeting in order to evaluate the quality of the meeting. This is one of the most powerful means to ensure that future meetings will be high quality. The following technique not only assesses the quality of the meeting, but also ensures that all participants take strong ownership in this and future meetings. Have each member privately write down a rating of the overall quality of the meeting, with 1 representing "very poor" and 5 "very good." Then, one at a time, out loud, each member:

1.   Shows other members the rating that he/she wrote down.

2.   Very briefly explains why he/she gave that rating.

3.   Says what he/she could have done *during that meeting* to earn a rating of 5 now for the meeting.

The facilitator(s) or members of senior management should provide their evaluation last.

Having the members write down their rating ensures that you do not get "group think" in the ratings. Naming what the member could have done to improve the meeting during the meeting results in a greater sense of freedome and accountability to take that type of action in future meetings.

How to Capture Learning During and From Meetings

1.   **Ask to hear from a few participants about what they have learned during the meeting.**
      Remind them that learning is enhanced knowledge, skills and perceptions.

2.   **Ask them about what spawned that learning during the meeting.**
      Was it a comment someone said? Was it an insight that came to them? New knowledge?

3.   **Share your own learning, as well.**
      Show your learning after others have had an opportunity to speak up.

4.   **Document participants' learnings in the minutes of the meeting.**
      Ask each participant if his/her learning can be documented in the minutes.

How to Close Meetings

1.   **Review decisions, assignments and actions from the meeting.**
      The value of meetings usually is in the decisions, assignments and actions from a meeting. Therefore, it is very important to review them at the end of the meeting to be sure that everyone is aware of, and understands, them.

2.   **Ensure that someone will be distributing minutes from the meeting.**
      This is extremely important. Regardless of how useful a meeting was, if the decisions, assignments and actions are not documented and distributed to all those who will be interested, then the meeting's participants tend to forget these highlights altogether.

3.   **Establish the time and location for the next meeting, if necessary.**
      The scheduling of meetings is often the most challenging and frustrating aspect of having meetings. Therefore, use the opportunity when all participants are together now with their calendars to schedule the next meeting.

4.   **Ask who should be at the next meeting and ensure that someone invites them.**
      Now, when the important topics have been discussed and addressed, is an appropriate time to consider who else plays an important role with those topics and, therefore, should be in attendance at future meetings.

5. **Ask for agenda items for the next meeting.**
   Attendees to a meeting are much more likely to participate in the meeting if they had strong involvement in designing the agenda for that meeting. Now is a appropriate time for them to make suggestions for the agenda.

How to Manage Conflict and Come to Decisions

If there seems to be prolonged conflict among several members of a group, then consider the following guidelines.

1. **First, verify if members indeed are in conflict. Ask the members. Listen for 3 minutes.**
   They might not be in destructive conflict, at all. Name or describe what behaviors you are seeing that might indicate destructive conflict. Do not try to "diagnose" causes of those behaviors, just name what you are seeing or hearing. Acknowledge that conflict is natural in healthy groups, but why you conclude that conflict has become destructive.

2. **If members are in destructive conflict, then select approaches to resolve conflict.**
   Take a 5-minute break. Ask one or two other members (a subgroup) to step aside with you. Ask them to suggest approach(es) to address the conflict, and then read the ideas listed immediately below. Ask them which approach(es) are most likely to move things along.

3. **Use the approaches selected by the subgroup, with the entire group.**
   Explain that the approaches were selected by several of you, not by just one person. Ask that members set aside 10-15 minutes on the agenda to try them out. The more the members are in destructive conflict, the more likely they will be willing to try out the approaches.

Possible Approaches to Conflict Resolution

Depending on the situation and duration of the conflict, there are a variety of approaches that might support resolution of destructive conflict. Here are some possible approaches:

- Focus on what members agree on, for instance by posting the mission, vision and/or values statements to remind people of why they are there.

- Ask members, "If this disagreement continues, where will we be? How will it hurt our organization?"

- Have members restate their position. If it will take longer than three minutes, allow opportunities for others to confirm or question for understanding (not disagreement).

- Shift to prioritizing alternatives, rather than excluding all alternatives but one.

- Take a 10-minute break in which each member quietly reflects on what he/she can do to move the group forward.

- Take 5-10 minutes and in pairs of two, each person shares with the other what he/she is confused or irritated about. One person in the pair helps the other to articulate his/her views to the larger group. Then switch roles and repeat the process.

- Propose an "agree to disagree" disposition.

- If disagreement or lack of consensus persists around an issue, have a subgroup select options and then report back to the full group.

- Tell stories of successes and failures in how group members operate, including how members got past their differences and reached agreement.

- Call for a vote on a stated question or decision.

How to Get Your Group Members Unstuck

Sometimes, even if there is a lot of participation from members and no prolonged conflict, a group might not seem to be making any progress on group activities. Members may simply be stuck, for example, during planning or when needing to make a major decision. Consider a similar general process as when a group seems in prolonged conflict (listed above). You could:

1. **First, verify if members indeed are stuck. Ask the members. Listen for 3 minutes.**
    They might not be stuck, at all. Name or describe what behaviors you are seeing that might indicate they are stuck. Do not try to "diagnose" causes of those behaviors, just name what you are seeing or hearing.

2. **If members are stuck, then select approaches to move the group forward.**
    Take a 5-minute break. Ask two other members to step aside with you. Ask them to suggest the approach(es) to move things along, and then read the ideas listed immediately below. Ask them to choose which approach(es) would be most likely to move things along.

3. **Use the approaches, selected by the subgroup, with the entire group.**
    Explain that the approaches were selected by several of you, not by just one person. Ask that members set aside 10-15 minutes on the agenda to try them out. The more the members are stuck, the more likely they will be willing to try out the approaches.

Possible Approaches to Get Unstuck

Depending on the situation, there are a wide variety of actions that might be helpful in moving the group forward. Possible approaches that members can use to become unstuck include:

- Ask the group, "If we continue to be stuck, where will we be? How will we be hurting our organization?"

- Take a five-minute break to let members do whatever they want.

- Resort to some movement and stretching.

- Ask for five examples of "out of the box" thinking.

- Resort to thinking and talking about activities in which resources do not matter.

- Play a quick game that stimulates creative thinking.

- Use metaphors, such as stories, myths or archetypal images. For example, ask each person to take five minutes to draw or write a metaphor that describes his/her opinions and position in the meeting.

- Have each or some of the planners tell a story and include some humor.

- Use visualization techniques, for example, visualize reading an article about the organization's success some years into the future. What does the article say about how the success came about?

- Play reflective or energizing music (depending on the situation).

- Restructure the group to smaller groups or move members around in the large group.

- Have a period of asking question after question after question (without answering necessarily). Repetition of questions, "why?" in particular, can help to move planners into deeper levels of reflection and analysis, particularly if they do not have to carefully respond to each question.

- Establish a "parking lot" for outstanding or unresolved issues, and then move on to something else. Later, go back to the stuck issue.

- Turn the problem around by reframing the topic and/or issue. Usually, questions help this reframing happen.

- Ask key questions, for example, "How can we make it happen? How can we avoid it happening?"

- Focus on what the group agrees on, for instance by posting the mission, vision and/or values statements to remind people of why they are there.

PART VI:

HOW TO LEAD

EMPLOYEES

How to Ensure Fair and Equitable Treatment of Your Employees

As mentioned near the beginning of this guide, the practices of leadership and supervision must be in close accordance with the Board-approved personnel policies and procedures of the organization. Previous sections in this Guide were primarily about non-personnel practices, for example, leading and managing yourself, leading and changing the organization, and leading teams. PART VI is primarily about leading and supervising employees. Consequently, guidelines about personnel policies are provided early in PART VI.

How to Develop and Update Your Personnel Policies

Role and Need for Personnel Policies

Numerous laws and regulations regulate the nature of the relationship between an employee and his or her organization. They are intended primarily to ensure that everyone is treated fairly and equitably regardless of their race, creed, color or sexual orientation. They are intended to ensure that the treatment of employees is based primarily on their job performance. Common types of activities guided by the laws and regulations are, for example, hiring and firing, benefits and compensation, affirmative action, rights of privacy, discrimination and harassment, and wrongful termination.

One of the fastest growing types of lawsuits brought by employees against their organizations is wrongful termination of employment. Other common types of lawsuits are in regard to allegations of discrimination and harassment. It is far better for organizations first to ensure that these types of improper types of behaviors do not occur, than to have to defend themselves later in courts of law. The best way to ensure proper behaviors is to enact comprehensive guidelines regarding how employees should be treated in the workplace. These general guidelines are called personnel policies. Specific sequences of activities resulting from the guidelines are often called procedures.

Note the difference between operational policies and personnel policies. Operational policies are to guide how employees conduct the ongoing activities of the organization, ranging from how customers receive services to making sure the coffee maker is unplugged at the end of the day. Operational policies are not about the nature of the relationship between the employee and the organization.

Developing Personnel Policies

Each organization should carefully consider what policies it requires and how they should be worded. When developing policies, always consult an expert who is knowledgeable about federal, state/provincial and local laws regarding employment practices. For example, in the USA, consider the Civil Rights Act of 1964, Americans with Disabilities Act of 1992, and Occupational Safety and Health Acts. In Canada, some major employment laws are, for example, Employment Insurance Act, Canada Pension Plan, Old Age Security Act and Canada Labour Code. Personnel policies might also be governed by union rules or other contractual agreements.

Many organizations develop their policies first by closely reviewing policies of organizations with similar products and services. While that practice is a good start, you still should have an authority on employment practices review your policies. Finally, the Board should formally approve the policies and the approval should be documented in Board meeting minutes.

The University of California lists examples of topics in policies at http://nature.berkeley.edu/ucce50/ag-labor/7labor/16.htm .

Training on Policies

If employees' behaviors do not conform to the written personnel policies for your organization, and if an employee sues your organization, then courts will consider your written policies to be superseded (or replaced) by your employees' actual behaviors that you appeared to be permitting to occur. For example, if policies specified that employees should not discriminate on the basis of race, creed or color, yet there was a history of your employees clearly discriminating against other employees on that basis, then courts will conclude that your policies are to permit discrimination. Therefore, it is critical that all employees have a clear understanding of each personnel policy and that their behaviors conform to those policies. The best way to accomplish that understanding is for employees to be trained on the policies and for their supervisors to always be sure that policies are followed. Training about policies can be carried out by ensuring that:

- All employees receive an orientation that includes an overview of the policies and procedures.

- All employees sign a document that indicates that they have reviewed the policies and will act in accordance with them.

- Supervisors regularly issue reminders to employees about key policies.

- All supervisors themselves act in accordance with the policies.

Any violation of terms of the policies should be immediately addressed with appropriate response. This might range from reprimand to termination of the employee, depending on the nature of the violation. The method of response should be documented so that the organization has verifiable evidence of how it handled the employee matter in case the employee files a lawsuit. The evidence might be useful in the courts with any other employee litigation because the evidence will indicate that the organization indeed does try to comply with its policies.

Recommended Personnel Policies

Table VI:1 on the following page lists many examples of types of personnel policies.

Table VI:1 – Sample List of Personnel Policies

Work Schedule

Work day hours
Lunch periods and break times
Holidays
Vacation
Sick Time
Personal Leave
Leave of Absence
Severe Weather
Jury Duty

Hiring Procedures

Interviewing job candidates
Conducting background checks
Offering employment

New Employee and Internal Orientation

New employee orientation – general information
Intern orientation
New employee and internal orientation checklist

Compensation

Paydays
Overtime and compensation time
Classifying employees as exempt or non-exempt
Salary ranges
Positioning pay within a salary range
Maintaining competitive salary information
Reclassifying positions
Salary review policy
Promotional increases
Withholding salary increase due to performance
Withholding salary increase due to leave of absence

Payroll Information & Timekeeping Procedures

Payroll information – General
Payroll information – Direct deposit procedures
Payroll information – Required and voluntary payroll deductions
Timekeeping – salaried and hourly employee classifications
Supervisor's signature

Benefits

Eligibility and general information
Types of available benefits
Medical insurance
Dental insurance
Disability insurance
Supervisory communication of benefits
Life insurance
Confidentiality note
Retirement plan
Social security (in USA)
Employee advisory resource

Workers' Compensation Information and Procedures

When there is an injury or accident on the job
What is covered under Workers Compensation
Type of injury covered by Worker's Compensation Insurance
Medical expenses resulting from a work-related injury
Resources available

Employee Performance Management

Performance assessment cycle
Performance assessment process
Dealing with performance issues
Discipline: when the positive approach does not work
Separation from employment checklist
Communications by the supervisor regarding personnel issues
COBRA (in USA)
Leave-taking procedures

Data Practices

Policy
Procedures
Definitions
Security of Records
External releases
Internal releases
Use of data
Legal procedures
Destruction of records
Employee access

How to Use an Employee Manual

All personnel policies and procedures should be organized into a manual commonly referred to as an employee manual, employee handbook or personnel handbook, which each employee retains. As mentioned in the above paragraphs, all employees should be oriented to the policies in the manual and have signed an agreement that they will follow the policies.

Each manual should have a cover page which specifies that the Board has authorized the policies to be followed in the workplace, that policies can be changed at any time, that notice of changes will be communicated to employees, and that the policies do not constitute a contract between the organization and the employee. The following suggested language is not to be interpreted as legal advice. Consider the following wording on the cover of your policies manual:

> "Nothing contained in or implied by this manual creates or shall be deemed to create or constitute a contractual obligation to employees on the part (of the organization). The policies, procedures and guidelines contained in this manual are subject to change at any time, do not confer any obligation (on the part of the organization) and do not create any right to employment on the part (of the organization)."

How to Ensure Fair Compensation of Your Employees

Basics of Benefits and Compensation

Benefits

Benefits are forms of value, other than payment, that are provided to employees in return for their contribution to the organization, that is, for doing their jobs. Some benefits, such as Workers Compensation in the USA and Canada, are required by law for certain sized organizations. (Some people see Worker's Compensation as a worker's right, rather than a benefit.)

Prominent examples of benefits are insurance (medical, life, dental, disability, worker's compensation, etc.), vacation pay, holiday pay, maternity leave, contribution to retirement (pension pay), profit sharing, stock options and bonuses. Some people would consider profit sharing, stock options and bonuses as forms of payment or compensation.

You might think of benefits as being tangible or intangible. The benefits listed previously are tangible benefits. Intangible benefits are less direct, for example, appreciation from a boss, likelihood for promotion and a nice office. People sometimes talk about fringe benefits, usually referring to tangible benefits, but sometimes meaning both kinds of benefits.

You might also think of benefits as company-paid and employee-paid. While the company usually pays for most types of benefits (holiday pay, vacation pay, etc.), some benefits are often paid, at least in part, by employees, either because of high costs or because they only appeal to part of the employee population. For example, medical insurance costs might be shared between the company and employee because the costs are high, while day care assistance, fitness center memberships and life insurance costs might be shared or covered by the employee because not all employees place a priority on that coverage.

For the purposes of estimating personnel costs, you might consider the cost of fringe benefits to be about 40% of the cost of the wages or salaries, although this percentage continues to increase. Note that fringe benefits are usually higher for salaried personnel than for personnel who are paid hourly wages.

Compensation

Compensation is payment to employees in return for their contributions to the organization, that is, for doing their jobs. The most common forms of compensation are wages, salaries and tips.

Compensation is usually provided as base pay and/or variable pay. Base pay is usually based on the role in the organization and the market value for the expertise required to conduct that role. Variable pay is based on the performance of the person in that role, for example, for how well that person achieved his or her goals for the year. Incentive plans, for example, bonus plans, are a form of variable pay. (Some people might consider bonuses as a benefit, rather than a form of compensation, depending on the criteria for determining the amount of the bonus.)

Organizations usually associate compensation/pay ranges with job descriptions in the organization and on salary surveys about similar jobs in similar organizations. The ranges include the minimum and the maximum amount of money that can be earned per year in that role. Documentation of the pay range associated with each job descriptions is an important part of a fair compensation policy.

Employers have to pay various payroll-related payments. For example, in the USA, employers pay Workers Compensation and FICA (social security). In Canada, employers pay Workers Compensation and Employee Health Tax.

Employees have certain monies withheld from their payroll checks. For example, in the USA, employees have deductions taken from their paychecks for state and federal income taxes, FICA (social security) and optionally, employee contributions to the costs of certain benefits, such as supplementary life, medical insurance and retirement. In Canada, employees have deductions from their paychecks for various provincial and federal taxes, Canada Pension Plan, employment insurance and optionally, employee contributions to the costs of certain benefits, such as supplementary life and medical insurance.

Salaried and Hourly Job Roles

In various countries, job roles in organizations often have two primary classifications based on the approach to computing compensation. These classifications include "salaried" and "hourly" jobs. The compensation of salaried jobs is usually based on a bi-weekly (once every two weeks) or monthly, fixed amount. The compensation of hourly jobs is usually based on an hourly rate. In the USA, salaried jobs are referred to as "exempt" jobs and hourly jobs are referred to as "non-exempt" jobs, meaning whether they are exempt or not exempt from certain requirements of the Taft-Hartley Act.

- Production-related, many entry-level and most unskilled jobs are usually referred to as hourly jobs (non-exempt in the USA). Hourly jobs also usually get paid over-time (at least, in the USA and Canada), that is, extra pay for hours worked over 40 hours a week or on certain days of the week or on holidays.

- Professional, management and other types of skilled jobs are usually referred to as salaried jobs (or exempt in the USA). It is not uncommon for salaried positions to receive higher compensation rates and benefits than hourly jobs, although hourly (non-exempt) workers sometimes can make more money than salaried (exempt) workers overall simply by working more hours.

Each job must have the same pay range for anyone performing that job, that is, one person cannot be eligible for a higher maximum pay in that job than someone else doing that same job.

How to Establish Benefits and Compensation Programs

Nature of Programs Vary

The various forms of benefits and compensation that an organization chooses to provide and how it chooses to provide them are often referred to as the organization's benefits and compensation program. The nature of the program depends very much on the size of the organization (usually its headcount), where it is located and the nature of its mission. For example, a small business in a low-population area would usually have a smaller, less complex program than a medium or large business with many people in a large, urban area.

The nature of the program often changes as the organization grows. For example, the program might offer a wider range of benefits to meet the increasingly diverse needs of its increasing number of employees. An organization that has very limited financial resources might offer an attractive set of benefits to offset its limited ability to provide high compensation. Likewise, an organization that has strong financial resources might offer rather high compensation, yet rather limited benefits.

Developing Benefits and Compensation Programs

A new business often develops its program by getting help from local expertise, example, from an association of businesses having similar products, or from specialists in benefits and compensation. The benefits and compensation program must be clearly described in the organization's personnel policies. The Board must approve the policies; thus, the Board must approve the forms of benefits and compensations and how they are delivered to employees.

- A new business usually starts by offering a base-pay compensation program and a rather limited list of benefits, including standard forms of paid leave, including vacation pay (usually two weeks per year for new employees), holiday pay (usually the major holidays), funeral leave and maternity/paternity leave.

- Salary ranges for a position are often established by doing some basic research, including contacting other businesses in the area to see what they pay their people. Another useful approach is to reference various salary surveys.

The following site has numerous salary surveys at http://jobstar.org/tools/salary/index.php .

- Organizations must be sensitive about their compensation programs in order to ensure that there is not any appearance of exorbitant pay, that is, of pay that is much more than reasonable for a particular role in the organization.

- Considering the rising cost of medical insurance, many employees would rather have medical insurance than life insurance as their only insurance benefit.

A new or small business might have a variety of informal or intangible benefits, such as flexible work hours or comp time practices. As the organization grows, these benefits should be formalized and incorporated into the Benefits and Compensation Program that apply uniformly to all employees. This will ensure fair treatment of all employees and ensure that the practices are not abused as the organization grows. Without such a Program, managers might consciously or unconsciously resort to highly subjective approaches to deciding informal or intangible benefits for employees, such as granting benefits based on which employees the managers seem to like the most. That subjective approach is not only unfair, but is very open to lawsuits for discrimination – lawsuits the company is likely to lose.

How to Hire the Best Employees

How to Identify the Best Candidates

It is very important that your activities of hiring an employee are based, as much as possible, on the person's match to the specifications and requirements in a written job description, rather than on your subjective impression of the person's personality or nature. The latter approach leaves you open to losing a lawsuit that alleged that you discriminated against (that you did not hire) a potential employee because you did not like the person's race, creed, color or orientation.

 Consider "How to Develop and Update Your Personnel Policies" on page 171.

1. **Encourage current employees to apply for the job.**
    Whether internal candidates would be leaving another job in the organization that is critical or not, all internal candidates deserve equal opportunity to apply for new jobs in the organization.

2. **Advertise the position. The ad should be based on content of the job description.**

    a. Post ads in classified sections of local major and neighborhood newspapers. In the ads, include the job title, general responsibilities, minimum skills and/or education required, whom they should send a resume to if they are interested and by when. Consider having a closing date after which you will not accept resumes.

    b. Mention the open position to customers.

    c. Send cover letters and job descriptions to professional organizations.

    d. Be sure to mention the open position to all employees to see if they can recommend any favorite candidates.

    e. Consider online ads with general job listing sites or sites associated with professional organizations.

    f. Ask candidates to send a resume to your organization (to whomever is designated to collect the resumes).

    g. Consider searching online resume listings for appropriate candidates, either with general job sites or specialized sites based on skills, experience, desired work or associations.

3. **Screen resumes.**

    a. When screening resumes, notice the candidate's career objective – or the lack of it. If an objective is not specified, then the candidate may not have considered what he/she really wants to do in the future, which may impact the candidate's commitment to your new role.

b. Notice if the candidate stayed at jobs long or left quickly. Are there unaccounted for periods in the work history? If so, are there acceptable explanations for that period?

c. Notice the candidate's education and training. Is it appropriate for the new role?

d. Consider what capabilities and skills might be evidenced in the person's past and current work activities.

e. If you have many resumes, then create one document on which to summarize and compare the "highlights" and "concerns" about each of the candidates; otherwise, after about 10 resumes, they will all seem to read the same.

How to Interview Candidates

The thoroughness and professionalism you use to interview candidates can make a strong, positive impression on candidates. It also conveys to them that you expect the same thoroughness and professionalism from them if they are hired by your organization.

Preparation

1. **Schedule interviews with all candidates that meet the minimum qualifications.**
    Those qualifications were specified in the job description. This practice helps to make sure that you are not excluding candidates because of any unfair biases on your part.

2. **When inviting them for an interview, also send them the job description.**
    That ensures they have reasonable preparation for the interview. Also mention who will interview them.

Use Multiple Interviewers Per Interview

1. **Consider having multiple people at the interview.**
    Although this can be intimidating to the interviewee, this practice can ensure them a more objective and fair consideration for the job because several perspectives (among the interviewers) will be considered, rather than only one. Have the same interviewers in all of the interviews, if possible, to ensure that each candidate received equal treatment.

Questions to Pose During Interviews

When posing the following types of questions, always be courteous and respectful to the candidates. Do not share reactions between interviewers until after all interviews are complete.

1. **Do not rely on your memory – ask permission from the candidate to take notes.**
    Be sure that you include the name of the candidate and the date on the notes.

2. **While interviewing candidates, always apply the same questions to all candidates.**
    That approach ensures the fair treatment and comparison of all candidates.

3. **All questions should be primarily in regard to performing the duties of the job.**
    Do not ask questions about the candidate's race, nationality, age, gender, disabilities (current or previous), marital status, spouses, children and their care, criminal records or credit

records. Asking those types of questions leaves you open to losing lawsuits that allege discrimination.

4.   **Ask open-ended questions and try to avoid questions answered with "yes" or "no."**
Open-ended questions tend to generate more useful information and provide the opportunity for the interviewer to observe how well the candidate articulates answers to questions.

5.   **Consider asking some rather thought-provoking and challenging questions.**
Ask, "What skills do you bring to this job?", "What concerns do you have about filling this role?" and "What was your biggest challenge in a past job and how did you meet it?"

6.   **Talk for at most 25% of the time – listen for the rest.**
This often is a challenge for new interviewers who feel that silence is somehow to always be avoided. The more time that the interviewer talks, the less time to learn about the candidate.

7.   **If it is clear that the candidate is not suitable for the job, then "sell" the organization.**
If he/she does not meet the minimum qualifications, after all, or there are other stronger candidates, then use the time in the interview to enlighten the candidate about the positive attributes of the organization in case the candidate chooses to spread the word to others.

Administrative / Human Resource Questions

1.   **Ask the candidate about what he/she expects for compensation and benefits.**
Even though the job description might specify the pay ranges and benefits, the candidate might have strong preference for other provisions that suit his/her nature.

2.   **Find out when the candidate can start work, if offered the job.**
Allow him/her at least two weeks to get his/her affairs in order. Expecting a candidate to start sooner might convey to the candidate that the organization operates in a crisis mode, which can be unattractive to good candidates.

3.   **Explain to the candidate when you will be getting back to them.**
Then always do get back to each person soon regarding whether he/she got the job. If your first choice for candidate does not work out, you might have to resort to choosing the second-best candidate. He/she might not accept the job if offended that you did not get back to him/her.

4.   **Ask if you can get, and check, any references from the candidate's previous jobs.**
Always contact at least three references that the candidate offers from his/her past work history. Share the results of these activities with the interviewers. If your employees will be directly involved with children, adults and the elderly, then seriously consider conducting background checks on the most preferred candidates for the job.

5.   **Be sure to tell candidates of any relevant conditions from your personnel policies.**
For example, tell the candidate whether there is a probationary period for the job. (The best way to deal with a poor performer is not to hire him or her in the first place. It is often wise to have a probationary period of, for example, six months, wherein if the employee does not meet the responsibilities of the position, you can quickly terminate the employee.)

How to Choose the Best Candidate

At this point, usually one or two candidates clearly stand out as the most qualified for the job. However, it is surprising how much interviewers' impressions can change once they all have an opportunity to carefully discuss and consider all of the candidates. Be sure your approach to selecting the best candidate is a comprehensive and consistent approach.

1.   **Soon after interviews are completed, interviewers together select the best candidate.**
Within one or at most two weeks after all interviews have been completed, convene the interviewers. Consider a consistent method to select the best candidate from among the interviewers. For example, mention the name of a candidate, and allow 15 minutes total for all interviewers to share their impressions of that candidate. Also share results of any comments from references and/or background checks. Repeat the process for each candidate. After all candidates have been discussed, then list the candidates again, this time having interviewers vote for the best candidate from the list.

2.   **If there does not seem to be a suitable candidate, then consider the following:**

   a.   Are the job requirements too stringent or an odd mix? For example, the job might require someone with strong technical skills and also someone with strong clerical skills. Those two types of skills are sometimes unusual to expect to mix together.

   b.   Reconfigure the job so that the nature of the required skills and training are somewhat similar and so that the overall nature of the job becomes more common.

   c.   Hire the candidate who most closely matched the requirements of the job and then plan for dedicated training to bring that person's skills up to needed levels.

   d.   Re-advertise the position.

   e.   Get advice from a human resources professional. At this point, your need for their advice is probably quite specific, so they might provide services on a pro bono basis.

   f.   Hire a consultant for the position on a short-term basis, but only as a last resort as this may be quite expensive.

How to Hire the New Employee

You send a strong message to the candidate in the way that you provide the job offer to them. It is best to be both business-like and personal in your approach.

1.   **Provide a written job offer to the most qualified candidate.**
The letter should come from the person who will be supervising the new employee. In the letter:

   a.   Convey that you are pleased to offer the job to the candidate.

   b.   Specify the exact amount of compensation offered to him/her.

   c.   Specify the benefits offered to him/her.

d.   Specify the date on which to start the job.

e.   Include a signature line that the candidate can sign.

f.   Ask him/her to sign a copy of the offer letter and return it to you by a certain date. Give them at least one week to consider the job offer.

g.   Mention if there is a probationary period and the length of the period.

h.   Mention who he/she can contact if there are any questions.

i.   Attach a copy of the job description to be sure that the offer is associated with the correct job.

2.   **If everyone declines the job offer, then consider the following:**

a.   Ask the best candidates why they declined the offer. Usually, you will hear the same concerns, for example, the pay is too low, the benefits incomplete, the organization seems confused about what it wants from the role, or the interview process seemed hostile or contentious.

b.   Reconvene the interviewers and consider what you heard from the candidates. Recognize what went wrong and correct the problem. Contact your favorite candidate, admit the mistake, describe what you did to correct it, and explain why you would like to make an offer to him/her again.

c.   Go to the second choice. Sometimes the process of re-examining the candidates can bring a second-choice candidate to the front.

d.   Re-advertise the position.

3.   **Otherwise, start a personnel file for the new employee.**
The personnel file with contain all of the job-related information and material, for example, the employee's resume, job description, job offer, signed offer letter, completed tax withholding forms and signed forms for benefits.

4.   **Do not forget to send letters to the candidates who did not get the job.**
They deserve a sincere letter from you thanking them for their consideration and for interviewing for the job. Clearly explain that another candidate most closely matched the qualifications specified in the job description. If you plan to retain their job applications, mention that to them so they are aware that they still might be considered for other jobs that arise in the organization.

How to Train Your Employees

Most workplace training is on-the-job training, which, many times, is inadequate. Also, it is common for leaders and supervisors to not really understand how to design and conduct effective employee training – even though a primary role of supervisors is to ensure effective training and development of employees. This section gives a useful, overall perspective on training, and includes guidelines to help you to fully train your employees to do their jobs.

Many Forms of Job Training You Can Use

Reasons for Job Training

Employee job training can be initiated for a variety of reasons, for example:

1.   To equip the employee who is new to the job or task.

2.   As part of an overall professional development program.

3.   To "benchmark" the status of improvement in a performance improvement effort.

4.   When a performance appraisal indicates performance improvement is needed.

5.   As part of succession planning to help an employee be eligible for a planned change in role in the organization.

6.   To "pilot," or test, the operation of a new performance management system.

Major Types of Training

When planning the training for your employees, it helps to understand some basics about training and development. There are four major types of training:

1.   **Self-Directed Versus Other-Directed Learning**
      Self-directed learning is where the learner decides what he or she will learn and how. Other-directed learning is where other people decide what the learner will learn and how.

2.   **Informal Training Versus Formal Training**
      Informal training has no predetermined form. Examples are reading books to learn about a subject, talking to friends about the subject and attending a presentation. Formal training has a predetermined form. The form usually includes specification of learning results, learning objectives and activities that will achieve the results, and how the training will be evaluated. Examples might be college courses, workshops and seminars. Note that because formal training has a form, it does not necessarily mean that formal training is better than other forms. Informal training is probably the most common type of training and includes, for example, on-the-job training, coaching from supervisors, using manuals and procedures, and advice from peers.

Other-directed, formal training is typically more expensive than other approaches, but is often the most reliable to use for the learner to achieve the desired knowledge and skills in a timely fashion.

Self-directed, informal learning can be very low-cost; however the learner should have the capability and motivation to pursue his/her own training. Training may take longer than other-directed forms.

Highly specific and routine tasks can often be trained without complete, formal approaches. On the other hand, highly complex and changing roles often require more complete and formal means of development, which can be expensive as a result.

If training is needed right away, then other-directed training is often appropriate, for example, a training course at a local university, college or training center. Or, training professionals can be brought in. Again, other-directed training is usually faster and more reliable, but more expensive.

Self-directed forms of training require that the learner be highly motivated and able to conceptualize his/her approach to training, particularly in formal training.

Common Forms of Training

Training methods are either on-the-job, implemented outside the organization or a combination of both. The following is a brief overview of rather typical methods of development (in alphabetical order). Knowledge of the forms can be useful when designing training programs for employees.

1. **Apprenticeships**
    For centuries, apprenticeships were the major approach to learning a craft. The apprentice worked with a recognized master craftsperson. Particularly during times of low unemployment, businesses are eager to get any kind of help they can find. Seeking an apprenticeship may be an appropriate and effective way to eventually develop a new skill.

2. **Career counseling**
    Hopefully, learners have the opportunity to work with their supervisors to develop career plans that identify areas for improvement or advancement, how those areas can be addressed and when.

3. **Coaching**
    Coaching is becoming a popular means of development, and often includes working one-on-one with the learner to conduct a needs assessment, set major goals to accomplish, develop an action plan, and support the learner to accomplish the plan. The learner drives these activities and the coach provides continuing feedback and support.

4. **Continuing professional development**
    Many professions require verification of ongoing training to retain certification, for example, social workers, some fields of law and nurses. Professionals must stay up-to-date in the views and practices necessary to lead and manage in today's organizations. There seems to be an increasing number of universities, colleges and training centers associating continuing education units (CEUs) with their courses and workshops.

5. **Courses**
    Universities, colleges and training centers often have a large number of courses in management, professional and personal development. If the learner is looking to build a skill, then he or she must actually apply new information from these courses – otherwise, the learner is collecting information (hopefully, knowledge), rather than building skills.

6. **Distance learning**

   This typically includes learning by getting information and / or guidance from people who are not face-to-face with the learner, for example, learning via satellite broadcast, broadcast over the Internet, and e-mail or postal mail correspondence. Some people consider online learning (for example, information and tutorials available on diskette, CD-ROM and over the Internet) to be distance learning, as well.

7. **Internships**

   Internships are offered usually by organizations to college students wanting to find work experience during the summer months. The internships offer precious, real-life job experience and the organizations often get skilled, highly dedicated service. Many times, interns go on to be hired by the organizations, as well.

8. **Job assignments**

   Job assignments are wonderful opportunities from which to learn. We just are not used to thinking of them that way. To cultivate learning, consider having employees write short reports, including an overview of what they did, why they did it, what areas of knowledge and skills were used, how the job might have been done better, and what areas of knowledge and skills would be needed to improve the job.

9. **Job rotations**

   This can be one of the most powerful forms of development, allowing learners to experience a broad range of managerial settings, cultures and challenges.

10. **Lectures**

    Lectures, or focused presentations by experts on subject matter, are held in a wide variety of locations, not just in classrooms. Professional associations often bring in speakers. Guest lectures are often sponsored by local universities, colleges and training centers, and announced to the public. Many times, the lectures are repeated over local radio and television.

11. **Management development programs**

    Local universities, colleges and training centers usually offer these programs. Carefully review their program content and design to ensure that training includes real-life learning activities during which learners can develop skills for the workplace.

12. **Mentoring**

    Hopefully, learners find experienced managers in the workplace who are willing to take learners "under their wing" and provide ongoing coaching and mentoring.

13. **Online training**

    There are now numerous sources of online training (learning information from computer diskette, CD-ROM or over the Internet). This form of learning is sometimes called Web-based-training. Various forms of distance learning involve learning over the Internet as well.

14. **On-the-job training**

    This form helps particularly to develop the occupational skills necessary to manage an organization, for example, to fully understand the organization's products and services and how they are developed and carried out.

15. **Other-directed learning**
    This includes having someone other than the learner identify the training goal, methods to achieve the goal, and approaches to evaluating the training and progress toward achieving the training goal.

16. **Orientation to new jobs or roles**
    A carefully developed procedure for orienting new employees is helpful for getting employees "off on the right foot" when starting their jobs.

17. **Peer-based methods**
    This includes formats where peers focus on helping each other learn, for example, by exchanging ongoing feedback, questions, supportive challenges and materials. Perhaps the best example is the action learning process, originated by Reginald Revans.

18. **Professional organizations**
    A wide variety of professional organizations often offer courses, seminars, workshops and sessions from conventions.

19. **Self-directed learning**
    Highly motivated learners can usually gain a great deal of knowledge and skills by identifying their own learning objectives, how to meet those objectives and how to verify they have met the objectives, as well.

20. **Television**
    Various television networks often have a wide variety of enlightening shows about basic job skills, such as computer basics and business writing.

21. **Tutorials**
    Tutorials include guidance to proceed through learning some technique or procedure, for example, a tutorial on using a computer software package. There are an increasing number of online tutorials (tutorials available on diskette, CD-ROM and over the Internet).

22. **Training courses and seminars**
    Courses, seminars, convention sessions, etc., are useful for highly focused overviews of a particular subject or training about specific procedures.

23. **University and college programs**
    It seems there is an exponential number of management development programs in universities and colleges.

24. **Workshops**
    Workshops typically include some hands-on practice by the learner, and can be a very practical means to learn a certain technique or procedure.

Most Basic Form of Training – Tell, Try, Adjust, Repeat

Probably the most common form of informal training is a form of on-the-job-training. The approach is rather straightforward and includes:

1.   The supervisor, or some other expert at the subject matter or skill, tells the employee how to do something.

2.   The employee does what he/she was told to do.

3.   The expert watches and promptly shares feedback.

4.   The employee tries it again until he/she does it right.

The above approach works best in straightforward tasks. However, as jobs become more complex, employees often require more formal training.

How to Orient Your New Employee

Employee orientation is a form of training. Develop an orientation checklist and consider the following activities for inclusion on the list. The employee's supervisor should conduct the following activities.

1.   **When the employee starts in the organization, meet with him/her.**
       Explain how he/she will be trained, introduce him/her to other employees, give keys to facilities, get him/her to sign any needed benefit and tax forms, explain the time-recording system (if applicable), and provide copies of important documents (an organization chart, last year's final report, the strategic plan, this year's budget, and the personnel policies and procedures manual).

2.   **Show him/her the facilities.**
       Describe the layout of offices, bathrooms, storage areas, kitchen use, copy and fax systems, computer configuration and procedures, telephone usage, and any special billing procedures for use of office systems.

3.   **Schedule any needed computer training.**
       Include use of passwords, overview of software and documentation, location and use of peripherals, and where to go to get questions answered.

4.   **Review any policies and/or procedures about use of facilities.**
       Be sure to explain procedures to minimize damage to themselves or facilities, for example, what to unplug from electrical connections and where to go in case of fire.

5.   **Assign an employee as a "buddy" who is available to answer questions.**
       This simple practice goes a long way toward making new employees feel much more comfortable in his/her new surroundings.

6.   **Take him/her to lunch on the first day and invite others along.**
       Similar to assigning a buddy, this simple practice also really helps to make the new employee feel much more accepted and welcome in their new role.

7. **Meet with him/her at the end of the day to hear any questions or comments.**
Ask him/her is there is anything else you can do to help him/her feel comfortable and more equipped to do the job. Be sure to follow up on any requests that you hear.

8. **Meet with the new employee during the first few days of work**.
Review the job description again. Remind them to review the employee manual and to sign a form indicating they have reviewed the manual and that they will comply with its contents. Review any specific goals for the position, for example, goals from the strategic plan. In the same meeting, explain the performance review procedure and provide them a copy of the performance review document.

9. **Hold one-on-one meetings on a weekly basis for the first six weeks.**
Discuss the new employee's transition into the organization, get status on work activities, hear any pending issues or needs, and establish a working relationship with the supervisor.

How to Carefully Design and Implement Training Plans

The guidelines in this section are to help leaders and supervisors to design and implement focused and systematic training plans for their employees.

A. Determine the Overall Goals for Your Training Plan

When getting started with your training plan for your employee, first think about answers to the following questions:

1. What knowledge, skills and abilities (competencies) are needed by your employee to best do the job?

2. Are there others in the organization who can suggest what competencies the employee should learn for the job?

3. Should you have the employee conduct some form of self-assessment, for example, a questionnaire or interview to discern what competencies that he/she still needs for the job?

4. Write down your training goals as what competencies that the employee should achieve.

5. Are you providing training and development for your employee in order to address:

   a. A performance gap where he/she seems to have the capability, but somehow is not fully using it?

   b. A growth gap where he/she needs to learn more in order to progress in his/her career?

   c. An opportunity gap where he/she needs to gain certain learning to take advantage of an opportunity?

 Consider "How to Set Relevant and Realistic Goals With Your Employees" on page 191.

6. Think about what kind of gap that employee has and then about when the employee should achieve the competencies? A performance gap might be filled in time for the next performance review. A growth gap might be filled in time for him/her to evolve to the next stage in his/her career. An opportunity gap might be filled in time to take advantage of the opportunity.

B. *Identify Learning Objectives for Your Employee*

7. Learning objectives are the necessary accomplishments that the person must achieve in new knowledge, skills and abilities. For example, you might want the person to learn certain information about a software application (new knowledge), and then how to use that application (skills) to generate useful financial statements (capabilities). There might be several learning objectives each for new knowledge, skills and abilities.

8. In what sequence should the learning objectives be attained? Usually people must learn new knowledge before they can develop new skills to accomplish overall capabilities. Therefore, objectives should probably be organized in that order.

C. *Identify Learning Strategies for Your Employee*

9. What are the best learning activities (methods) for the person to use to achieve each of his/her learning objectives, for example, reading a book, working with a mentor or using an online tutorial? Do the learning activities include ongoing reflections about what the person is learning?

D. *Identify What Resources Are Needed to Implement Strategies*

10. Now that you know what learning activities will be conducted, think about what resources will be needed, for example, tutorial software, tuition in courses or self-study books. Think about what funding will be needed to obtain those resources.

E. *Identify What Tangible Results Can Be Evaluated*

11. What observable results, or evidence of learning, will the person produce from the learning activities that can be reviewed for verification of achieving the learning objective, for example, will the person show his/her supervisor that he/she can do the job?

12. Who will verify that each of the learning objectives was reached, for example, will the supervisor evaluate the person's progress? If an evaluator will be needed from outside of the organization, think about what funding will be needed to pay that evaluator.

F. *Budget Funds for Resources and Services for Training Program*

13. Consider costs of trainers, consultants, room rental, books, tuition, travel expenses and labor to pay the employee while attending training. Also consider the cost for any materials that need to be developed, as listed below.

G. Develop Any Training Materials They May Need

14.   Consider if the learner needs to obtain, or start:

      a.   Enrolling in courses.

      b.   Buying books.

      c.   Scheduling time with experts.

      d.   Getting a mentor.

      e.   Scheduling time with the supervisor.

H. Implement Their Training Plan and Evaluate During Implementation

15.   During the training, how will you be sure that the employee understands the new information and materials?

16.   Will the learning be engaging and enjoyable? This is important for sustaining your investment in the employee's training.

17.   Are you sure that the employee will receive the necessary ongoing feedback, coaching and mentoring during training and development activities? Identify resources you can call on for this and check in with the employee throughout the implementation of the plan.

18.   Where will the employee get the necessary administrative support and materials?

19.   Regularly collect the learner's impressions of the training experiences and any evidence how he/she is doing in the program. Does your employee understand the learning methods as they are being applied? Is he/she regularly providing feedback about how well he/she understands the materials?

I. Evaluate Their Learning When the Plan Has Been Implemented

20.   Was the employee able to sufficiently display the competencies necessary for the tasks, job or role?

21.   Are there any plans for follow-up evaluation, including assessing results several months after the employee has completed the training plan?

How to Ensure Maximum Performance From Your Employees

The term "supervisor" is referred to throughout this section. Remember that supervisors exist throughout the ranks of management. A supervisor is someone who has at least one person reporting to him/her and, therefore, is responsible for the progress and productivity of that person. For example, a CEO supervises middle managers who supervise entry-level supervisors who supervise individual contributors.

How to Set Relevant and Realistic Goals With Your Employees

Supervisors Often Lack Understanding of Performance

Performance is when an employee is achieving a goal in a highly effective and efficient manner and when that goal is closely aligned with achieving the overall goals of the organization. A common problem for new supervisors is having no clear, strong sense of whether their employees are high performing or not.

Employees can be very busy in their roles, but that does not mean they are high-performing if their roles are not directly contributing toward achieving the overall goals of the organization. The first step toward solving this problem is to establish clear performance goals. Some people have a strong negative reaction toward setting goals because they fear goals as "the law" that must be maintained and never broken. Some people fear they will never achieve the goals. Others have disdain for goals because goals seem to take the "heart" out of their work.

Advantages of Using Goals in the Workplace

Despite the negative views that one can have about goals, they hold certain strong advantages in the workplace. They:

1. Provide clear direction to supervisors and employees.

2. Form a common frame of reference around which they can effectively communicate.

3. Clearly indicate success, and can cultivate a strong sense of fulfillment for those working toward achieving the goals.

4. Help clarify the specific expectations of the supervisor and employee.

Performance Gaps, Growth Gaps, Opportunity Gaps and Training Gaps

Goals can be valuable for specifying expectations and for setting measurements of progress in working to fill four types of gaps:

1. **Performance gaps**
    These gaps are identified during the employee performance management process. Ideally,

performance gaps are addressed by performance improvement plans. Performance improvement plans are sometimes a last-ditch effort at helping a person to improve his/her performance. Ideally, the performance problem is addressed through ongoing feedback and adjustments during regular one-on-one meetings. In these plans, goals are established to improve performance, and may include, for example, increased effort on the part of the employee, support from his/her supervisor, and certain training and resources to assist the person in his/her development. Dedicated employees can greatly appreciate having specific performance goals for them to achieve in order to keep their jobs, verify their competence to their supervisor and accomplish overall professional development.

2. **Growth gaps**
   These gaps are identified during career planning. Employees perceive certain areas of knowledge and skills that they would like to accomplish in order to qualify for certain future roles and positions. Employees often appreciate having clear-cut goals that mark what they need to do to advance in their careers.

3. **Opportunity gaps**
   These gaps are identified when a sudden opportunity arises for the employee. If the person is highly interested in taking advantage of the opportunity, then he or she will appreciate knowing exactly what goals must be achieved to take advantages of the opportunity. Growth gaps and opportunity gaps are very similar.

4. **Training gaps**
   These gaps are identified when hiring a new employee, during performance management planning or career planning. Gaps are usually in terms of areas of knowledge, skills or abilities (competencies). Training plans can be designed with clear-cut training goals to give direction to the employee or trainer.

Whatever the type of goal, it is critical that the employee have strong ownership and commitment to achieving the goal.

Goals Should Be SMARTER

You can help ensure that goals are agreeable to supervisor and employee by ensuring that they are highly involved in identifying the goals. When setting goals with others, strive to describe them to be "SMARTER." This acronym stands for goals that are:

1. **Specific**
   For example, a goal to generate three types of financial statements, including cash flow, budget-versus-actual and income statement.

2. **Measurable**
   For example, to be able to assess if the three types of statements were generated or not.

3. **Achievable**
   For example, the goal would be irrelevant if the person had no access to the financial information from which to generate the statements.

4. **Relevant**
   For example, the goal would not be useful if the organization has no plans to ever make decisions based on the financial statements.

5. **Timely**
   The statements should be generated by a certain deadline, for example, in time for the Board to review and approve the statements.

6. **Extending capabilities**
   Ideally, the goal involves the person's learning more than they already knew about generating statements.

7. **Rewarding**
   Ideally, the activities of generating the financial statements would be fulfilling for the person to accomplish.

If goals seem insurmountable to the employee, then break goals down into smaller goals, or sub-goals or objectives until they are SMARTER.

How to Delegate For Growth and Performance of Your Employees

Delegation is when supervisors give responsibility and authority to their subordinates to complete a task by a certain date, and generally let the subordinates figure out how the task can be accomplished. Effective delegation develops people who not only are more productive in the workplace, but also who are more fulfilled. Supervisors become more fulfilled and productive themselves as they learn to rely more on their employees and, thus, are freed up to attend to more strategic matters in their own jobs.

Delegation is often difficult for new supervisors, particularly if they have had to scramble to start the organization or a major new product by themselves. Many supervisors want to remain comfortable, making the same decisions the same way that they always have – doing the same jobs the same way they have always done those jobs. These supervisors believe they can do the jobs better than anyone else so why ask anyone else to do them. New supervisors often do not want to risk losing any of their new power and stature by sharing them with others (ironically, those supervisors do lose these if they do not soon learn to delegate effectively). Sometimes, supervisors do not want to risk giving authority to subordinates in case the subordinates fail and somehow impair the organization.

However, supervisors do not progress in their careers and do not develop their people if they do not learn how to effectively delegate to others. There are basic approaches to delegation that, with practice, become the backbone of effective supervision and development. Thomas R. Horton, in *Delegation and Team Building: No Solo Acts Please* (Management Review, September 1992, pp. 58-61) suggests the following general steps to accomplish delegation:

1. **Delegate the whole task to one person.**
   This gives the person complete responsibility for doing the task and increases the person's motivation to do the task, as well. It also provides more focus for the supervisor when working with the person to understand that the desired results should look like.

2. **Select the right person to delegate to.**
   Assess the skills and capabilities of the person to be sure that individual can actually accomplish the task. Does he/she have the knowledge, skills and abilities to do the task? If not, the person might need training. Or, perhaps the task should be delegated to someone else.

3.   **Clearly specify your preferred results.**
     Provide information on what the results should look like, why those results are desired, when the results should be accomplished, who else might help the person, and what resources the person has to work with. You might leave the "how to accomplish the task" to be decided by the person. It is often best to write this information down.

4.   **Delegate responsibility and authority – assign the task, not the method to accomplish it.**
     Let the person complete the task in the manner that he/she chooses, as long as the desired results are likely to be what the supervisor specifies. Let the person have strong input as to the completion date of the project. Note that you may not even know how to complete the task yourself – this is often the case with higher levels of management. Make sure that others in the organization understand that this person has both the responsibility and the authority to complete the task.

5.   **Ask the person to summarize back to you, a description of the results you prefer.**
     Explain that you are requesting the summary to be sure you effectively described the results to the person, not necessarily to be sure that the person heard you. That explanation helps the person to not feel as if he/she is somehow being treated as if he/she is untrustworthy.

6.   **Get ongoing non-intrusive feedback about progress on the project.**
     This is a good reason to continue to get weekly, written status reports from the person. Reports should describe what he/she did last week, plans to do next week, and any potential issues that might arise. Regular meetings with the person provide feedback, as well.

8.   **Maintain open lines of communication.**
     Do not hover over the person to monitor his/her performance, but do sense what he/she is doing and do support the person's checking in with you while doing the task.

9.   **If you are not satisfied with the progress, do not do the task yourself!**
     Continue to work with the person to ensure that he/she perceives that the task is his/her responsibility. Look for the cause of your dissatisfaction. For example, is it lack of communication, training, resources or commitment of the person?

10. **Evaluate and reward the person's performance.**
     Evaluate achievement of desired results more than the methods used by the person. Address insufficient performance and reward successes. (Upcoming topics in this section will help you to evaluate the performance, including addressing performance problems and rewarding performance.)

How to Support Your Employee's Self-Motivation

Clearing Up Some Common Myths About Motivation

The topic of motivating employees is extremely important to supervisors. Despite its importance, several myths about motivation persist – especially among new supervisors. Before looking at what management can do to support employee motivation, it is important to clear up these common myths.

Myth #1 – "I can motivate people."
Not really – they have to motivate themselves. You cannot motivate people anymore than you can empower them. Employees have to motivate and empower themselves. However, you can set up an

environment where they best motivate and empower themselves. The key is knowing what environment will work for each of your employees.

Myth #2 – "Money is a good motivator."
Not necessarily. Certain things like money, a nice office and job security can help people from becoming less motivated, but they do not always help people to become more motivated. A key goal is to understand the motivations of each of your employees.

Myth #3 – "Fear is a good motivator."
Fear is a great motivator – for a very short time. That is why a lot of yelling from the boss might seem to "light a spark" under employees, but not for very long.

Myth #4 – "I know what motivates me, so I know what motivates others."
Different things motivate different people. I may be greatly motivated by earning time away from my job in order to spend more time my family. You might be motivated much more by recognition of a job well done. Again, a key goal is to understand what motivates each of your employees.

Myth #5 – "Increased job satisfaction means increased job performance."
Research shows increased job satisfaction does not necessarily mean increased job performance. Employees might be satisfied just sitting at their desks and playing games on their computers. However, that does not produce high-performing employees.

Myth #6 – "Motivation is a complex social science. I cannot understand it."
Not true. There are some basic steps you can take that will go a long way toward supporting your employees to motivate themselves toward increased performance in their jobs. (More about these steps is provided later on in this section.)

Basic Principles to Remember

1.   **Motivating employees starts with motivating yourself.**
It is amazing how, if you hate your job, it seems like everyone else does, too. If you are very stressed out, it seems like everyone else is, too. Enthusiasm also is contagious. If you are enthusiastic about your job, it is much easier for others to be, too. Also, if you are doing a good job of taking care of yourself and your own job, then you will have much clearer perspective on how well others are taking care of themselves and their jobs, too.

2.   **Key to supporting motivation of others is understanding what motivates each of them.**
Different things motivate each person. Before you take steps to support the motivation of your employees, be sure to find out what it is that really motivates each of them.

3.   **Recognize that supporting other's motivation is a process, not a task.**
Organizations change all the time, as do people. Indeed, it is an ongoing process to sustain an environment where people can strongly motivate themselves. If you look at this as an ongoing process, then you will be much more fulfilled and motivated yourself.

4.   **Support motivation by using organizational systems – not just good intentions.**
Do not just count on cultivating strong interpersonal relationships with others in order to help them to motivate themselves. The nature of these relationships can change greatly, for example, during times of stress. Instead, use reliable and comprehensive systems in the workplace to help motivate employees. For example, establish fair and equitable personnel policies about employee performance management, and about benefits and compensation.

5. **Always work to align goals of the organization with goals of employees.**
    As mentioned above, people can be excited about their work and be working very hard. However, if the results of their work do not directly contribute to the goals of the organization, then the organization is not any better off than if they were just sitting on their hands – maybe even worse off because you are paying them to not be productive! Therefore, it is critical that supervisors know what they want from their employees. These preferences should be worded in terms of SMARTER goals. Whatever steps you take to support the motivation of others, ensure that they have strong input to identifying their goals and that these goals are aligned with the goals of the organization.

Steps You Can Take

The following specific steps can help you go a long way toward supporting your employees to motivate themselves in your organization.

1. **Do more than read this Guide – actually apply what you are reading here.**
    This maxim is true when reading any management publication.

2. **Write down motivational factors that sustain you and how to keep them.**
    This little bit of "motivational planning" not only helps your motivation, but also can give you strong perspective on how to think about supporting the motivations of others.

3. **Make of list of three to five things that motivate each of your employees.**
    Have each of your employees complete the checklist on page 199. Then meet with each of them to discuss what he/she thinks are the most important motivational factors to him/her. Lastly, take some time alone to write down how you will modify your approaches with each of them to ensure that his/her motivational factors are being met.

4. **Work with each person to include his/her motivations in how he/she is rewarded.**
    For example, the employee's job might be redesigned to be more fulfilling. You might find more means to provide recognition, if that is important to the person. You might develop a personnel policy that rewards the person with more family time.

5. **Use one-on-one meetings with each person to build a relationship with him/her.**
    In the workplace, people often are more motivated by your care and concern for them than by your attention to their work. Get to know each of your employees, and a bit about their families, their favorite foods and names of their children. This can sound manipulative – and it will be if not done sincerely.

6. **Cultivate strong skills in delegation.**
    Delegation includes conveying responsibility and authority to your employees so they can carry out certain tasks. However, you usually should leave it up to your employees to decide *how* they will carry out the tasks. This also allows employees to take a stronger role in their jobs, which usually means more fulfillment and motivation in their jobs, as well.

Consider "How to Delegate for Growth and Performance of Your Employees" on page 193.

7. **Implement at least the basic principles of performance management.**
    Good performance management includes identifying goals and measures to indicate if the goals are being met or not, providing ongoing attention and feedback about measures toward the goals, and suggesting corrective actions to redirect activities back toward achieving the desired goals when necessary. Good performance management techniques provide strong motivation for employees because they clearly understand what is expected of them, feel that they are being treated fairly and equitably, and rewarded for when they have done a good job.

8. **Establish goals that are SMARTER.**
    SMARTER goals are: specific, measurable, achievable, relevant, timely, extending of capabilities, and rewarding to those involved.

     See "How to Set Relevant and Realistic Goals With Your Employees" on page 191.

9. **Clearly convey how your desired results contribute to organizational results.**
    Employees often feel strong fulfillment from realizing that they are actually making a difference in the organization when they achieve your desired results. This realization requires clear communications from you about organizational goals and how the desired results are directly aligned with those goals.

10. **As much as possible, reward desired behaviors when you *see* the behaviors.**
    A critical lesson for new supervisors is to learn to focus on employees' behaviors, not on their personalities. One of the best ways to ensure that you maintain focus on behaviors, rather than on personalities, is to use your eyes more than your feelings when assessing performance. You can get in a great deal of trouble (legally, morally and interpersonally) by focusing only on how you *feel* about others' performance, rather than primarily on what you are actually *seeing* or reading regarding their performance.

11. **Or, reward the desired behaviors soon after you see them.**
    This helps to reinforce the notion that you highly prefer the behaviors that you are currently seeing from your employees. Often, the shorter the time between an employee's action and your reward for that action, the clearer it is to the employee that you indeed highly prefer that action.

12. **Celebrate achievements!**
    This critical step is often forgotten. Celebration of achievements is not direct means of motivating employees; rather it cultivates an environment where employees can more readily feel a sense of accomplishment, and thus, fulfillment, in their jobs. New supervisors are often focused on getting "a lot done." This usually means identifying and solving problems. Experienced supervisors have come to understand that acknowledging and celebrating a solution to a problem can be every bit as important as finding the solution itself. Without ongoing acknowledgement of success, employees can become very frustrated, skeptical and even cynical about their efforts in the organization.

13. **Let employees hear from their customers (internal or external).**
    Let them hear how they have benefited the organization's customers or other employees in the organization. For example, if the employee is working to keep internal computer

systems operating well, then have other employees express their gratitude for how well the computers are operating. Similarly, if an employee is helping to provide a service to a customer, then bring in the customer to express his/her appreciation to the employee.

14. **Admit to yourself (or to someone else) if you do not like an employee.**
Supervisors are people. You may find that you just do not like someone who works for you. That someone could, for example, look like an uncle you do not like. In that case, admit to yourself that you do not like the person. Then talk about your dislike confidentially with a confidant (someone else who is appropriate to talk to, for example, a peer, your boss or your mentor). Indicate to the confidant that you want to explore what it is that you do not like about the person who works for you and that you would like to come to a clearer perception of how you can accomplish a positive working relationship with that person. It often helps a great deal just to talk out loud about how you feel and to get someone else's opinion about the situation. As noted above, if you continue to focus on what you *see* about the person's performance, you will go a long way toward ensuring that your treatment of person remains fair and equitable.

Table VI:2 – Checklist of Categories of Typical Motivators

To help you identify what motivates you, consider from among the following categories of typical motivators. Rank the categories, starting with "1" as the highest. You might have several categories that rank a "1". Do not worry about getting your ranking to be "perfect." The point is to go through the process of thinking about what motivates you. Consider discussing the results with your supervisor, friends or family.

__ Career Development / Success

__ Comfort / Relaxation

__ Health / Balance / Energy

__ Influence / Leadership

__ Learning / Knowledge / Discovery

__ Materials / Possessions

__ Recognition / Praise (It is OK to seek this.)

__ Security / Money / House

__ Social / Affiliation / Popularity / Acceptance

__ Status / Prestige / Stand Out / Reputation (It is OK to seek this.)

__ Task Accomplishment / Problem Solving / Achievement

__ Teaching / Guiding Others

__ Vitality / Energy

__ Others? _____

__ Others? _____

__ Others? _____

Are there other comments you could make that would help you (and maybe others) to more clearly understand what motivates you? Take a moment to consider this question and write down your answers.

How to Know What Role to Play – Facilitate, Coach, Direct or Train?

As a leader, you might perform a variety of roles when leading others, primarily the roles of facilitator, coach, expert or trainer. There are no specific indicators as to when you should fill a certain role. However, there are general guidelines from which you can get an indication as to which roles you might fill based on current conditions in the organization or in a project.

When You Might Fill the Facilitator Role

Facilitating is helping a person or group of people to decide what results they want to achieve, how they want to achieve them and then helping them to achieve the results. Facilitation styles range from directive to indirectly suggestive. Conditions when a leader might want to act as a facilitator include:

1.   **When a project needs strong, ongoing trust, commitment and participation of others.** Ongoing ownership and commitment from others usually do not come from others during trainings or when receiving expert advice. Instead, the buy-in of others comes from knowing that their beliefs and opinions are being solicited and valued. The essence of facilitation is to bring out those beliefs and opinions and to help others decide what they want to do and how they want to do it.

2.   **When working to address complex problems or major goals with others.** The most accurate understanding of a situation often comes from considering the open and honest perspectives of everyone involved. Facilitation often is the most approach to make it safe for, and to solicit, the perspectives from others.

When You Might Fill the Coaching Role

You might choose to fill the coaching role when the following conditions exist:

1.   **An individual seems stalled or troubled.** Coaching can be a powerful means to guide and support an individual to clarify current challenges or priorities, identify suitable strategies to address the challenges, and then to actually implement the strategies.

2.   **To maximize an individual's learning from experience.** Individuals learn differently. Coaching can be a powerful means to guide and support individuals to reflect on their experiences and then use that learning to improve effectiveness in life and work.

 Consider "How to Coach for Deep Problem-Solving and Learning" on page 202.

When You Might Fill the Expert Role

You might choose to fill the expert role when the following conditions exist:

1.   **The situation requires knowledge that would likely be used the same in any context.**
There are certain types of general knowledge that would probably be used the same in any organization or project, for example, setting up and operating financial systems, and many of the practices in management.

2.   **The project needs knowledge that is highly specialized and proceduralized.**
For example, installing computers, conducting market research, conforming to laws and regulations, designing certain products or providing certain services, financial processes and procedures, or use of specific tools for problem solving and decision-making.

When You Might Fill the Trainer Role

Training includes activities to help a learner or learners to develop or enhance knowledge, skills and attitudes to improve performance on a current or future task or job. You might choose to fill the trainer role when the following conditions exist:

1.   **Expert knowledge needs to be conveyed in a concise and timely manner.**
There may be times where employees need to learn certain expert-based knowledge in a highly focused and efficient manner. The knowledge might be any form of expert-based knowledge as listed in the above topic about playing the expert role.

2.   **Knowledge needs to be conveyed to a group of people.**
Training is often most useful when a group of people need to learn expert-based knowledge. This can be quite common in projects, for example, when training project members about the nature of organizational change or the project's change plans or methods of data collection.

Guidelines for Switching Roles Between Facilitator and Expert

1.   **Be clear which "hat" you are wearing to your employee.**
You might even refer to your various roles as your wearing various "hats." Otherwise, your employee can become confused about your current priorities, how you are addressing them and how they should interact with you.

2.   **Be clear about the source of your advice.**
Be clear as to whether your advice is based on your expertise (your expert role), general knowledge in the field (other experts) or the learners' own wisdom. Facilitators often count on the wisdom of the participants in their groups.

3.   **Know your own expertise and the limits of that expertise.**
When you realize that you do not have sufficient skills to address a current issue or goal with another, then you are often more effective to adopt a facilitator role. That role more advantageously recruits the skills of others, in addition to your own.

4.   **Do not fall in love with one role.**
Leaders who value their own expertise and prefer to exhibit that expertise often resort primarily to the expert role. Similarly, leaders who have strong people skills often resort primarily to the facilitator role. Highly effective leaders can switch between roles depending on the needs of the current situation, rather than on their personal comfort levels.

How to Coach for Deep Problem-Solving and Learning

One of the primary goals of a leader is to help his/her employees to learn to be more effective at solving problems and learning. One of the most powerful approaches to do that is through the use of coaching to help others: a) closely examine their own perceptions, assumptions and conclusions about their current problem or goal; b) take relevant and realistic actions; and c) learn by continuing to reflect on those actions and experiences. You can use coaching at almost any time when your employees seem to be struggling to address an issue or achieve a goal. Coaching is powerful means to delegate to employees.

What Is Coaching? How Is It Useful in Leadership?

There are a variety of different perspectives on coaching due to the dramatic increase in popularity of the field of personal and professional coaching. For the context of leading others in the workplace, coaching could be described as using skills in listening, questioning and support to help another to:

1. **Take a complete look at his/her current situation.**
   This includes asking the person useful questions to clarify his/her assumptions and perceptions about the current situation.

2. **Set relevant and realistic goals for themselves.**
   Based on insights from answering the questions, the person sets relevant, realistic and specific goals based on his/her own nature, needs, capabilities and timelines.

3. **Take relevant and realistic actions toward reaching the goals.**
   A hallmark of good coaching is supporting others to take ongoing actions toward his/her goals, rather than only to reflect and think about the situation.

4. **Learn by continuing to reflect on useful questions and results of actions.**
   The person who gets coached often learns a great deal from reflecting on the questions posed to him/her and on the results of the actions that he/she is taking.

Coaching is highly adaptable to the nature of the person being coached because it works from the person's answers to the coach's questions, rather than working at the person by asserting directives to him/her. It helps the person to closely examine his/her own style, thinking and approaches to problem solving.

Guidelines for Designing a Coaching Session

The nature of a coaching conversation can be distinctly different from a typical workplace conversation. A typical conversation is usually a spontaneous exchange of information that almost seems to "ping pong" casually back and forth among the participants. The focus of the conversation can move with whatever comments are offered by participants. In contrast, coaching is usually a much more focused conversation in which the nature of exchange is based, in large part, on asking powerful questions to another, while using effective listening and feedback skills, as you support the person in thoughtfully answering the questions.

You need to intentionally prepare yourself and your employee for a coaching session. Consider the following guidelines:

1. **Briefly describe the nature of coaching and its benefits to your employee.**
   Mention that one of the most powerful ways to help someone solve a problem or clarify plans to achieve a goal is through use of a coaching session. Explain how coaching helps the person closely examine the situation, carefully think about action plans, and learn at the same time. Explain the role of questions during coaching.

2. **Ask the employee if he/she would like you to coach him/her.**
   You should always get the person's permission to be coached. Otherwise, the person may feel uncomfortable, manipulated and distrusting during questioning.

3. **Consider any culturally specific conventions.**
   Depending on the conventions in the particular culture of your organization and on the personality of the person you plan to coach, the person might not appreciate getting questioned by you. In some cultures, questions might be perceived as disrespectful.

Consider "How to Lead in Multicultural Organizations" on page 91.

4. **Focus on organizational issues, not just on the individual's issues.**
   Your role is to facilitate organizational change, not only to facilitate change in one individual. Thus, you should maintain focus on the desired results for the organization in addition to the current challenges of the person whom you are coaching.

5. **Use the guidelines for effective listening.**
   For example, be sure that you can hear the person, listen more than talk, and acknowledge the person's responses.

Consider "How to Really Listen to Others" on page 89.

6. **Respectfully and supportively offer probing questions.**
   Questions are the heart of the coaching session. The rest of this section on coaching provides numerous guidelines about traits of useful and not so useful questions, along with examples of powerful questions.

7. **Limit advice during the questioning.**
   Sometimes, you might feel an urge to answer a question that the person seems to be struggling to answer. The person might be struggling because he/she is searching for the best answer. That search can yield a great deal of learning for the person.

8. **Limit general discussion during the questioning.**
   A general discussion can diffuse the focus on the questioning. Instead, keep focused on asking questions. Each question might be based on answers to the previous question. There can be other times in the project for general discussion.

9. **Avoid lecturing your employee.**
   This guideline is relevant to probably any supportive and respectful communication with

another. Lecturing can be detected by regular use of phrases, such as "you should" or "you have to." Lecturing often leaves others feeling judged and angry.

10. **Use questions to help the person develop action plans.**
Often, it is helpful to help your employee come to conclusions by helping him/her to decide whether to take action and what those actions should be. Often, actions "shake loose" solutions and generate learning.

11. **Use questions to help your employee learn from the coaching session.**
Your employee can generate valuable insights from thinking about and responding to useful questions from you. It is important for you to help the person to identify and take ownership for that learning.

12. **Close the coaching session.**
Always use some means for specifically ending the coaching session. For example, thank the person, ask what they have learned, mention the value of the coaching session to you, or physically move to a different location. Ask the person to summarize his/her learning and ask him/her about next steps.

Why Questions Are So Important in Coaching

The primary tool in coaching is your respectfully and supportively posing powerful questions to your employee. There are several advantages to questioning when coaching a person.

1. **It helps the person to recognize his/her own perceptions and assumptions.**
Usually, a coaching session starts with the person describing some issue or goal that is important to him/her. For example, the person might explain to you that he or she believes that he/she has a significant problem with time management. The person might add that he/she has tried hard to address the problem, but does not seem to be getting anywhere. The person might suggest that he/she needs to take a time management course.

2. **It helps the person to clarify his/her own assumptions.**
As the person continues to think about the questions posed by you, he/she usually provides more information about the reasoning that led to the conclusion that there's a time management problem, for example, the person might mention that other leaders seem to get more done, and feel much less frustrated.

3. **It helps the person to verify his/her own assumptions.**
As you pose more questions (for example, about whether others really do get much more done and really do not feel frustrated), the person might question him/herself about whether the person is being realistic about the amount of tasks to get done in a day, and ultimately, whether the time management problem might be a symptom of another larger problem.

4. **It helps the person to modify their views on the issues.**
Many times, finding the right problem is at least as important as finding the right answer. As the coaching session progresses, the person might seem to be talking about another problem or goal. For example, the person might mention that he/she wishes for more guidance from you about setting priorities and providing more resources, but that he/she is reluctant to ask you for help for fear of appearing incompetent.

5. **It helps the person to arrive at realistic conclusions about what to do.**
   Many times, leaders in organizations are faced with so many challenges and options for meeting those challenges that they do not know what to do. Other times, leaders are so inspired and driven that they struggle to be realistic. Coaching helps people to move on to action-oriented conclusions that are relevant and realistic.

6. **It helps the person to develop powerful skills in inquiry and reflection.**
   In our example, over several coaching sessions, the person often begins to develop his/her own skills in asking useful questions to others and themselves. Conversations become more focused, particularly on useful actions and learning. The person is learning to solve his/her own problems and identify learning, too.

7. **It allows you to help your employee without extensive background.**
   One of the major advantages of using questions during coaching is that often you can help another person without having to know a great deal of history about the particular issue or goal faced by that person. Actually, the more that you know about how the person got stuck on a particular issue, the more that you can sometimes get as stuck as that person during coaching. Many times, people struggle because of strong misperceptions. The more that you closely examine the background and thinking about those misperceptions, the more that you might adopt those misperceptions yourself. You can avoid that trap by asking questions during coaching sessions.

Traits of Destructive Questions

Before suggesting guidelines to conduct supportive questioning, it is important for you to know what types of questions to avoid. Consider these guidelines:

1. **Avoid asking questions that can be answered simply with "yes" or "no."**
   You and your employee gain little understanding or direction from such pointed questions that have such short answers. Instead, consider questions that start with "What," "How," "When" and "Where."

2. **Avoid leading questions.**
   Leading questions are questions that are asked to lead another to a certain pre-determined conclusion or insight. Those questions can be perceived by the other as manipulative and dishonest. Leading questions often can be answered with "yes" or "no," for example, "You did what I suggested, right?"

3. **Avoid frequently asking questions that begin with "Why."**
   Those types of questions can leave others feeling defensive, as if they are to be accountable to you to justify their actions. That feeling of defensiveness can damage feelings of trust and openness between you and your employees.

Traits of Useful Questions

Consider these guidelines:

1. **Where possible, use open-ended questions.**
   Open-ended questions are those that are not answered with "yes" or "no." They generate thinking and reflection on the part of the person you are coaching. They also ensure that the person keeps focused in the coaching session.

2. **Focus questions on the here-and-now.**
   The goal of coaching is to help the person to go forward by changing how he/she looks at the problem, identifying realistic actions to take, and learning from those actions.

3. **Ask questions to clarify what the other is saying.**
   Clarifying questions help you and the person you are coaching to understand the key point or "bottom line" of what he/she is saying. They often lead to discovering the root cause of issues.

4. **Ask questions about the person's perspectives, assumptions and actions.**
   Adults can learn a great deal by closely examining their own thinking. Often, they struggle because of inaccurate perceptions or assumptions. Therefore, ask questions about their thinking, assumptions and beliefs about current priorities. Do not ask lots of questions about other people – you cannot coach people who are not with you.

5. **Ask the other person for help.**
   It can be powerful when you show enough trust and confidence in the relationship with your employee that you can ask him/her for help with helping them. For example, you might ask, "What question should I ask you?" or "What additional questions should I be asking now?"

Examples of Powerful Questions for Coaching

It is common that a coaching session goes through a certain life cycle. Initially, the person you are coaching will report some major problem, goal, challenge or priority. Your questions can be useful at that time to help the person to report the problem or goal, and then to closely examine and clarify that priority. Next, you can help the person to identify appropriate actions to take to effectively address the priority. Lastly, you can help the person to learn from the coaching session itself. Consider the questions in the following table when coaching an employee. Notice the grouping of the questions into the four stages of a useful coaching session.

Table VI:3 – Useful Questions to Ask When Coaching Others

1. To Help Another Report a Priority:

- What do you want to work on today?
- What is wrong? What is missing?
- What would be exciting to achieve?
- What would you like from me today?
- How would you like to get it?

2. To Help Another Clarify the Priority:

- What is important?
- How is this issue important?
- What do you think the real problem is?
- What is your role in this issue?
- Where do you feel stuck?
- Is what you are doing getting what you want?
- What is the intent of what you are saying?
- Where are those strong feelings coming from?
- What would you like me to ask?

3. To Help Another Move to Action(s):

- Have you experienced anything like this before? What did you do? How did it work out?
- What do you hope for?
- What is preventing you from...?
- What would you be willing to give up for that?
- If you could change one thing, what would it be?
- Imagine a point in the future where your issue is resolved. How did you get there?
- What can you do before the next meeting?
- Who will do that action? By when? What will it look like when done? How will you know it is done?

4. To Help Another Deepen Learning:

- Have you said everything that you want to say?
- How did this coaching session go for you?
- What is the learning in this for you?

How to Share Useful – and Respectful – Feedback

Feedback to employees is information regarding their performance and also is information they can act on. Feedback must be shared in a manner that is understandable to them and is perceived by them as being provided in a highly respectful manner. Sharing feedback involves skills in effective listening, verbal and non-verbal communications, and working in multi-cultural environments. Consider the following guidelines, as well.

1. **Be clear about what you want to say before you say it.**
    You might have already sensed what feedback you want to convey. However, you should be clear to yourself about what you want to convey and how you want to convey it.

2. **Share your feedback in a concise and specific manner, then you can embellish.**
    People often lose specificity when they speak because they say far too much, rather than not enough. Or, they speak about general themes and patterns. When giving feedback, first share what you saw or heard, what you want instead, and how the person can achieve it. Then you can add more descriptive information if necessary.

3. **Avoid generalizations.**
    Avoid use of the words "all," "never" and "always." Those words can seem extreme, lack credibility and place arbitrary limits on behavior. Be more precise about quantity or proportion, if you address terms of quantities, at all.

4. **Be descriptive rather than evaluative.**
    Report what you are seeing, hearing or feeling. Attempt to avoid evaluative words, such as "good" or "bad." It may be helpful to quickly share your particular feeling, if appropriate, but do not dwell on it or become emotional.

5. **Own the feedback.**
    The information should be about your own perception of information, not about the other's perceptions, assumptions and motives. Use 'I' statements as much as possible to indicate that your impressions are your own.

6. **Be careful about giving advice.**
    When giving feedback, it is often best to do one thing at a time – share your feedback, get the person's response to your feedback, and then, when he/she is more ready to consider additional information, share your advice with him/her.

How to Understand and Manage Conflict

Clarifying Confusion About Conflict

Conflict occurs with two or more people who, despite their first attempts at agreement, do not yet have agreement on a course of action, usually because their values, perspectives and opinions are contradictory in nature. Conflict can occur:

1. Within yourself when you are not living according to your values.

2. When your values and perspectives are threatened.

3.   When there is discomfort from fear of the unknown or from lack of fulfillment.

Conflict is inevitable and often necessary when forming high-performing teams because they evolve through "form, storm, norm and perform" periods. Getting the most out of diversity often means addressing contradictory values, perspectives and opinions.

Conflict is often needed. It:

- Helps to raise and address problems.

- Energizes work to be focused on the most important priorities.

- Helps people "be real" and motivates them to fully participate.

- Helps people learn how to recognize and benefit from their differences.

Conflict is not the same as discomfort. The conflict is not the problem – poor management of the conflict is the problem. Conflict is a problem when it:

- Hampers productivity.

- Lowers morale.

- Causes more and continued conflicts.

- Causes inappropriate behaviors.

Types of Managerial Actions That Cause Workplace Conflicts

1.   **Poor internal communications.**

   a.   Employees experience continual surprises, for example, they are not informed of major decisions that affect their workplaces and lives.

   b.   Employees do not understand the reasons for the decisions – they are not involved in the decision-making.

   c.   They trust the "rumor mill" more than their management.

2.   **The alignment or the amount of resources is insufficient.**

   a.   There is disagreement about "who does what."

   b.   There is stress from working with inadequate resources.

3.   **Poor "personal chemistry," including conflicting values or actions.**

   a.   Interpersonal natures among workers do not seem to match.

   b.   Employee conflicts in the workplace are so frequent that it becomes toxic.

4. **Leadership problems.**
   For example, inconsistent, missing, too-strong or uninformed leadership (at any level in the organization), evidenced by:

   a. Employees avoiding conflict, "passing the buck" with little follow-through on decisions.

   b. Employees seeing the same continued issues in the workplace.

   c. Supervisors not understanding the jobs of their subordinates.

Key Managerial Actions / Structures to Minimize Conflicts

1. **Regularly review job descriptions.**
   Get your employee's input to them. Write down and date job descriptions. Ensure:

   a. Job roles do not conflict.

   b. No tasks "fall in a crack."

2. **Intentionally build relationships with all subordinates.**

   a. Meet at least once a month alone with them in office.

   b. Ask about accomplishments, challenges and issues.

3. **Get regular, written status reports that describe:**

   a. Accomplishments.

   b. Currents issues and needs from management.

   c. Plans for the upcoming period.

4. **Conduct basic training about:**

   a. Interpersonal communications.

   b. Conflict management.

   c. Delegation.

5. **Develop procedures for routine tasks and include the employees' input.**

   a. Have employees write procedures when possible and appropriate.

   b. Get employees' review of the procedures.

   c. Distribute the procedures.

   d. Train employees about the procedures.

6. **Regularly hold management meetings with all employees.**
    For example, every month, communicate new initiatives and status of current products or services.

7. **Consider an anonymous suggestion box in which employees can provide suggestions.**
    This can be powerful means to collect honest feedback, especially in very conflicted workplaces.

Ways People Deal With Conflict

There is no one best way to deal with conflict. It depends on the current situation. Here are the major ways that people use to deal with conflict:

1. **You can avoid it.**
    Pretend it is not there or ignore it. Use this approach only when it simply is not worth the effort to argue. Be aware that this approach tends to worsen the conflict over time.

2. **You can accommodate it.**
    You can give in to others, sometimes to the extent that you compromise yourself. Use this approach very sparingly and infrequently, for example, in situations when you know that you will have another more useful approach in the very near future. Usually this approach tends to worsen the conflict over time, and causes conflicts within yourself.

3. **You can compete with the others.**
    You can work to get your way, rather than clarifying and addressing the issue. Competitors love accommodators. Use this approach when you have a very strong conviction about your position.

4. **You can compromise.**
    You can engage in mutual give-and-take. This approach is used when the goal is to get past the issue and move on together.

5. **You can collaborate.**
    You can focus on working together. Use this approach when the goal is to meet as many current needs as possible by using mutual resources. This approach sometimes raises new mutual needs. Collaboration can also be used when the goal is to cultivate ownership and commitment.

To Manage a Conflict with Another Person

1. **Know what you do not like about yourself, early on in your career.**
    We often do not like in others what we do not want to see in ourselves.

    a. Write down 5 traits that really bug you when see them in others.

    b. Be aware that these traits are your "hot buttons."

2. **Manage yourself.**
    If you and/or another person are getting upset, then manage yourself to stay calm:

    a. Speak to the person as if the other person is not upset – this can be very effective!

  b. Avoid use of the word "you" – this avoids your appearing to be blaming the person.

  c. Nod your head to assure the person that you heard him/her.

  d. Maintain eye contact with the person.

3. **Move the discussion to a private area, if possible.**
Many times, moving to a new environment invites both of you to see or feel differently.

4. **Give the other person time to vent.**
Do not interrupt the person or judge what he/she is saying.

5. **Verify that you are accurately hearing each other.**
When the other person is done speaking:

  a. Ask the person to let you rephrase (uninterrupted) what you are hearing to ensure you are hearing it correctly.

  b. To understand the person more, ask open-ended questions (avoid "why" questions – those questions often make people feel defensive).

6. **Repeat the above step, this time for the other to verify that he/she is really hearing you.**
When you describe your perspective:

  a. Use "I", not "you."

  b. Talk in terms of the present as much as possible.

  c. Quickly mention your feelings.

7. **Acknowledge where you disagree and where you agree.**
One of the most powerful means to resolve conflict is to mention where you both agree.

8. **Discuss the matter on which you disagree, not the nature of the other person.**
When the person is convinced that you understand him/her:

  a. Ask "What can we do fix the problem?" The person might begin to complain again.

  b. Then ask the same question. Focus on actions you both can do.

  c. Ask the other person if they will support the action(s).

  d. If the person will not, then ask for a "cooling off period".

9. **Thank the person for working with you.**
It takes patience for a person to engage in meaningful conversation during conflict. Acknowledge and thank the other person for his/her effort.

10. **If the situation remains a conflict, then:**

a.   Conclude if the other person's behavior violates one of the personnel policies and procedures in the workplace and if it does, then follow the policy's terms for addressing that violation.

b.   Otherwise, consider whether to agree to disagree.

c.   Consider seeking a third party to mediate.

How to Conduct Meaningful Performance Appraisals

Yearly formal performance reviews for each employee are extremely important to ensuring their strong performance and fulfillment in their jobs. Performance appraisals have come under fire recently as not being effective in improving performance of employees. Appraisals are not effective – if they are not done well.

Well-done performance reviews help supervisors feel more honest in their relationships with their subordinates and feel better about themselves in their supervisory roles. Subordinates are assured a clear understanding of what is expected from them, their own personal strengths and areas for development, and a solid sense of their relationship with their supervisor. Avoiding performance issues ultimately decreases morale, decreases credibility of management, decreases the organization's overall effectiveness and wastes more of management's time.

The process used to evaluate the performance of employees should be clearly specified in the personnel policies and procedures, which are approved by the Board. The appraisal process should be a mere formality with no surprises for the employee, if the supervisor has been doing his/her job all along, including: a) sharing the written job description, performance goals, and the personnel policy which guides the appraisal process; and b) sharing useful feedback with the employee during the appraisal period. Consider the following, additional guidelines.

1.   **Design a legally compliant and valid performance review process.**
     Patricia King, in her book, *Performance Planning and Appraisal* (McGraw-Hill, 1984), mentions that the law requires that performance appraisals be: job-related and valid; based on a thorough analysis of the job; standardized for all employees; not biased against any race, color, sex, religion, or nationality; and performed by people who have adequate knowledge of the person or job.

     You can use the suggestions in this section to design your process. Be sure to build in the process a route for recourse if an employee feels he or she has been dealt with unfairly in an appraisal process, for example, that the employee can go to his or her supervisor's supervisor and/or file a written response with the appraisal for the personnel file. The process should be clearly described in a personnel policy.

2.   **Design a standard form on which to document the person's performance. Include:**

     a.   Name of the employee.

     b.   Date the form was completed.

     c.   Dates specifying the time over which the person's performance is being evaluated.

d. Section to describe the major work roles and activities conducted by the employee during the appraisal period.

e. Section to write opinions about the employee's: major accomplishments during the appraisal period, exhibited strengths and weaknesses according to the dimensions on the appraisal form, and suggested actions and training or development to improve performance. The form should ask for examples of observed behaviors during the appraisal period that substantiate comments about where performance needs to be improved.

f. Reference to the duties and responsibilities on the person's job description, any additionally assigned performance goals that were previously provided to the person in writing.

g. Rating system (for example: "poor," "average," "good" and "excellent;" or "does not meet," "meets" and "exceeds expectations"). Next to the description of each rating should be brief explanation of that rating.

h. Space for the supervisor's commentary next to each rating.

i. Final section for overall commentary from the supervisor.

j. Final section for specifying action plans for the employee to address to improve performance and/or progress in his/her career.

k. Lines for signatures of the supervisor and employee. You can design the form so that the signatures either indicate that the person accepts the comments on the appraisal, or contests certain comments on the form.

3. **Schedule the first performance review for six months after the employee starts.**
    The timing of the review depends on the terms specified in the Board-approved personnel policies and procedures, and if there is a specific probationary period associated with the employee's job.

4. **Initiate the performance review process with the employee.**
    By now, the person should have received his/her written job description, performance goals and procedure for performance appraisals well in advance of the upcoming performance appraisal process. In a one-on-one meeting with the employee:

    a. Tell him/her that you are initiating a scheduled performance review process.

    b. Remind the person of what is involved in the process. You might reference the personnel policy that directs how appraisals are done.

    c. Schedule a meeting to occur with the two of you about two weeks out.

    d. Share the standard performance appraisal form with the person and ask him/her to provide opinions about his/her performance on the form. Ask to get the opinions 2-3 days before the upcoming meeting. Mention that you will consider the employee's opinions when you write your own on opinions on the form. Mention that you will share your opinions in writing on the form at least three days before the appraisal meeting.

e. Ask the person to review the job description and to share comments in the upcoming meeting.

5. **Before the upcoming meeting, document your (the supervisor's) input on the form.**

   a. When writing your opinions, do not just rely on your memory. Reference your files to remind you of the person's activities, any major accomplishments and any concerns that you have observed.

   b. Also reference the person's opinions on the appraisal form that the person shared with you several days before the appraisal meeting.

   c. Mark the appraisal form as "draft" to indicate that it is not the final version. (The version becomes final when the supervisor and employee have agreed on the information on the form or the employee has attached descriptions of his/her disagreements to the form.)

   d. Share the draft with the employee several days before the upcoming appraisal meeting.

6. **Conduct the one-on-one performance appraisal with the employee.**

   a. State that the goals of the meeting are to understand each other's perceptions about the person's performance and about his/her priorities during the next appraisal period.

   b. In the meeting, let the employee speak first about his/her reactions to the content of the appraisal. Then respond with your own opinions. Then discuss areas where you disagree. Then discuss where you agree. Strive for balance of praise and constructive feedback.

   c. Avoid becoming defensive – the process should focus on observed behaviors, not on character traits of each other.

   d. Discuss behaviors, not personalities. Avoid final terms such as "always" and "never." Encourage participation and be supportive.

   e. Come to terms on actions to enhance performance or evolve the person's career, where possible.

   f. End the meeting on a positive note. Thank the person for his/her participation.

   g. Ask the employee to sign the form in a section that indicates his/her agreement to the information on the form, or whether he/she disagrees and will add an attachment explaining his/her disagreement.

   h. Update the form with any information that you both agreed upon or with the employee's attachment about disagreement. Be sure the employee has signed the form. Share copies of the form with the employee, and with the supervisor's immediate supervisor. If the organization has a Human Resources department, it will need a copy of the signed form, as well.

7. **In one-on-one meetings with the employee, review status of actions.**
    One of the most powerful approaches to accomplishing meaningful appraisals is to meet
    with the employee in one-on-one meetings at least once every two or three months to discuss
    the employee's progress on the actions listed on the appraisal form. That practice makes the
    appraisal much more relevant and important to all persons involved in the process.

How to Reward and Retain High-Quality Employees

Major Myths About Rewarding Employees

Myth #1: "Money is the best reward."
No. Research shows that money does not constitute a strong, ongoing reward in and of itself. It is
like having a nice office; it can give a temporary boost in morale and energy. The key roles for
money and nice offices are that they can stop people from feeling worse.

Myth #2: "Employees are professionals. They should just 'suck it up' and do their jobs."
That view is outdated. Times have changed dramatically. Workers can no longer be treated like
machines. They come at a high price and can cost as much to replace. Workers expect to be valued
as human beings. Today, the rewarding of workers is done as a partnership between the supervisors
and their workers.

Myth #3: "If I reward every time they do something useful, I will have to reward all the time."
Employees are mature adults. They do not need to be, and do not expect to be, rewarded for every
useful thing they do in the workplace. One of the most important outcomes from regularly
rewarding workers is that they believe that their supervisors fully acknowledge their value to the
workplace.

Myth #4: "We're working to address critical problems, not to make our workers happy."
That is like saying, "This is a wood saw. It should be able to saw wood all the time. It should not
ever have to be sharpened!"

Guiding Principles of Effective Reward Systems

There are a variety of ways to reward people for the quality of the work they do in the workplace.
For example, rewards can be in the form of money, benefits, time off from work, acknowledgement
for work well done, affiliation with other workers or a sense of accomplishment from finishing a
major task.

1. **Rewards should support behaviors directly aligned with accomplishing strategic goals.**
    This principle may seem so obvious as to sound trite. However, the goal of carefully tying
    employees' behaviors to strategic goals has only become important over the past decade or
    so. Recently, the term "performance" is being used to designate behaviors that really
    contribute to the "bottom line." An employee can be working as hard as anyone else, but if
    his/her behaviors are not tied directly to achieving strategic goals, then the employee might
    be engaged only in busy-work.

2. **Rewards should be tied to passion and purpose, not to pressure and fear.**
    Fear is a powerful motivator, but only for a short time and then it dissipates. For example, if
    you have initially motivated employees by warning them of a major shortage of funds unless
    they do a better job, then they will likely be motivated to work even harder. That approach

might work once or twice, but workers soon will realize that the cause of the organization's problems is not because they are not working hard enough. They might soon even resent management's resorting to the use of fear. If, instead, management motivates by reminding workers of their passion for the mission, the motivation will be much more sustainable.

3.   **Workers should be able to clearly associate the reward to their accomplishments.**
     Imagine if someone told you "Thank you" and did not say what for. One of the purposes of a reward is to reinforce the positive behaviors that earned the reward in the first place. If employees understand what behaviors they are being rewarded for, they are more likely to repeat those behaviors.

4.   **Rewards should occur shortly after the behaviors they are intended to reinforce.**
     The closer the occurrence of the reward to the occurrence of the desired behavior in the workplace, the easier it is for the employee to realize why he/she is being rewarded. The easier it is for him/her to understand what behaviors are being appreciated.

Importance of Sense of Purpose and Feeling Appreciated

Finding and training new employees is a substantial cost, no matter the size of the organization. One of the best ways to retain employees is to reward them for their work. One of the primary rewards for working adults is to feel a sense of meaning or purpose in their work. If employees feel that they are serving a useful purpose, they are much more likely to stay at their current job.

A common complaint from employees in small- to medium-sized organizations is that they feel burned out. A common symptom of burnout is to feel unappreciated. One of the best ways to address burnout, and retain employees, is to ensure that they feel appreciated for their work.

Thus, it is critical that organizations give careful consideration as to how they reward their employees. Organizations do not need huge sums of money in order to reward them (besides, the belief that money is the major reward is just a myth). Guidelines in this section will help you to think about what might be the best rewards for your employees and to take steps to ensure that you are providing those rewards.

Guidelines to Rewarding Employees

There is not a set of standard rewards to be used for employees everywhere. Instead, each person has his/her own nature and needs. The following guidelines will help you to determine what might be the best ways to reward your employees.

1.   Reward employees by letting them hear positive comments from customers about how the employees' activities benefited the customer.

2.   Occasionally have a Board member come to an employee meeting to thank them. This usually means a lot to employees, almost as much as having customers provide positive feedback about the employees' activities.

3.   Understand what motivates each of your employees. You can do this by applying the "Checklist of Categories of Typical Motivators" in the previous subsection about supporting employee motivation on page 199. A major benefit of this approach is that each employee is afforded the opportunity to explain what motivates him or her.

4.   In each monthly staff meeting, take a few minutes to open the meeting by mentioning major accomplishments of various employees.

5.   Present gift certificates to employees who have made major accomplishments. Guidelines for determining who gets this reward should be clearly explained in your personnel policies in order to ensure all employees perceive the practice as fair and equitable. Allow employees to recommend other employees for awards.

6.   Probably the most fulfilling for employees is to be able to do useful work. Be sure that each employee understands the mission of the business and how his/her work is contributing to that mission. Post your mission statement on the walls. Discuss the action-planning section of your strategic plan with employees so that they see how their activities tie directly to achieving the strategic goals of the organization.

How to Effectively Address Performance Issues

If your organization's personnel policies about performance management indicate a specific procedure for handling performance issues, that procedure should be followed very carefully. Otherwise, a court may interpret your official personnel policies to be modified by how you actually handled a performance issue rather than as specified in your policies and you may lose protection from your related policies in court. In the absence of a personnel policy about addressing performance issues, the following steps are suggested.

Note that performance issues should always be based on behaviors that you see, not on how you felt about the characteristics of the person's personality.

Note that any person deserves to have clear directions about what constitutes appropriate behavior, for example, clearly specified in a job description, personnel policies or in performance goals. It would be grossly unfair to notify an employee that he/she has a performance problem if the individual had no idea of what performance was expected of him/her in the first place.

 Consider "How to Focus on Real Causes of Problems, Not Just Symptoms" on page 131.

1.   **Convey performance issues to employees when you see first see the issues!**
Do not wait until the annual performance review! Worse yet, do not ignore the behaviors in case they "go away."

2.   **When you first convey an issue to an employee, say what you noticed and want instead.**
Consider this to be a verbal warning.

    a.   Be specific about what you saw that you consider a performance problem.

    b.   Ask the employee for feedback.

    c.   Ask the employee if there is any special training or resources needed to do the job.

    d.   Explore if the job is configured for success or if most people would probably fail, and so the job needs to be redesigned.

e. Tell him/her that the behavior needs to improve. In most cases, the person will understand your assertion. If he/she reacts strongly, for example, the person says that he/she is quitting the job, then provide a day to think it over. In any case, remind the person that you support him/her in the role.

3. **Consider special circumstances.**
You can usually fire someone if they committed certain gross acts, such as theft, blatant insubordination, a major impropriety, for example, telling information to competitors or spreading confidential information about customers. However, if there is poor performance or chronic absenteeism because of a physical or mental illness, then it is best to consult an expert to deal with this situation.

4. **If the problem recurs, immediately issue them a written warning.**

a. In the written warning, clearly specify what you saw that you do not like, refer to the previous meeting and verbal warning and its date, say the behaviors have not improved, warn them that if the behaviors occurs again over some specific time period (for example, over the next month), they will be promptly terminated. Meet with them to provide them the written warning. Attempt to have this meeting on a day other than Friday; otherwise, employees are left to ruminate about the situation without ready access to you during the weekend.

b. If you are convinced that the employee is trying hard, but cannot improve, consider placing him or her elsewhere in the organization.

5. **Consider creating a performance improvement plan.**
This plan details the necessary areas of improvement with specific actions and timelines for addressing those areas. This type of plan is usually developed by the employee's supervisor and the supervisor's supervisor and presented to the employee in a face-to-face meeting. The employee's feedback on the plan might be used to revise it, depending on the nature of the feedback and the criticality of the issues being addressed. The employee, the supervisor and optionally the supervisor's supervisor should sign and date the plan. The signed copy should be placed in the employee's personnel file. Lack of progress on a performance improvement plan is sometimes considered grounds for firing but this should be made clear in the plan if that is the intention.

6. **Make notes about the first warning, meeting and results, and keep in a file.**
Continue this for any subsequent meetings and communications. The notes may come in handy later on if the performance problem persists. You might mention the situation to your Board if the person is in a management role. The Board will likely be a precious and objective asset to dealing with this situation, especially if things with the employee get worse.

7. **On the third occurrence of seeing problem behaviors, consider firing the employee.**
(See the next section, "How to Fire an Unsuitable Employee.")

How to Fire an Unsuitable Employee

Prerequisites to the Fair Firing of an Employee

The firing of an employee is primarily one official action, rather than a long and drawn out process, if the supervisor has done the following activities before the firing became necessary:

1. **You have clear, provable evidence that you conveyed performance requirements.**
    The requirements came to the employee by means of the following, which were provided to the employee before you first began warning him/her of any performance issue:

    a. Written job description provided to him or her.

    b. Any written performance goals.

    Ideally, you also have evidence of your attempting to further equip the employee with resources to improve his/her performance, for example, with training.

2. **You have evidence that the individual was fully aware of procedures for firing.**
    You have clearly written personnel policies, which specify conditions and directions about firing employees, and you can prove that the person was aware of the policy; for example, the person initialized a copy of the policy handbook that contained that policy. Those policies should have been reviewed and updated by an expert on employment laws and also the Board should have approved the policies.

3. **You warned the person in successive stages as specified in personnel policies.**
    For example, the policies might have specified that an employee should:

    a. First be warned of a performance issue with a verbal warning that clearly explained the nature of the performance issue, and that referenced what he/she was supposed to be doing, but was inappropriately doing instead.

    b. Then be warned in writing with explanation again of the nature of the same performance issue, including what the person should be doing instead.

    c. Be eligible to be fired if he/she again failed to meet the specified standard of performance.

Note that if the employee is being fired within a probationary period that was specified in your personnel policies, then you may not have to meet all of the above prerequisites.

Take a day or so to consider what you are about to do. Consult with members of your Board.

Taking Action and Meeting With Employee

If you still decide to fire the employee, then do so promptly in order to maintain your credibility with other employees, and so as not to begin procrastinating about this sometimes painful, upcoming event.

1. **Write a letter of termination to give the employee in an upcoming meeting.**
    As with the previous letters of warning, be clear about the observed behaviors, when you

saw them, earlier warnings and their consequences, what you did in response, and the consequence that must now be enacted according to your personnel policies. In the letter, specify when the firing is to take effect (hopefully it takes effect immediately). Also mention your proof that the employee was aware of the policies.

2. **Meet with the person. Provide him/her the letter. Explain how termination will occur.**
    Have another person in the meeting, for example, a Board member. Give the person several minutes to read the letter. Answer any questions to help the person understand the content of the letter, but do not begin justifying your actions to fire the person. Ask the employee for any keys to facilities. Give the person half an hour or so to remove personal items. You may choose to monitor the person during this removal, depending on the nature of the grounds for dismissal.

3. **As with other meetings, make notes of what was said and exchanged.**
    Keep the notes in your records.

Follow-Up

1. **Tell the computer system administrator to change the person's password.**
    Assert that this action should be done promptly and in complete confidence.

2. **Change any locks on facilities.**
    This action may seem somewhat drastic, but if you do not change the locks, you will never know who can get into your facilities if he/she wishes.

3. **Inform other co-workers as necessary and appropriate.**
    Usually, you are better off not to explain everything about the situation to the employee's peers and subordinates. Despite the person's poor performance, the person deserves your respect and protection of his/her dignity. Otherwise, you expose yourself to losing a lawsuit that alleges libel or slander.

APPENDICES:

Appendix A: Glossary

Appendix B: Resources for Business

Appendix C: Useful, Free Organizational Assessments

Appendix D: Founder's Syndrome –
How to Detect It, How to Avoid It

Appendix A: Glossary

Accountability

Board members continually making their organization and themselves responsible to meet the expectations of stakeholders, and verifying with those stakeholders that their expectations are indeed being met. Also see **Stakeholders**.

Assessment

Systematic collection of data, followed by analysis to generate findings and conclusions, for example, an organizational assessment to detect the strengths and weaknesses of all of the organization's most important operations.

Best practices

Practices conducted by individuals, groups or organizations that are widely respected for some particular expertise or activity that involves those practices, for example: best practices in Board operations, personnel management and financial management. There can be wide disagreement about what constitutes a best practice, depending on the context of the practices and the values of those in observance of the practices.

Board development

Raising the performance of the Board of Directors up another level, either to resolve major issues on the Board (restoring the Board) or to make sufficient performance even better. Can include a variety of activities to enhance Board operations, for example, a Board self-evaluation, producing a Board development plan, orienting Board members, training Board members, coaching the Board Chair and re-assessing the Board's performance. (Contrast to **Board orientation** and **Board training**.)

Board model

Structure by which Board members organize themselves and work together, including their level of involvement in management functions, if any. The model can be developed in a proactive, planful manner or emerge as Board members work together and with employees. There are a wide variety of models for governing Boards.

Board of Directors

Group of people legally charged to govern the corporation. Board members are responsible to ensure the business meets the needs of stockholders. See **Governance.**

Board orientation

Orienting Board members to the unique features of the organization, for example, to other members on the Board, where the Board meets, and the organization's products and services. (Contrast to **Board training** and **Board development**.)

Board policies

General guidelines and sometimes specific procedures by which Board members choose to operate amongst themselves and sometimes with employees, for example, policies to staff the Board, conflict-of-interest, attendance and evaluation of members.

Board training

Training Board members about the roles and responsibilities of a governing Board of Directors. (Contrast to **Board orientation** and **Board development**.)

Business planning

Activities to clarify the demand for a product or service in the market, specific groups of people comprising the markets, how the product or service meets each group's particular expectations, resources needed to develop and provide the product or service, how the resources will be organized and managed, costs to obtain and support use of the resources, and how communications between the organization and potential markets will be coordinated. (Contrast to **Strategic planning**.)

By-Laws

Board members' comprehensive, primary policy that specifies how the Board chooses to operate themselves and the organization, including, for example: Board structure, roles, committees, meetings, membership and attendance requirements. The contents of the By-Laws are determined by statute in some states.

CEO

See **Chief Executive Officer (CEO)**.

Chief Executive Officer (CEO)

(Usually) the singular, organization-wide, employee position that is primarily responsible to carry out the strategic plans and policies established by the Board of Directors. The extent of authority and the scope and level of activities depends on the Board model preferred by the business. Not all organizations have employees, including a CEO. Particularly in small or new businesses, the Board members and CEO often seem to work in partnership to oversee and manage the organization's operations, even though the Board has the ultimate authority for governance and operations.

Corporate Board

Phrase used to refer to a Board of a for-profit corporation. Also see **Board of Directors**.

Corporation

Organization that is chartered (or incorporated) by the appropriate governmental agency in order to exist as a legal entity separate from the members of the organization. Corporations require a Board of Directors to govern the corporation. There are certain advantages to chartering an organization as a corporation, including limited liability of organization members for the operations of the organization. Also, the corporation can own property, hold its own bank account, enter into contracts, and conduct tax-exempt activities. Also see **Governance**.

Culture (of an organization)

The "personality" of an organization as defined by the aggregate of values, assumptions, opinions, behaviors, etc., by which members act in the organization.

Evaluation

Systematic collection and analysis of data to make a decision. Usually includes generation of findings and recommendations to address findings.

Financial management

Activities to ensure the organization's finances are effectively accounted for, legally allocated, utilized in an optimum manner and at minimum risk. Includes operating according to fiscal policies and procedures, bookkeeping to monitor and record transactions, generating and analyzing financial statements, and actions to improve financial management.

Founder's Syndrome

Exists when an overall organization operates more to the personality of one person in the organization than to its mission. Could be according to the founder or another prominent person in the organization.

Governance

Board of Director's activities to ensure that the business operates effectively and efficiently, according to its mission and strategic priorities. New perspectives consider governance to include stakeholders affiliated with the business.

Inputs (products or services)

Items that are used by the various processes in order to achieve the overall outputs and desires outcomes of the products or services. Types of inputs are people, money, equipment, facilities, supplies, people's ideas and people's time.

Leader

Person who sets direction and directs or influences other individuals or groups to follow that direction. An individual can be a leader by the nature of the authority in their role, their expertise and/or their personality.

Leadership

Nature of activities or the capacity to establish direction and influence another person or group to follow that direction. Can also refer to leadership traits or leadership roles.

Logic model

The overall conceptual "system" of an organization by depicting the inputs, processes (or activities), outputs and outcomes from a product or service. Outcomes might be listed as short-term, intermediate or long-term.

Management (in organizations)

Traditionally, refers to the activities involved in the four overall, general practices: planning, organizing, leading and coordinating. The four functions recur throughout the organization and are highly integrated.

Marketing

The wide range of activities involved in making sure that you are continuing to meet the needs of your customers and getting sufficient value in return. These activities include market research to find out, for example, what groups of potential customers exist, what their needs are, which of those needs you can meet and how you should meet them. Marketing also includes analyzing the competition, positioning your new product or service (finding your market niche), pricing your products and services, and promoting them through continued advertising, promotions, public relations and sales.

Minutes (of Board meetings)

The official documentation of the meeting's date of occurrence, attendance, topics and results from discussions (for example, decisions, resolutions and delegations). Board members approve the minutes, thereby making the document an accurate and official representation of the results of the meeting.

Mission

The overall purpose of the organization. A mission statement describes that mission, for example: the values that the organization aspires to, what products are offered to what markets and how the organization stands apart from others. Mission statements vary widely in their focus, scope and length.

Policy governing Board

One model of a governing Board where members attend primarily to developing and enforcing top-level plans and policies, usually delegating implementation of those plans and policies to employee. These Boards often use a variety of committees, some with employees on them. Sometimes referred to as a "traditional" Board. (Contrast with **Working governing Board**.)

Product evaluation

Systematically collecting and analyzing information regarding product design, development and delivery in order to make a decision about the product.

Product planning (also see Business Planning)

Activities to carefully identify needs and wants among a certain market, what products might meet the needs of that market, how the product could be developed and delivered, what management and staffing resources will be needed, and the finances needed to develop and deliver the product.

Promotions (marketing)

Methods to keep products in the minds of the customers and help stimulate demand for the products. The ongoing activities of advertising, sales and public relations are often considered aspects of promotions.

Public relations

Ongoing activities to ensure the organization has a strong public image. Public relations activities include helping the public to understand the organization and its products and services. Often, public relations are conducted through the media, that is, newspapers, television, magazines, internet, etc. As noted above, public relations are often considered as one of the primary activities included in promotions.

Publicity

Mention in the media. Organizations do not control the message in the media, at least not as much as they do in advertising. Reporters and writers decide what will be said, though press releases often influence what is published.

Revenue

Refers to the money earned (sales or fees) by the product or service during operation of the business.

Sales

Involves most or many of the following activities, including cultivating prospective buyers (or leads) in a market segment; helping leads to understand how the features and benefits of a product or service can be beneficial to the lead; and closing the sale (or coming to agreement on pricing and services).

Stakeholders

People or groups of people who "have a stake," or strong, vested interest in the operations of the business, for example: Board members, employees, customers, investors, and stockholders.

Strategic planning

Activities to clarify the overall mission and most important priorities for the business to address, and how to address those. There are many different ways to conduct strategic planning, ranging from: 1) formal, explicit and systematic, including intentional and comprehensive analyses of external and internal environments, identification of critical priorities, and the goals, objectives, responsibilities and resource needs to address those priorities, to 2) informal, implicit and non-systematic, including ongoing and occasional clarification of priorities, along with what seems most reasonable to address the priorities for now. Also see **Business planning**.

Supervision

Activities by a supervisor to oversee the progress and productivity of people who report directly to the supervisor. Includes staffing analysis, specification of duties and responsibilities (job description), recruitment and selection of employees, assignment of goals, feedback on achievement of goals, rewarding achievement of goals and addressing performance problems.

Supervisor

Someone who has at least one person reporting to him/her and, therefore, is responsible for the progress and productivity of that person, for example, a CEO supervises middle managers who supervise entry-level supervisors who supervise individual contributors.

Team building

Activities to form and develop a small group of people to effectively work toward a common purpose and achieve specific goals. There are a wide variety of means to build teams, ranging from enhancing members' feelings about each other to improving structures (plans, roles and policies) in the teams.

Transparency

Board members always providing full disclosure and explanation of the organization's governance, finances and effects on communities, and also willingly supporting stakeholders' efforts to understand that information.

Work plan (in Board committees or task forces)

Specification of the goals, along with associated objectives, responsibilities and timing to achieve the objectives, in order to achieve the overall goal.

Working governing Board

One model of a governing Board where members attend both to strategic and hands-on matters. Often used early in the life of a business when it has few employees. (Contrast to **Policy governing Board**.)

Appendix B: Resources for Business

Free Management Library[SM]

The Free Management Library includes extensive free materials about personal, professional and organizational development. From its online roots in 1995, the Library has grown to over 675 topics that are organized into the following popular categories. It draws over 1 million visitors per month. The list of topics is located at http://www.managementhelp.org/ on the Web.

Advertising and Promotion	Benefits and Compensation	Boards of Directors
Career Development	Chief Executive Role	Communications (Interprsnl)
Communications (Writing)	Computers, Internet & Web	Consultants (using)
Coordinating Activities	Creativity and Innovation	Crisis Management
Customer Satisfaction	Customer Service	E-Commerce
Employee Performance	Employee Wellness Programs	Ethics - Practical Toolkit
Evaluations (many kinds)	Facilities Management	Finances (For-Profit)
Finances (Nonprofit)	Fundraising (Nonprofit)	General Resources
Group Performance	Group Skills	Guiding Skills
Human Resources Mgmnt	Insurance (Business)	Interpersonal Skills
Interviewing (all kinds)	Jobs	Leadership (Introduction)
Leadership Development	Legal Information	Management (Introduction)
Management Development	Marketing	Operations Management
Organizational Alliances	Organizational Change	Org'l Communications
Organizational Performance	Organizations (Introduction)	Organizing (many kinds)
Performance Management	Personal Development	Personal Productivity
Personal Wellness	Planning (many kinds)	Policies (Personnel)
Product Selection & Dev.	Program Management	Project Management
Public and Media Relations	Quality Management	Research Methods
Risk Management	Sales	Social Entrepreneurship
Staffing	Starting an Organization	Supervision (Introduction)
Supervisory Development	Systems Thinking	Taxation
Training Basics	Volunteers	----------------

Free Micro-eMBA^{SM} Organization Development Program

This state-of-the-art, online, self-study training program includes 10 highly integrated courses that can be taken for free by anyone, anywhere, at any time. At the end of the program, each learner will have all of the basic systems and processes needed to start and operate a business. Learners are encouraged to work with their supervisors or Boards of Directors (in the case of corporations) while going through the program. Participants going through the program together can share plans, policies and procedures.

Any of the 10 courses in the program can be taken separately. The courses, along with links to their supporting materials and their learning objectives, are located online in the Free Management Library at http://www.managementhelp.org/fp_progs/org_dev.htm in the Course Catalog. (Your organization may also have a wide range of materials around which you could organize courses.) Courses include:

1. Program Orientation – Getting The Most From This Program

2. Starting and Understanding Your Business Organization

3. Understanding the Role of Chief Executive

4. Developing Your Basic Leadership and Management Skills

5. Building and Training Your Board of Directors (in corporations)

6. Developing Your Strategic Plan

7. Marketing Your Products/Services and Promoting Your Organization

8. Managing Your Accounting and Finances

9. Staffing and Supervising Your Employees

10. Practical Guide to Managing Ethics in the Workplace

Sources of Assistance to Businesses

There are many sources of assistance to businesses. One of the best places to start is by calling the Small Business Center (SBC), sponsored by the Small Business Administration. Call 402-595-2387.

1. Contact your Secretary of State and/or your state's Attorneys General office and ask for a list of resources.

2. Look in the Yellow Pages of your local telephone directory for professional associations. Look for networks or associations of organization development practitioners, facilitators or trainers.

3. Look in the Yellow Pages of your local telephone directory under the categories "Consultant".

4. Call a local university or college and speak to someone in the college of Human Resources, Training and Development, or Business Administration.

5. Ask a retired businessperson if they are interested in mentoring or coaching you.

6. SCORE - Service Corps Of Retired Executives. They have many retired business people available who have many years of experience in business. Call 800-827-5722.

7. Small Business Answer Desk. Call 800-827-5722.

8. Small Business Administration (SBA). The SBA has a vast amount of resources available for helping small businesses, at http://www.sba.gov

9. Small Business Development Center, in conjunction with the SBA, is often a local source of assistance to businesses. Call 402-595-2387.

10. Business Assistance Service (with Department of Commerce). Call 202-483-3176.

11. National Business Association. Call 800-465-0440.

Business Publications

Schedule a half hour every other week to go to the local public library. Glance through the *Wall Street Journal*, *U.S. World News* and *Business Week*. Also glance through the business section of your local newspaper or local business publications. The following Web sites reference 100s of other business journals.

1. *Wall Street Journal* at
   http://online.wsj.com/public/us

2. NewsLink at
   http://newslink.org/biznews.html

3. Bizjournals at
   http://www.bizjournals.com/journals.html

4. Research journals, magazines and newspapers at
   http://www.brint.com/ISJournal.htm

5. Regional business journals on the Web at
   http://www.bibliomaven.com/businessjournals.html

Major Organizations and Associations for Business

It will be well worth your time to stop in at your local Chamber of Commerce. Chances are that that office will give you many listings of sources for assistance. The Web address for the national Chamber is listed below.

1. Chamber of Commerce at
   http://www.uschamber.org/default.htm

2. American Management Association at
   http://www.amanet.org/index.htm

3. National Business Association. Call 800-465-0440.

4. American Small Business Association at
   http://www.asbaonline.org/

Lists of Free, On-Line Newsletters

There has been an explosion of on-line newsletters in regard to business and management, many of them from various consultants across the country. The following newsletters are a good place to start.

1. Free Management Library's Blogs at
   http://managementhelp.org/blogs/

2. About.com's management newsletter at
   http://management.about.com/

3. Yahoo!'s list of newsletters at
   http://dir.yahoo.com/News_and_Media/Business/Newsletters/

4. NewsletterAccess list of newsletters at
   http://www.newsletteraccess.com/

5. SmallBizSmarts list of newsletters at
   http://www.smallbizsmarts.com/

6. IOMA.com's list of newsletters at
   http://www.ioma.com/

7. InfoWorld list of newsletters at
   http://www.infoworld.com/newsletters

On-Line Discussion Groups

There are a vast number of on-line groups about business. The following groups are a good place to start.

1. HRNET about human resource management at
   http://groups.yahoo.com/group/HRNET/

2. TRDEV about training and development at
   http://groups.yahoo.com/group/TRDEV

3. ODNET about organizational development at
   http://www.odnetwork.org

4. Academy of Management Online list of groups at
   http://www.aom.pace.edu/lists/

5. EnterWeb list of groups at
   http://www.enterweb.org/discuss.htm

6. Discussion groups on your favorite social media site, such as LinkedIn, FaceBook, etc.

Appendix C:
How to Use Organizational Assessments

Leaders are responsible to ensure that their business provides products and services that continue to meet the needs of the customers in a highly effective manner. This means that leaders should know what is required to operate as a high-performing organization. One of the best ways leaders can learn what is required to be high-performing – and one of the most useful ways to measure if the business is indeed high-performing – is through use of organizational assessment tools.

How to Select Best Organizational Assessment Tools

Considerations When Selecting

Before you begin reviewing tools to use, be sure that you are aware of the major types of tools, the advantages and disadvantages of using each, and general guidelines for applying each type of tool.

1. **Focus**
   Does the tool focus on a broad range of functions, including operations of the Board, strategic planning, Chief Executive Officer, employees, marketing, finances, or evaluations?

2. **Purpose of the tool**
   For example, does it detect strengths and weaknesses of the organization, and compare them to certain "best practices?"

3. **Values and assumptions**
   For example, does the tool assume a specific Board structure or top-down leadership?

4. **Languages**
   English? Other(s)?

5. **Audiences for the tool**
   To whom will the tool be applied?

6. **Administrator of the tool**
   Who will guide the application of the tool? An outside person? Self-assessment? Will the data collection be participatory?

7. **User guide**
   Are there adequate descriptions of procedures to use the tool and analyze the results?

8. **Duration and frequency**
   How long will it take to use the tool? Is the tool to be applied at certain times? More than once?

9. **Cost**
   What are any costs to obtain the tool? Use the tool?

10. **Availability**
    How soon can the tool be made available?

11. **Technical support for the tool**
    If you have questions or need guidance, can anyone help you?

12. **Modification**
    You might need permission if you seek to modify the tool.

Organizational Assessment Tool with Best Practices

The following tool is available free, online at
http://www.surveymonkey.com/s.asp?u=88982454855 .

Description

Note that the following checklist, or assessment tool, originally developed by the Greater Twin Cities United Way of Minnesota (USA), has been modified by the author to make it relevant to for-profit organizations in Canada, as well as the United States.

This checklist includes the following topics:

- How to Use the Tool
- Disclaimers
- Legal
- Governance (Board)
- Human Resources
- Strategic Planning and Evaluation for the Entire Organization
- Business Planning and Evaluation for Each Product or Service
- Financial

How to Use the Tool

Six of the above-listed topics include a variety of indicators for that topic. Each of the many indicators in this tool suggests a management practice needed to have a healthy, well-managed organization. Since it is a self-assessment tool, organizations should evaluate themselves honestly against each indicator and use the response to change or strengthen its operations.

Ratings of Each Indicator

Each indicator is rated based on its importance to the operation and effectiveness of the organization. Thus, the ratings could be interpreted as representing "best practices." The ratings are:

1. **E** – Indicators marked with an "E" are essential or basic requirements to the operations of all organizations. Organizations that do not meet the terms of these indicators could be placing their organizations in jeopardy.

2. **R** – Indicators marked with an "R" are recommended as standard practices for effective organizations.

3. **A** – Indicators marked with an "A" can enhance and strengthen operations.

Possible Responses to Each Indicator

Organizations can respond in one of three ways to each indicator used:

1.   **Met** – Each indicator marked as "Met" indicates that the organization has met the terms of that indicator. However, the organization should review this indicator again in the future to be sure that their management remains healthy in view of the many internal and external changes, which constantly occur in all organizations.

2.   **Needs work** – Each indicator marked as "Needs Work" indicates that work is yet to be done towards meeting the terms of that indicator. The organization is aware of the terms for that indicator, and is working towards meeting those terms.

3.   **N/A** – An indicator marked as "N/A" can indicate several conditions, including:
   - the indicator is not applicable to the management operations of this organization.
   - the organization is not sure of the need to meet the requirements of this indicator.
   - the organization has not met, nor is working on this indicator presently, but may address it in the future.

Analysis of Responses to Indicators

All responses to indicators should be reviewed carefully to see if they could improve management operations. Indicators checked "N/A" due to uncertain applicability to the organization must be further reviewed to determine if they should become a part of "doing business." If the assessors simply do not know what the indicator means, further information may be needed to accurately assess the feasibility of its application. Indicators marked "N/A" because they have not been met but that apply to the organization, may require immediate attention. Technical assistance, consulting or training may be required to implement these indicators.

The indicators in this checklist should be informative and thought provoking. The checklist can be used to achieve a beginning level of good management or to improve management to provide the organization with greater stability, reliability and success. It is particularly useful if an organization is experiencing management problems, to help pinpoint any weaknesses so action can be taken or assistance sought to improve the organization's health. All organizations should use the checklist to re-assess themselves periodically to ensure compliance with established rules and regulations, and to continue improving administrative health through the indicator's helpful suggestions.

Disclaimer

As advised throughout this Guide, you should be careful when selecting and applying assessment tools so as not to convey that the tool is somehow a pre-determined, standard "solution" to your client's issues. Information gleaned from assessments should be informed by your knowledge of organizations and causes of issues in them. The assessment tools should be selected in collaboration with your client and according to the nature and needs of your client's organization.

This checklist is designed to provide accurate and authoritative information regarding the topics covered. Legal requirements and non-legal administrative practice standards reflected herein are subject to change due to new legislation, regulatory and judicial pronouncements, and updated and evolving guidelines. The checklist may be utilized only with the understanding that the provision of this checklist does not constitute the rendering of legal, tax or other professional services. If the organization requires professional assistance on these or other legal, governance or management issues, please contact your own professional advisors.

Legal

Rating *	Indicator	Met	Needs Work	N/A
E	1. All relevant legal filings are current and have been made according to the laws and regulations of the organization's country. (For example, in the USA, requirements might include: Annual Registration, Articles of Incorporation with all amendments, Change of Corporate Name, Change of Corporate Address.)			
E	2. The organization is registered with and has filed its annual report with the appropriate governmental agency. (For example, in the USA, the report might be filed with the state's Attorney General's office.)			
E	3. Tax reports are filed on a regular basis.			
E	4. Federal and state (or provincial) payroll tax withholding payments are current. (This requirement applies to organizations with employees.)			
E	5. Quarterly and annual payroll report filings are current. (This requirement applies to organizations with employees.)			
E	6. If the organization has qualified employee health and/or welfare and/or retirement benefit plans, they meet with all the federal and state/provincial laws. (For example, in the USA, COBRA; initial IRS registration; plan documents; annual filings of the 5500 C/R with copies available to employees.) This requirement applies to organizations with employees.			
E	7. Organization acknowledges and discloses to their Board and auditor any lawsuits or pending legislation which may have a significant impact on the organization's finances and/or operating effectiveness.			
E	8. When the Board of Directors makes decisions, a quorum is present and minutes are maintained.			
E	9. All federal, state/provincial and/or city, tax filings and payments are current.			
E	10. Organizations with employees represented by a union must have copies of the union contracts on file.			
Indicators ratings: E=essential; R=recommended; A=additional to strengthen organizational activities				

Governance

Rating *	Indicator	Met	Needs Work	N/A
E	1. The roles of the Board and the Chief Executive Officer are defined and respected, with the Chief Executive Officer delegated as the manager of the organization's operations and the Board focused on policy and planning.			
R	2. The Chief Executive Officer is recruited, selected and employed by the Board of Directors. The Board provides clearly written expectations and qualifications for the position, as well as reasonable compensation.			
R	3. The Board of Directors acts as governing trustees of the organization on behalf of the stockholders, while carrying out the organization's mission and goals. To fully meet this goal, the Board of Directors must actively participate in the planning process (as outlined in planning sections of this checklist).			
E	4. The Board members receive regular training and information about their responsibilities.			
E	5. New Board members are oriented to the organization, including the organization's mission, bylaws, policies and products and services, as well as their roles and responsibilities as Board members.			
A	6. Board organization is documented with a description of the Board and Board committee responsibilities.			
A	7. Each Board member has, and is familiar with, the Board operations manual.			
E	8. The organization has at least the minimum number of members on the Board of Directors as required by their bylaws or federal and state/provincial statute.			
R	9. If the organization has adopted bylaws, they conform to state/provincial statutes and have been reviewed by legal counsel.			
R	10. The bylaws should include, at a minimum: a) how and when notices for Board meetings are made; b) how members are elected/appointed by the Board; c) what the terms of office are for officers/members; d) how Board members are rotated; e) how ineffective Board members are removed from the Board; and f) a stated number of Board members to make up a quorum which is required for all policy decisions.			
R	11. The Board of Directors reviews the bylaws at least yearly.			
A	12. The Board has a process for handling urgent matters between meetings.			
R	13. The organization maintains a conflict-of-interest and Board attendance policy and all Board members and executives review and sign the policies to acknowledge compliance with the policies.			
R	14. The Board has and implements an annual calendar of Board activities. The Board also achieves at least a quorum of Board members in each meeting.			
A	15. Meetings have written agendas, and materials relating to significant decisions are given to the Board in advance of the meeting.			

Indicators ratings: E=essential; R=recommended; A=additional to strengthen organizational activities

Human Resources

Rating *	Indicator	Met	Needs Work	N/A
E	1. The organization has a written personnel handbook/policy that is regularly reviewed and updated, and at a minimum: a) describes the recruitment, hiring, termination and standard work rules for all employees; b) and maintains compliance with government employment laws and regulations. (For example, in the USA, this includes Fair Labor Standards Act, Equal Employment Opportunity Act, Americans with Disabilities Act, Occupational Health and Safety Act, Family Leave Act, Affirmative Action Plan if required, etc.)			
R	2. The organization follows nondiscriminatory hiring practices.			
R	3. The organization provides a copy of or access to the written personnel policy to all members of the Board, the Chief Executive Officer and all employees. All employees acknowledge in writing that they have read and understand the personnel handbook/policies.			
R	4. The organization has job descriptions including qualifications, duties, reporting relationships and key indicators of performance.			
R	5. The organization's Board of Directors conducts an annual review/evaluation of its Chief Executive Officer in relationship to a previously determined set of performance expectations.			
R	6. The Chief Executive Officer's salary is set by the Board of Directors in a reasonable process and is in compliance with the organization's compensation plan.			
R	7. The organization requires employee performance appraisals to be conducted and documented at least annually.			
A	8. The organization has a compensation plan, and a periodic review of salary ranges and benefits is conducted.			
A	9. The organization has a timely process for filling vacant positions to prevent an interruption of products and services or disruption to organization operations.			
A	10. The organization has a process for reviewing and responding to ideas, suggestions, comments and perceptions from all employees.			
A	11. The organization provides opportunities for employees' professional development and training within their job skill area and also in such areas as cultural sensitivity and personal development.			
Indicators ratings: E=essential; R=recommended; A=additional to strengthen organizational activities				

Strategic Planning and Evaluation for the Entire Organization

Rating *	Indicator	Met	Needs Work	N/A
E	1. The organization has a clear, meaningful written mission statement which reflects its purpose, values and customers served.			
R	2. The organization has a values statement that is reflected in the organization's activities and is communicated to its constituents.			
A	3. The values statement includes standards of ethical behavior and respect for other's interests.			
R	4. The Board members and employees periodically review the mission statement and modify it to reflect changes in the environment.			
E	5. The Board members and employees develop and adopt a written Strategic Plan to achieve its mission.			
A	6. Board and key employees participate in the planning process.			
E	7. The plan was developed after researching the internal and external environments.			
R	8. The plan identifies changes in the external and internal environments.			
R	9. The planning process identifies the critical issues facing the organization (including strengths, weaknesses, opportunities and threats).			
R	10. The plan sets goals and measurable objectives that address these critical issues.			
E	11. The plan integrates all the organization's activities around a focused mission.			
R	12. The plan prioritizes the organization's goals and develops timelines for their accomplishment.			
A	13. The plan establishes an evaluation process and performance indicators to measure the progress toward the achievement of goals and objectives.			
R	14. Through work plans, human and financial resources are allocated to ensure the accomplishment of the goals in a timely fashion.			
A	15. The plan is communicated to all stakeholders of the organization – Board, key employees and investors.			
A	16. Implementation of the plan is monitored on a regular by the Board and senior management.			
A	17. Adjustments to the organization's strategic priorities and policies are made, based on learning from implementation of the plan.			
Indicators ratings: E=essential; R=recommended; A=additional to strengthen organizational activities				

Business Planning and Evaluation for Each Product or Service

Rating *	Indicator	Met	Needs Work	N/A
E	1. Market research has verified there are target market(s) that have verified need(s) for the product or service.			
E	2. Market research has verified that each target market is willing to pay for the product or service.			
E	3. Market research has verified the optimum pricing structure for each target market for the product or service.			
E	4. Market research has verified the optimum packaging, or method of providing the product or service, for optimum access and convenience for each target market.			
E	5. Market research has identified all or most of the competitors for the product or service for each target market.			
E	6. The organization has established a unique value proposition for each product or service, or statement of why each target should buy the product or service from that organization, rather than from a competitor.			
E	7. The organization has developed a powerful description of the product or service that conveys the benefits of the product or service to each target market.			
E	8. Descriptions of the product or service are customized and delivered in the media or channels that are most accessible and preferred by each target market.			
E	9. Development of the product or service is with the most effective and efficient manner possible for each target market. This includes consideration of all needed resources, and the organization and management of those resources.			
E	10. Provision of the product or service is with the most effective and efficient manner possible for each target market. This includes consideration of all needed resources, and the organization and management of those resources.			
R	11. Performance indicators exist for each product or service.			
R	12. Progress toward each indicator is evaluated at least on an annual basis.			
R	13. Adjustments are made to production and delivery of the product or services as based on the results of the evaluation.			
R	14. All products and services are highly integrated to accomplish the optimum cost effectiveness in production and delivery to customers.			
Indicators ratings: E=essential; R=recommended; A=additional to strengthen organizational activities				

Financial Activities

Rating *	Indicator	Met	Needs Work	N/A
E	1. The organization follows accounting practices which conform to generally accepted accounting standards.			
E	2. The organization has systems in place to provide the appropriate information needed by the Board and management to make sound financial decisions and to fulfill government requirements (for example, in the USA, the Internal Revenue Service).			
R	3. The organization prepares timely financial statements including the balance sheet, income statement and cash flow statement which are clearly stated and useful for the Board members and employees. (Note that these statements might be referred to by different names in various countries.)			
R	4. The organization prepares financial statements on a budget-versus-actual and/or comparative basis to achieve a better understanding of their finances.			
E	5. The organization develops an annual comprehensive operating budget. This budget is reviewed and approved by the Board of Directors.			
R	6. The organization monitors unit costs of products and services through the documentation of employee time and direct expenses and use of a process for allocation of management and general expenses.			
E	7. The organization prepares cash flow projections.			
R	8. The organization periodically forecasts year-end revenues and expenses to assist in making sound management decisions during the year.			
E	9. The organization reconciles all cash accounts monthly.			
E	10. The organization has a review process to monitor that they are receiving appropriate and accurate financial information whether from a contracted service or internal processing.			
E	11. If the organization has billable contracts or other service income, procedures are established for the periodic billing, follow-up and collection of all accounts, and the documentation that substantiates all billings.			
E	12. Government contracts and purchase of service agreements are in writing and are reviewed by a member of the organization to monitor compliance with all stated conditions.			
E	13. Payroll is prepared following appropriate federal and state/provincial regulations and organizational policy.			
E	14. Persons employed on a contract basis meet all federal and state/provincial requirements for this form of employment. (In the USA, disbursement records are kept so 1099's can be issued at year-end.)			
E	15. Organizations that purchase and sell merchandise take periodic inventories to monitor the inventory against theft, to reconcile general ledger inventory information and to maintain an adequate inventory level.			

Continued on next page

Financial Activities (Cont.)

Rating *	Indicator	Met	Needs Work	N/A
E	17. The organization has documented a set of internal controls, including handling of cash and deposits, statement reconciliation, approval over spending and disbursements.			
E	18. The organization has a policy identifying authorized check signers and the number of signatures required on checks in excess of specified dollar amounts.			
E	19. All expenses of the organization are approved by a designated person before payment is made.			
R	20. The organization has a written policy related to investments.			
R	21. Capital needs are reviewed at least annually and priorities established.			
R	22. The organization has established a plan identifying actions to take in the event of a reduction or loss in funding.			
R	23. The organization has established, or is actively trying to develop, a reserve of funds to cover at least three months of operating expenses.			
E	24. The organization has suitable insurance coverage which is periodically reviewed to ensure the appropriate levels and types of coverage are in place.			
E	25. Employees and Board members who handle cash and investments are bonded to help assure the safeguarding of assets.			
R	26. The organization has an annual, independent audit of their financial statements, prepared by a certified public accountant.			
R	27. In addition to the audit, the auditor prepares a management letter containing recommendations for improvements in the financial operations of the organization.			
R	28. The Board of Directors, or an appropriate committee, is responsible for soliciting bids, interviewing auditors and hiring an auditor for the organization.			
E	29. The Board of Directors, or an appropriate committee, reviews and approves the audit report and management letter and with management input and support, institutes any necessary changes.			
A	30. Training is made available for Board and management on relevant accounting topics and all appropriate persons are encouraged to participate in various training opportunities.			
Indicators ratings: E=essential; R=recommended; A=additional to strengthen organizational activities				

Appendix D:
Founder's Syndrome –
How to Detect It, How to Avoid It

What is Founder's Syndrome?

Blindly Following the Leader – Not Mission, Plans and Policies

Often the first major challenges in the "maturing" process for a Board – or for an entire organization – is to move away from always following the nature of certain personalities in the organization and instead work according to its mission, plans and policies. That challenge is common to any type of Board model, whether it is a working Board or policy Board. The maturing process does not mean that members cannot choose any of these models. It means that members must use the model for the betterment of the organization, not for the betterment of the leader.

It is common for members of new Boards to follow the lead of whoever seems to be the most persuasive person in the organization. Often that person is the founder of the organization and the person who goes on to become its first Chief Executive, Board Chair or both. Other times, it can be a variety of people on the Board and/or among employees. In any case, the Board is not referencing the mission, policies and plans to guide the organization; rather it is just playing "follow the leader."

The problems inherent in working according to personalities, rather than according to the mission, have become so common, especially in new and small organizations, that some experts refer to the problems collectively as Founder's Syndrome. That phrase can be misleading, though, because the people having undue influence are not always the founders of the organizations. The "founder" can be one person on the Board or an employee or, at times, a certain group of people in the organization.

Typical Problem in New and Small Organizations

To continue to reliably meet the needs of their customers, organizations must evolve through a particular life-cycle change, just like people must do in order to mature. This change is usually from a highly reactive and seat-of-the-pants approach to growth to a well-planned and managed approach. Plans do not have to be constricting plans that are full of unnecessary paperwork – the business does not have to become highly bureaucratic. However, there should be enough plans and policies to provide a stable and efficient infrastructure from which to continue to grow.

This necessary evolution often requires a change in the nature of the founder's leadership from a highly reactive, individualistic style to a more proactive, consensus-oriented style. Many charismatic and visionary founders cannot make this transition – whether the founder is the CEO, someone on the Board or a group of people on the Board. They might have more confidence in their own grand plans and intuition than in what they often perceive as unnecessary "paperwork." As a result, more detailed plans and policies are not made, if at all.

As these organizations continue to grow and the demand for their services continues to grow as well, the need for more efficiency and resources continues to increase. As a result, the founder demands that people work even harder to take on more roles. Yet, the problem is not from lack of effort. It is from people's confusion about their purpose, direction and roles. It is from constant pressure from the leader – pressure that does not really seem to be solving any of the problems in the organization. Soon, Board members and employees become so frustrated that they leave – and the organization continues to struggle from one crisis to another.

No one really seems to know what is going on. Those who remain in the organization continue to look to the leader who seems to be doing the same things as before, but now even harder. Things just get worse. As a result, the organization remains managed, not in a manner that reliably provides services to customers, but in a manner that suits the personality of the increasingly frustrated founder.

Eventually, stakeholders confront the founder about the organization's recurring problems. Without ongoing coaching and support, it is likely that the founder will be replaced, or even worse, the organization will fold. Founder's Syndrome is no one's fault – no founder sets out to intentionally damage the organization. Besides, the syndrome does not occur without members of the Board and employees blindly following the leader.

Leadership and Founder's Syndrome – the Good and Bad

Troublesome Traits Among Founders and Boards

Whether the founder is the CEO, someone on the Board or a group of people on the Board, founders are dynamic, driven and decisive. They carry clear vision of what their organization can be. They know their customer's needs and are passionate about meeting those needs. Often these traits are strong assets for getting the new organization off the ground. However, other traits of founders too often become major liabilities. For example, founders often:

- Are highly skeptical about planning, policies and procedures. They claim "plans and procedures are overhead and just bog me down." They often believe they have found a new way to get things done.

- Make reactive, crisis-driven decisions with little input from others. They react to most problems with the lament "if only I had more money."

- Attend mostly to generating new ideas for products and services.

- Handpick their Board members and employees. See these people as working for the founder as much as working for the organization's mission.

- Attract Board members through the founder's dynamic, often charismatic personality – not through focus on the organization's mission.

- Hold occasional staff meetings to report crises and rally the troops.

- Count on whoever seems most loyal and accessible, and motivate by fear and guilt, often without realizing it.

- See their Boards mostly as a source for support, and work to remove Board members who disagree with the founder.

- Have a very difficult time letting go of the strategies that worked to quickly grow the organization, despite evidence that the organization can no longer absorb this rapid growth without major changes.

Ultimately, Founder's Syndrome sets in because the organization becomes dependent, not on the systems and structures of the organization, but on the unique style of the leader – whether the leader is consistently decisive or consistently indecisive.

Typical Traits of Well-Developed Leaders

The following traits are important for the Board members and Chief Executive to have if they are to effectively lead their organization. They are in sharp contrast to leaders with Founder's Syndrome. Traits include:

- Appreciating plans and budgets as guidelines, and realizing that these ultimately make the organization more responsive to the needs of their customers.

- Making proactive decisions based on mission and affordability.

- Making staffing decisions based one employees' responsibilities, training and capabilities.

- Valuing Board members and employees for their strong expertise and feedback.

- Sustaining strong credibility among customers and service providers.

Basic Principles in Developing Leadership

Eventually, most founders realize they must change the way they operate. Many go on to evolve their leadership style to the next level. First, they realize they must change from within. They:

- Understand that the recurring problems are not their fault – they are doing the best they can.

- Are willing to ask for and accept help.

- Communicate often and honestly (often difficult for crisis-driven, "heroic" leaders).

- Engage in stress management, especially forms not related to their jobs.

- Are patient with themselves, their Boards and employees.

- Regularly take time to reflect and learn, particularly about their value to others.

The following guidelines assume that the founder is the person who founded the organization and is also the Chief Executive, reporting to the Board. The Board model includes use of committees well. The CEO has employees reporting to him or her. However, as you read the following guidelines, adapt them to the particular model used by the Board and employees of your organization.

For more information about Boards, see the recommended books about Boards in the Bibliography on page 255.

Actions Your Board Members Must Take

If the organization seems stuck in a highly reactive way of doing things, addressing the same problems over and over again, then it may be facing Founder's Syndrome. This requires a major change in the way that the Board and Chief Executive operate together. Making this change in leadership style is usually confusing, lonely and stressful for the founder, whether the founder is the CEO, someone on the Board or a group of people on the Board. The Board can be the founder's greatest source of help if they:

1. **Understand and take full responsibility for the role of Board member.**
   Insist on highly condensed and focused Board training sessions on an annual basis in order to review the roles and responsibilities of a governing Board. Undertake a yearly self-evaluation of the Board to ensure it is operating effectively.

2. **Once a year, conduct a key risk management exercise.**
   Pretend the founder suddenly left the organization. Who will/can quickly step in? Are you sure? What activities are the employees doing? What is the cash flow situation? What stakeholders must be contacted? Where are the files/records?

3. **Know what is going on in the organization or how to quickly come up to speed.**
   Ensure job descriptions are up-to-date. Have employees complete weekly or biweekly written status reports. Ensure yearly written performance reviews are completed. Ensure regular staff meetings are held and actions are written. Is an employee being cultivated as an assistant Chief Executive? Is this needed?

4. **Strategic planning is one of the best ways to engage the Board and take stock.**
   Conduct regular and realistic strategic planning with the Board members and employees. Ensure the planning is carried out according to the nature of the organization, in a realistic and practical fashion. Focus on the top three or four issues facing the organization. Although most organizations scope plans to the coming three years, focus careful planning on the next 6 to 12 months. Establish clear goals and strategies, and work hard to establish objectives and timelines.

5. **Develop a highly participative Audit Committee or task force.**
   You might need to do the same with a Audit Committee or task force. Too often, Boards are extremely reluctant to face the founder by getting involved in finances. However, organizational problems are often revealed as financial problems. If a founder struggles or eventually leaves the organization, the finances are usually the first area to show major problems. Therefore, closely review the financial statements, especially cash flow.

6. **Do not be part of the problem!**
   Do not take on the traits of the crisis-driven founder and employees, or worse yet, just "numb out." Meet consistently and make decisions based on mission, planning and affordability, not on urgency. Avoid the notion of any quick fixes, such as hiring an intermediary for the founder with "people skills." This does not address the problem and may make things even worse.

7. **Help Board members and employees to keep up their hopes.**
   Regularly communicate with each other (through appropriate channels). Remind each other that the recurring problems are the result of the organization's success and that current

changes are to best serve the needs of its customers. Employees' morale will improve as they perceive stability, security, and progress.

8. **Support the founder with ongoing coaching and affirmation.**
The founder will change to the extent that he or she feels safe, understands the reasons for change, and accepts help along the way. Consider a Board Personnel Committee or task force to provide ongoing coaching to the founder (but not to replace his or her responsibilities and accountabilities). Include at least one or two experienced organizational leaders on this committee. Note that the founder is not changing roles, but priorities.

9. **Carefully monitor implementation and deviations from plans.**
Do not hold the founder to always be doing what is in the plan or budget – but do hold the founder to be always explaining deviations and how they can be afforded.

10. **Implement development and evaluation plans for the founder.**
Include the founder's input. Focus on the founder's accountability to implementing the plans or explaining deviations from them. Evaluate the founder as to how well he/she met his/her strategic objectives and responsibilities in his/her job description.

11. **Consider policies to carefully solicit feedback from employees to the Board.**
Consider having employee representatives on Board committees or task forces. Consider a 360-degree evaluation process for the Chief Executive, wherein employees provide feedback about the Chief Executive's performance. Establish a grievance procedure where employees can approach the Board about concerns if they can prove they have tried to work with the Chief Executive to resolve these issues.

12. **Closely monitor key indicators of successful change.**
Ensure ongoing communications between Board members and the founder, sound financial management, implementation of plans and policies, and stable turnover of employees. Perhaps the most useful indicator is continued positive feedback from customers.

13. **If problems recur, take action.**
If, after attempting to follow the above suggestions, the same major problems recur over the next six to nine months, then take major actions regarding the founder's position in the organization. The Board should have been highly involved in strategic planning, financial management, authorizing policies, reviewing product plans, and evaluating the Chief Executive. If the founder's leaving would cause the organization to fold, then the Board has not been doing its job all along.

Actions Your Founder Must Take

The major actions mentioned below are intended to help the organization to retain focus and direction, and become more stable and proactive. Each organization follows the practices according to its own nature and needs. The practices are not developed overnight and are never done perfectly. They should be followed to the extent that they are supportive, not restrictive. Start simple, but start! The following guidelines assume that the founder is the CEO, which, of course, is not always the case.

1. **Accept a mentor outside the organization and an advocate within.**
   Founder's Syndrome comes from doing what is natural for you. Changing your leadership approach may be rather unnatural. Seek and accept help.

2. **Ensure a customer-driven organization.**
   Always focus on the needs of customers. Regularly ask customers what they need and how the organization can meet their needs. Establish straightforward and realistic means to evaluate services. Start with basic questionnaires to gather customers' impressions. Interview some customers to get their "story."

3. **Set direction through planning.**
   Support the Board to carry out strategic planning. Ensure employees' input as well. Conduct regular staff meetings to hear employees' input. Cultivate a strong Finance Committee or task forces and help them to fully understand the organization's financial plan.

4. **Organize resources to meet goals.**
   Develop job descriptions with employees' input to ensure mutual understanding of responsibilities. Develop staff-driven procedures for routine, but critical tasks.

5. **Motivate leadership and employees to meet goals.**
   Delegate to employees by helping them understand the purpose of tasks. Get their input as to how the tasks can be completed. Give them the authority to complete the tasks. In regular staff meetings, celebrate successes! Bring in customers to tell employees how the organization helped address their challenges or advance their goals. Conduct regular performance reviews with employees to ensure organizational and employees' needs are being met. In regular staff meetings, share status information and conduct day-to-day planning.

6. **Guide resources to meet goals.**
   Share management challenges with the Board and ask for policies to guide management. Work from the strategic plan and develop an associated budget to earmark funds.

7. **Think transition!**
   Help the Board to regularly undertake contingency planning, including thinking about what the organization will do if/when you are gone. Have the Board members pretend that, for some unknown reason, you were suddenly gone. What would they do? How?

Actions Your Employees Might Take

If the founder is on the Board or is the CEO, then other employees still might play a major role in helping the organization to recover. However, employees may be in somewhat of a high-risk situation because the founder (who often values loyalty at least as much as effectiveness) may perceive employee actions as hurting the organization, rather than helping it. Therefore, employees are advised to proceed with caution.

The syndrome can be quite stressful for employees. They can lose perspective amidst the continued confusion and anxiety in the workplace. If they have been in the organization long enough, they, too, become part of the problem. Therefore, it is important for employees to get perspective on the nature and extent of the problem.

1. **Work hard to identify an external mentor and an internal employee advocate.**
   Bounce ideas off someone else whose judgment you highly revere.

2. **Get clear perspective by privately writing down a list of problems you perceive.**
   Privately record your concerns. In order to minimize your own biases, record only what you have seen with your eyeballs, not just felt with your heart. Document only those problems that seem to be persistent and/or which various people have tried to resolve.

3. **Match your list with previous section, "Some Troublesome Traits Among Founders."**
   How many of the symptoms match those recorded in your list? Consider sharing your list and results with someone whom you trust. Do they agree with your approach and results? It is up to you to conclude if the organization has the syndrome or not. Whether the organization has the syndrome or not, if there are enough other persistent problems, you may still want to take action.

4. **Assess if you want to stay in the organization and help it recover.**
   This requires that you carefully reflect on why you are in the organization, what you can do to help the organization recover, the likelihood of it recovering and how well you manage your own stress.

5. **If you stay in the organization and help it to recover, use the organization's structure.**
   That is, communicate your suggestions with peers and your immediate supervisor, whether that is the founder or not. Give them a chance to address your concerns. Promptly go to the Board only if symptoms of the problem result in discrimination or harassment of you and if your personnel policies include a grievance procedure for you to directly contact the Board. You might consider a letter to the Board if you resign, but this may hurt your career.

6. **Give suggestions from "Actions Board Must Take", "Actions Founders Must Take."**
   Do not provide all of the suggestions at once. Always associate your suggestions with a description of how they can constructively advance the mission of the organization. Do not personalize your descriptions of concerns by blaming them on someone. Make your suggestions in writing, for example, in status reports or in memos. Put a date on the suggestions so you can keep perspective on whether the suggestions are acted on or not.

7. **Monitor whether the organization is recovering or not.**
   Have you given the organization time to address concerns? Has the organization made substantial changes and symptoms have decreased? Or, do you see the same symptoms?

8.   **Update your resume and consider looking for another job.**
      Keeping your own health and happiness is the best thing you can do for yourself, the organization and the community. You may become ill if you stay in the organization. Your leaving may actually contribute to the organization's recovery if other employees realize why you left. Even if you decide to stay, the knowledge that you can leave might shift your attitude enough to approach the situation with fresh energy or perspective.

9.   **Do not "burn bridges."**
      It is extremely compelling to write a blistering letter to all members of the Board and various employees, explaining each and every problem in the organization. This may temporarily relieve you of your frustration, but it may also hurt your credibility with key members of the organization's community. If you communicate your concerns and reasons for leaving, be respectful and tactful.

Bibliography

Various categories of readings are included below. The following readings are by no means all of the important works in each category. However, the listed works will provide you a strong start to understanding information in that particular category. Also the bibliographies of many of the works listed below will help you to find related works from which you can continue to develop your knowledge about the particular category.

Boards of Directors

Corporate Boards: New Strategies for Adding Value at the Top, Jay Conger, et al., Jossey-Bass, 2001.

Thoughtfully written and research-based book that stresses that corporate Boards have a responsibility to stakeholders, not just to stockholders. Stresses the value of listening to employees and the communities served by the corporation.

Improving Corporate Boards: The Boardroom Insider Guidebook, by Ralph D. Ward, Wiley, 2000.

Provides extensive overview of the nuts and bolts of Board operations, including CEO and Board roles, structures, committees, meetings, evaluations and much more. The many tips and tools are provided on a CD-ROM, as well.

The Board Book: Making Your Corporate Board a Strategic Force in Your Company's Success, Susan Schulz, AMACOM, 2000.

Schulz writes from the perspective that the CEO helps the Board to do its job. She interviewed numerous CEOs and Board members to write about the strategic Board comprised of independent directors who have strong knowledge of the workings of the corporation.

Leadership and Supervision

First Time Supervisors Survival Guide, George Fuller, Prentice Hall Press, 1994.

An older, but seminal, book on the most important practices in supervision – practices that will be required regardless of where the reader is supervising, including overcoming initial anxieties of the job, delegating so employees take ownership in their job, and dealing with performance management issues.

Leadership for Dummies, Marshall Loeb, Wiley Publishing, 1999.

Like a typical "Dummies" book, this book provides very practical tips and tools to lead in a variety of situations. The book concisely explains the most important roles in leadership, how to build on your strengths to do those roles well, and how to lead in different contexts.

Management, Richard Daft, South-Western College Pub, 2002.

Rather than reading from among the vast range of new books on general leadership, the reader would be better served to read this book that provides clear descriptions of the foundations of management, including the roles of leadership and supervision.

Managing Change in Organizations

Changing the Essence, Richard Beckhard and Wendy Pritchard, Jossey-Bass, Inc., 1992.

> This is one of the seminal works on organizational change and written by the "father" of the field of Organization Development. It includes a comprehensive and strategic overview of key considerations in achieving successful organizational change.

Field Guide to Consulting and Organizational Development, Carter McNamara, Authenticity Consulting, LLC, 2005.

> This highly practical book combines the tools and techniques of the field of Organization Development with the power of systems thinking and principles for successful change in for-profits and government agencies. The book also addresses many of the problems with traditional approaches to consulting and leading. The result is a proven, time-tested roadmap for consultants and leaders to accomplish significant change.

Making Sense of Life's Changes, William Bridges, Addison Wesley, 1980.

> Bridge's book provides an excellent overview of the psychological and sociological aspects and considerations for successful organizational change. His book, combined with Block's (in the "Consulting" section in this Appendix) and Beckhard's (above), comprise a comprehensive "toolkit" for conducting successful organizational change.

Mastering the Challenges of Change: Strategies for Each Stage in Your Organization's Life Cycle, Leroy Jr. Thompson, Amacom Books, 1994.

> Provides top-level guidelines for managing change in organizations. Frequent case studies are cited to substantiate the guidelines. Suggests a set of life cycle changes that organizations evolve through and bases the guidelines on these life cycles. The author asserts that change management starts before the typical crises occur that so often cause change to occur.

Rx for Business: A Troubleshooting Guide for Building a High Performance Organization, Mark Graham Brown, Irwin Professional Publications, 1996.

> This book works as a quick reference guide, starting with identifying current problems and then considering a variety of tips and tools to solve those problems. Includes useful graphics that guide you through application of many of the recommendations in the book.

The Art of the Turnaround: How to Rescue Your Troubled Business from Creditors, Predators, and Competitors, Matthew L. Shuchman and Jerry S. White, AMACOM, 1995.

> The book is written for organizations that already find themselves in trouble and needing a turnaround. The content is focused especially on cash management and does a good job of digging deep into business activities to find causes and solutions for a turnaround. Includes checklists and guidelines for using consultants.

The Change Management Handbook: A Road Map to Corporate Transformation, Lance Berger and Martin Sikora, McGraw-Hill, 1993.

> Provides a roadmap for change in organizations, including specific tips and tools for leaders, managers and change agents to develop highly adaptable organizations that best survive change. Tips and tools are targeted for top-level and mid-level management, making it a comprehensive guide that can be used at all levels of the organization.

The Save Your Business Book: A Survival Manual for Small Business Owners, John Goldhammer, Lexington Books, 1998.

This is the book to read if things have gone from bad to worse in the company and it is facing the likelihood of bankruptcy. The book provides ideas to avoid bankruptcy, and for how you might reorganize, work with employees, creditors, suppliers and customers to recover. It also provides suggestions for getting through bankruptcy if that is the only course.

Strategic Planning

Simplified Strategic Planning: A No-Nonsense Guide for Busy People Who Want Results Fast!, Robert W. Bradford, Chandler House Press, 1999.

A good book for the reader who has little or no knowledge about strategic planning. Includes numerous tools and techniques for developing a plan based on sound marketing and financial analysis. Stresses how plans can be developed to be simple, but not simplistic.

Strategic Management: Formulation, Implementation, and Control, Fourth Edition, John A. Pearce II and Richard B. Robinson, Jr., Irwin Publishing, 1991.

Explains the strategic planning process in the overall context of strategic management. Explains complete strategic management cycle, primarily in reference to large for-profit corporations. However, the information applies equally as well to smaller businesses.

Strategic Planning for Dummies, Erica Olsen, Wiley Publishing, 2006.

The author does a great job of removing the mystique from strategic planning and making it seem like a process that a very busy person could do. The author also nicely integrates the business planning process into strategic planning, so the planning is relevant to products.

Index

Notes

Notes

Notes

Notes

Additional Titles for Business, Government and General Use

Field Guide to Consulting and Organizational Development

This highly practical book combines the tools and techniques of the field of Organization Development with the power of systems thinking and principles for successful change in for-profits and government agencies. The book also addresses many of the problems with traditional approaches to consulting and leading. The result is a proven, time-tested roadmap for consultants and leaders to accomplish significant change. You can use this book to accomplish change in small or large organizations, whether the organization is dealing with a variety of complex issues or striving to achieve goals for the future.

499 pp, softcover, 2006   Item #7480, ISBN 978-1-933719-20-7 / 1-933719-20-6 $58

Additional Titles About Action Learning and Peer Coaching Groups

Authenticity Circles Program Developer's Guide

Step-by-step guidelines to design, build, manage and troubleshoot an Action Learning-based, peer coaching group program. The program can be used by consultants or an organization's leaders for training enrichment, problem solving, support and networking among peers.

127 pp, comb-bound, 2002   Item #7730, ISBN 978-1-933719-10-8 / 1-933719-10-9 $25

Authenticity Circles Facilitator's Guide

This Guide describes how to organize, facilitate and evaluate peer coaching groups. Groups can be facilitated by an external facilitator or groups can self-facilitate themselves. It can also be used to recruit, develop and support facilitators of peer coaching groups. The Guide includes appendices with worksheets for the facilitator's use and a handy Quick Reference tool.

114 pp, comb-bound, 2002   Item #7720, ISBN 978-1-933719-11-5 / 1-933719-11-7 $20

Authenticity Circles Member's Guide and Journal

This Guide provides step-by-step guidelines for group members to get the most out of their Action Learning-based, peer coaching groups, including how to select goals to be coached on, how to get coached and how to coach others. The Guide includes a journal of worksheets to capture the learning of the group members and a handy Circles Quick Reference tool.

110 pp, comb-bound, 2004   Item #7710, ISBN 978-1-933719-12-2 / 1-933719-12-5 $15

Additional Titles Specific to Nonprofits

Field Guide to Developing, Operating and Restoring Your Nonprofit Board

This guide will help your Board to be highly effectively in all of the most important aspects of governance, including strategic planning, programs, marketing, staffing, finances, fundraising, evaluations, transparency, sustainability and lobbying. It includes guidelines to detect and fix broken Boards; select the best Board model for the nonprofit to implement; define how much the Board members should be involved in management, depending on the Board model; decide whether to use committees or not, and if so, which ones; establish specific, appropriate goals for Board committees; conduct comprehensive succession planning of the CEO position; ensure legal compliance to the Sarbanes-Oxley act; and ensure highly ethical behavior of Board members. Comprehensive guidelines and materials are written in an easy-to-implement style, resulting in a highly practical resource that can be referenced at any time during the life of a Board and organization.

296 pp, softcover, revised 2008   Item #7110, ISBN 978-1-933719-05-4 / 1-933719-05-2 $32

Field Guide to Nonprofit Strategic Planning and Facilitation

The guide provides step-by-step instructions and worksheets to customize and implement a comprehensive nonprofit strategic plan – that is relevant, realistic and flexible for the nonprofit organization. The guide describes the most useful traditional and holistic approaches to strategic planning. It also includes the most important tools and techniques to facilitate strategic planning in an approach that ensures strong participation and ownership among all of the planners. Emphasis is as much on implementation and follow-through of the plan as on developing the plan document. Hardcopy and online worksheets help you to collect and organize all of the results of their planning process.

284 pp, softcover, revised 2007   Item #7120, ISBN 978-1-933719-06-1 / 1-933179-06-0 $32

Field Guide to Leadership and Supervision for Nonprofit Staff

Top-level executives, middle managers and entry-level supervisors in nonprofit organizations need the "nuts and bolts" for carrying out effective leadership and supervision, particularly in organizations with limited resources. This guide includes topics often forgotten in nonprofit publications, including: time and stress management, staffing, organizing, team building, setting goals, giving feedback, avoiding Founder's Syndrome, and much more. It also includes guidelines to ensure a strong working relationship between the Chief Executive Officer and the Board.

303 pp, softcover, revised 2008   Item #7130, ISBN 978-1-933719-07-8 / 1-933179-07-9 $32

Field Guide to Nonprofit Program Design, Marketing and Evaluation

Nonprofits have long needed a clear, concise – and completely practical – guidebook about all aspects of designing, marketing and evaluating nonprofit programs. Now they have such a resource. This guide can be used to evolve strategic goals into well-designed programs that are guaranteed to meet the needs of clients, develop credible nonprofit business plans and fundraising proposals, ensure focused and effective marketing, evaluate the effectiveness and efficiencies of current programs in delivery of services to clients, evaluate program performance against goals and outcomes, and understand how a program really works in order to improve or duplicate the program.

252 pp, softcover, revised 2006   Item #7170, ISBN 978-1-933719-08-5 / 1-933719-08-7 $32

Additional Titles Specific to Nonprofits - continued

Field Guide to Consulting and Organizational Development With Nonprofits

This highly practical book combines the tools and techniques of the field of Organization Development with the power of systems thinking and principles for successful change in nonprofits. The book also addresses many of the problems with traditional approaches to consulting and leading. The result is a proven, time-tested roadmap for consultants and leaders to accomplish significant change in nonprofits. You can use this book to accomplish change in small or large nonprofit organizations, for instance organizations that 1) have a variety of complex issues, 2) must ensure a strong foundation from which to develop further, 3) must evolve to the next life cycle, 4) need a complete "turnaround," 5) must address Founder's Syndrome or 6) want to achieve an exciting grand goal.

517 pp, softcover, 2005   Item #7180, ISBN 978-1-933719-00-9 / 1-933719-00-1 $58

Coming in 2011 – Watch our website for news!

Field Guide to Strategic Planning and Facilitation

For business now too!

To order

To get your copies of these and other practical publications, contact us:

Online: http://www.authenticityconsulting.com/pubs.htm

Phone: 800.971.2250 toll-free in North America or +1.763.971.8890 direct

Fax: +1.763.592.1661

Mail: Authenticity Consulting, LLC
                 4008 Lake Drive Avenue North
                 Minneapolis, MN   55422-1508
                 USA